Untangle

Shirlee Scribner

D1127949

Scribner Media Inc.
Celebration, Florida

Published by: Scribner Media Inc.
Celebration, Florida
scribnermediainc@gmail.com

Scribner Media is committed to publishing works of quality and integrity. In that spirit, we are proud to offer this book to our readers; however, the story, the experiences, and the words are the author's alone.

Disclaimer
Every reasonable effort has been made to recreate events, locales and conversations from my memories of them and what I have experienced and what is true for me.

Library of Congress Cataloging-in-Publication Date
Untangle, Copyright 2013
Scribner, Shirlee
Untangle / Shirlee Scribner
ISBN 978-0-615-90646-1
© Shirlee Scribner

www.UntangleTheBook.com

Cover Design by Matt Ritter

"One must not conceal any part of what one has recognized to be true."

—Albert Einstein

To Carolyn
Live with Joy!
Shirlee Scribner
062814

Prologue

My parents met in the summer of 1945 and married after a whirlwind courtship. It was a jubilant time. World War II was over. We were triumphant. No other period had been as turbulent or tragic for so many lives. The end of the war marked a pivotal moment when an entire nation turned from despair to hope. But the war between my parents had just begun. Soon after my parents married, I was born into it.

CHAPTER ONE

Breaking all the Rules

Dad was driving at a high speed along a local highway. Even at the age of nine, I knew he was drunk, and I begged him to slow down. I held my baby brother Lynn in my lap, pressing him tightly against my chest. Dad had stormed out of the house after a fight with my mother, taking us kids with him, and he was still fuming. This was the way he drove when he didn't care if he slammed into a tree and ended it all.

The car was strong with the smell of cigarette smoke. Scattered empty beer bottles littered the floor of the car. Between his knees Dad held a brown glass beer bottle. With one hand he fondled the frosted bottle and quickly lifted it to his lips. He took a long sip before throwing it out the window. The wind outside sent a gush through the car, emphasizing the already strong smell of alcohol. Suddenly, Dad pressed wildly on the gas pedal.

The western sun seared my eyes as I held onto my one-year-old brother, bracing for the worse. With no seatbelts in the front seat, there was nothing to hold me securely to the seat. The speedometer needle rose. We were going 100 miles an hour. Dad's black Studebaker rode waves of dips and valleys as it careened over the unevenly paved road, throwing the car to and fro. Dad's hands swirled aimlessly to control the steering wheel. The car accelerated as the weight of his foot tightened harder on the gas pedal. We flew up into the air. My stomach lurched at the thrust of landing hard on the road. The sound of metal against the road ricocheted in my head. I still hung precariously onto Lynn.

"Please, Daddy, stop!" I cried.

He ignored me, and we proceeded down the highway at break-neck speed. The landscape out the window transformed from distinct varieties of trees to a blur. Dad sucked in his cigarette; it lit up his face and showed his nicotine lines and his anger. The speedometer needle rose even higher. Lynn started to wail. He was only a baby. *If we crash and die it would be my fault because I couldn't protect him. I would never see my brothers and sisters again. I would never see my precious Grandma.* My muscles tightening, I braced for the worst. My mind went blank as fear and panic took over.

Suddenly in the distance, a speed limit sign rose up from the ground. Dad pumped hard on the brakes until the car slowed to the speed limit. Up ahead a black-and-white police car crossed over the intersection. Dad blew out smoke from his nose and flicked the ashes of his cigarette out the car window. His jaw unclenched.

"Damn! It's a cop," he said, but he could not contain his sigh of relief, chuffing out his beery breath. The police car disappeared around the corner. Dad wiped his brow with his hand and turned onto Hazel Street, leading to our home.

I grew up in northeast Indiana. Albion is a small town whose residents seldom stray far. It has a sense of time, place, and measure; it's a place where people notice the humblest things that give pleasure. There, life moved at a slow and thoughtful pace. The heat of summer nights was consistent with the daytime temperature. The Sunday after my near brush with death, I awoke to a brilliant sun shining through my window, beads of sweat already forming on my skin. I quickly arose from my bed, fumbled to remove my nightgown, and placed my dress over my shoulders, struggling to pull it down over my moist body.

I tiptoed past my two sisters, still asleep in their bed, and walked to my brothers' bedroom to see if they were awake. The three of them lay limp on the bed from the burning heat. Church bells rang in the distance, and I rushed down the steep stairs to the living room. My parents were also still asleep in their bedroom. I reached for my bible on the nearby stand and pushed open the screen door to the outdoors, stepping onto the concrete porch. My shoes tripped over a crushed beer can, carelessly left from the night before. I kicked it hard to the edge of the street.

My tiny feet raced up the block toward Albion Wesleyan Church. Sunday school had started, and I was late. As I came closer to the church, I slowed my breathing and observed my surroundings. Tall leafy maples in a palette of greens graced the church lot. Sunlight filtered through the trees to illuminate an unkempt lawn and layers of fallen dried leaves dotted the landscape, creating a textured canvas. I stepped onto the lawn and ran toward the church entrance, scattering leaves and trampling the grass.

The red brick exterior of the church was accentuated by gothic-style stained glass windows boasting colorful biblical scenes, which were often studied by the churchgoers for their intricate patterns. One could get lost staring at those windows. I looked up, higher, exalting in the white steeple. I had been coming to this church since I could walk on my own.

My church was pure in its faith. It followed many traditions that were upheld by the church rules. Among those rules were no drinking, no makeup, no dancing, and no fornicating outside of marriage. Some rules I didn't understand. And I have little memory of words spoken about the sins of violence.

My parents broke all the rules.

There was a puritanical zeal among parishioners to live life according to the church doctrine. We practiced a staunch Christian religion that included threats of damnation. Every Sunday night, altar call was held. Self-proclaimed sinners humbly kneeled at the altar, loudly repenting their sins, begging for God's forgiveness. As a child, I sometimes witnessed testimonials that frightened me with their flailing passion.

But most of the time I could not wait to enter the peaceful confines of the church. Stepping through the white carved doors, my hand tightly clutched my bible. I looked around the sanctuary for a place to sit. The parishioners sat quietly as Pastor Kenny walked to the lectern. He raised his head up, examining the faces turned toward his.

"Please stand for prayer," he said. As the women stood up, the hems of their dresses dropped to their ankles. Then Pastor Kenny closed his eyes and began to pray. I closed my eyes, too, my lips moving in silent prayer.

Afterward, I opened my eyes and panned the room as the congregation dutifully sat down on the hard benches. The parishioners dressed in clothing that was pressed, starched, and simple, lacking ornamentation. My church thought it sinful to adorn one's body with jewelry; not even a watch could be worn. Women were discouraged from cutting their hair, so they wore it long or tied up in a knotted bun.

The temperature inside the sanctuary felt as hot as an oven. Even the frenetic wave of hand fans did little to ease my discomfort. Nevertheless, despite the heat, I loved being in church and sitting among its oak pews stacked in rows upon the shiny hardwood floor on both sides of the aisle. The sturdy hardback seats sat erect, facing the pulpit, symbolic of the orderliness and simplicity that was expected from every church member. I observed the rough-hewn oak chart that hung proudly, displaying the numbers of previous weeks' attendance.

As the parishioners got settled, I quietly tiptoed to the front of the church where Grandma was seated. She preferred to find God in the first pew. She always saved me a seat next to her. I sat down at her side. She placed her arms around me and pulled me closer to her, smiling with approval that I had made it to church. I studied her large nose, which sat prominently on her sharp-featured face. It securely anchored her wire rim eyeglasses. Grandma's hair was pulled back, tightly positioned in a circular bun with thin black pins. A ray of light from the stained glass window shone on her gray hair, highlighting thin yellow streaks.

I was proud to sit next to Grandma. She was highly respected by members of the congregation. Grandma—that was the name that everyone called her, including Pastor Kenny --- was a religious and loyal member of the church. People liked her. She was of even temperament, never raising her voice in anger, and she never spoke ill of anyone, nor made quick judgments about evil people. Despite the hardship and poverty that had marked her life, Grandma exuded joy. Her philosophy was that God made each day, and she was going to embrace His gift. But Grandma could be quiet and pensive, too. I hung onto every word she spoke, and I loved her more than I loved anyone in the world.

The choir began to sing the first song. Grandma lowered the hymnal book to her knee so I could follow along. Parishioners sang in unhurried unison, and traditional hymns filled the church. Sound spilled through the open windows to the world outside. We sang "The Old Rugged Cross," passionately, from the depths of knowing despair. As my voice bellowed out songs of worship, the slow methodical rhythms soothed me and lifted my spirit.

My church was only a block from my house, but the life inside the church and the life inside my home, were worlds apart. At church, I always felt a calm sense of belonging. Members knew me by name, and I kept them busy with questions, about everything. Some even affectionately called me a "question box." I always participated in the children's church recitals, memorizing bible passages for short biblical plays and songs, and reciting them before a full audience. They acknowledged me by patting my arm, and speaking soft and kind words that made me feel like a solid part of the church family. I felt loved and safe among them. But most of all, I loved being there with Grandma.

After we sang the hymnal, Grandma removed her arm from my shoulder and set her black leather bible securely on her lap. Pastor Kenney began his sermon with a scripture reading from the bible. Grandma gently flipped through the pages to the bible passage and secured it with a bookmark. Pastor Kenny adjusted his glasses and looked down at the scripture.

"Peter and John walked to the temple court where the man begged them for alms. Peter said, 'Silver and gold I do not have, but in the name of Jesus Christ of Nazareth, walk.' And the man jumped to his feet, and became strong and walked."

Grandma listened intently to Pastor Kenny as he described the beggar, born paralyzed at birth and sitting at the Gate of Beautiful, begging for handouts. Grandma shifted her body in my direction and put her arm around me again. I looked up at her face; she seemed moved by the preacher's message. The sermon ended, and the pianist played the final hymnal. Parishioners rose from their seats as Pastor Kenney walked to the back of the church, where he shook hands with departing members. I kissed Grandma and walked to the back doors. Before exiting, Pastor Kenny reached over, patted my head softly, and said he was glad to see me.

I bounced out the church doors into the sunlight, skipping toward home. The air was thick with humidity, and a sudden burst of strong wind attacked my face. I had put on my best clothes for church, and as I skipped, my black patent leather shoes clicked against the pavement, and my long brown hair whipped against the back of my cream-colored dress.

The entire town felt like an inferno. I could feel the sun's rays scorching my delicate skin. My feet met the paved asphalt and continued down Hazel Street towards my house. Skipping along, the tar of the street stuck to my leather soles with each step, releasing the bottom of my shoe with a cry. I slowed my skipping to a walk, and beads of sweat rolled down my forehead. Birds chirped in the background with an occasional fluttering of their wings. A blue jay roosting on the tree branch above me suddenly flew up and passed noisily over my head, letting me know I had interrupted the quiet.

My neighborhood was unusually quiet, even for a Sunday. I walked past neighbors who waved to me while lounging on their screened front porches. Hazel Street, where I lived, rolled along undulating hills that lead to the center of town. Shady maple trees lined both sides of the street, towering like umbrellas, and providing a welcome relief from the sun.

I looked up, admiring the black iron lampposts that lined the street and were topped by opaque lamps, statuesque in their style. They served as sculptures by day, and they lit the way at night. I picked up my pace again, skipping towards home. A block away, the paved street gently dipped to a slight recess, leading to our gray, shingled house.

Our property was situated in the middle of the block, which was divided in half by a narrow dirt alley, with tire tracks and uncut grass growing up the center. On one side of the alley, a plot of land flourished with a large vegetable garden, rhubarb and mulberry bushes, and cherry and peach trees. When our parents locked us kids out, we would gather our sustenance from there. On the other side of the alley sat our house. In front of our house, two maple trees created privacy from the neighbors across the street and provided us with a playground to climb and hide. Twenty feet from the back of the house sat an unpainted outhouse, precariously leaning backward from years of use, awaiting its ultimate destruction. A couple years before, my father had installed a new bathroom in the house, thankfully ending the dreaded trips to the outhouse.

On our front lawn, my brothers and sisters were playing with the garden hose. They were spraying each other, delighted with the blasts of cold water. I cut across the grass to join them in their folly. The oldest of my three brothers, Roger, turned the hose in my direction and giggled when he hit me, jubilant at having nailed his older sister. I tackled him and sprayed him back.

After we had exhausted this game, I walked around to dad's bike shop, which was attached to the house next to the alley, making it convenient for the occasional customers to park their cars. His shop looked like it was built without a level because the large room tilted slightly backward. Dad built bicycles to supplement his day jobs. Sometimes, he worked odd jobs at the local factories, when work was available, but he was out of work a lot. In the summer, Dad spent most of his time working in his shop building bicycles in hopes of making a sale.

Dad was kneeled over a bicycle in front of his shop. Bicycle handles, chains, wheels, and frames were strewn about the area, ready for assembly. His head was bent down, and his shock of white hair hung over his forehead as he assembled bike parts into a whole. The soil around him was streaked with yellow gobs of wet and dried spittle from his mouth. A random scattering of cigarette butts dotted the ground where he worked. A cigarette hung loosely from his lips; he inhaled, pursing his lips, and masterfully blew smoke circles in the air.

"Hi Dad!" I said, sidling up next to his crouched figure. Moving closer, I reached for the smoke circle and closed it tightly in my hand.

"Hello Sholo!" Dad greeted me, using his special nickname for me. Dad meant it in an affectionate way. Sholo was a foreign and exotic name that he had called me for as long as I could remember, and he singled me out from my siblings with this name. I never knew why he didn't call my brothers and sisters by similar nicknames. This afternoon, he seemed to be in a good mood, and asked me to hold a wrench while he made another adjustment on the bike. We talked for a while, and then I went into the house to find mom.

My parents met in my mother's native Hawaii, a world away from Albion. At the time, my mother was an 18-year-old beauty queen, her orchid white skin and auburn hair celebrated among the uniformed soldiers who passed through during the war. When the men left port, they passed her name on to the next group of arriving soldiers, just in case one of them might be lucky enough to get a date with her. My mother thrived on the attention. When my father arrived during the last days of the war, young and handsome in his uniform, they fell in love at first sight. Within a couple of months of their first meeting, my father proposed to my mother, and they moved back to Albion to begin their new life together.

But almost as soon as she landed in Albion, Mom began to miss her homeland, her family, and her culture. Mom said her parents told her that if she married Dad and moved to the mainland, they would never visit her. And they never did. Finances in their young marriage were tight, and there was never money for visits to see her family. So Mom stayed in Albion and became a baby machine, producing one child after another.

At twenty-nine years old, my mother had birthed three healthy baby boys and three girls. I was the oldest and took charge of my siblings. The next oldest, Sissy, was tiny for her age. Her sharply blended features displayed a pointed chin, thin lips, and a large nose similar to Grandma's, and she had a temper to match that of Dad's. She could get volatile at a moment's notice over the slightest provocation, and her face would redden in contrast to her white skin and pale blond hair. Then came Diane. Where Sissy was sometimes acerbic, Diane's disposition had the sweetness of honey. When light filtered through the window and hit her golden hair, it revealed the natural white gold and sunflower striping throughout. The next babies to come were the boys: Roger, Roland, and, of course, baby Lynn.

With so many children in a three-bedroom house, there was little privacy or quiet. My brothers shared a single bed. Lynn, because he was the smallest, slept sandwiched in the middle of the bed between Roger and Roland. The air in their bedroom was dank and suffocating; it stank with the tang of urine. In the middle of the attic, a wall with a door separated another bedroom for my sisters, Diane and Sissy, and me. A double-hung window faced Hazel Street, and the maple tree was within touching distance of the screen.

For my mother, the change from the Hawaiian Islands to the Bible belt had not been what she was expecting. There were no oceans or sandy beaches. There were no palm trees to sway in the wind. Swimsuit-clad girls didn't romp on the beaches. Women in Albion didn't show any skin; their clothes were buttoned to the neck, hems down to their ankles.

At first, Mom clung to reminders of her homeland. She hung a flowered drapery from the doorway to provide privacy to my parents' bedroom. When we were young, Mom liked to talk of Hawaii. Often, she bent over the kitchen dinette table, cutting thin strips of green crepe paper. She sewed together the long paper strips and attached them to a waistband, and she created leis to match the colorful hula skirts. She dressed my sisters and me in the hula costumes, and she taught us to dance the hula. After much practice, we were put on display to dance at the local veteran's hall in front of friends and neighbors, who found us utterly amusing.

Occasionally, in one of Mom's happier moods, she would break into a Hawaiian hula dance herself. Barefoot, she kicked her slender legs and feet rhythmically back and forth, her hand movements gracefully animating stories of ocean waves, palm trees, and love. I enjoyed seeing her express love for her culture. But the church people didn't approve of my mother's dancing. They thought my mother was sinful for wearing makeup and jewelry and dancing the hula. They ignored my mother. At times, she must have felt very lonely.

Nevertheless, she had her beauty. I remember being fascinated by the brass tray sitting on top of her dresser. A variety of cosmetics filled the tray: lipsticks, colorful compact cases, soft brushes, powders, and rouges. A three-strand pearl necklace lay loosely on the vanity top, and it glistened in a ray of light shining through the window. When there was enough money, mom would place a single fresh flower in her crystal vase. Plumeria, an exotic flower from the islands, was mom's favorite flower and fragrance. It was hard to get at the local florist shop. Almost always, the vase was empty.

Sometimes I would stand next to my mother's vanity as she readied for her day, attending to the construction of herself. Mom's sharply sculptured face and nose were chiseled to perfection. Her eyes were as bright as a budding leaf in the sunlight. She busied herself, dusting powder on her face and applying lipstick, full and red, and her face came alive with colors. Mom's thin arms lifted and extended as she combed her long auburn tresses.

Mom was consumed by her vanity. Her need for flattery never subsided. She would feed on it. Seek it out. She grew from it like a plant moving toward sunlight. She could never get enough. Everyone said I resembled

13

my Mom. When I was a little girl, I couldn't wait to grow up and become as beautiful as she was.

When I was 10 years old, Mom announced that she was going to have another baby. Baby number seven. That year, winter came sooner than expected. A light dusting of snow fell to the ground, and school was let out early. As I took the short walk home, a strong surge of wind rushed past me. My bare hand clasped the collar of my jacket tightly around my neck.

Upon reaching home, I ran up the porch steps, tapping my feet hard on the concrete. The porch was slick from the snow, and my foot slipped on the top step, tossing me hard onto the landing, where I dropped my schoolbooks to the ground. Those four steps to the front door had come to represent pain over the years. The permanent scars dug high on my forehead proved I had fallen too many times; my father refused to put in handrails.

I dusted the snow from my bruised knee and gathered my books. My right hand firmly grasped the screen door handle, and I entered the front door. The house was dead quiet. My parents were in their bedroom, probably sleeping.

Our sparse living room harbored only one piece of furniture, a blue velvet sofa that seemed out of place in a home filled with six small children and another baby on the way. A folded dirty diaper sat on the edge of the sofa. Strewn about the floor were empty baby bottles with chewed rubber nipples, dirty clothes, and an empty cereal box. A simple white rod exposed the framing of the double-hung windows. Heavy fabric hung from the windows, making the room feel dark and isolated from the outside.

All at once, a strong breeze swept through the front door and gave a whip and a snap to the curtains. I ran back to close the door tightly. My leather shoes echoed loudly over the linoleum, and my foot unexpectedly caught the torn edge of a tile worn by years of heavy traffic. I fell hard on the floor, my second spill of the day. If I woke my father, he might very well thrash through the bedroom curtains butt naked, yell profanities at me, and use his belt to strap me as punishment for disturbing his sleep. The thought terrified me. I stood up and softened my footsteps.

My brother Lynn sat in the corner of the living room, wheezing from chronic asthma. He suffered from allergies that made him weak and listless at times. With watery, pitiful eyes, he struggled for breath. Seeing me, Lynn gave a whimper and reached his arms up toward me. He needed to be held. I sat on the sofa with him. I loved holding him on my lap and burying my nose in his neck. My fingers played gently with his curly white hair, and he instantly fell asleep in my arms. I gently laid him on the sofa and covered him with a woolen blanket.

In the kitchen, I found my other brothers foraging for food. Roger had pushed the dining chair up to the steel cabinet and crawled onto the countertop in hopes of finding something to eat. Roland had opened the bottom cabinets, and he was rummaging through cans and bottles. Bellies aching with hunger, their tiny hands reached high and low in the metal cabinets for an unopened box of cereal, anything. I wrapped my arms around each of their tiny bodies and hugged them. Being the oldest child, I felt responsible for my brothers and sisters.

"Come down," I told them, "and I will make you something to eat."

I pulled out a slice of Wonder Bread, loaded it up with sugar, and topped it with sweetened condensed milk. Mom served this sweet concoction to fill our empty stomachs when there was no money for food. I reached for an opened cereal box and poured the contents into two small bowls. I used the last bit of milk sparingly to wet the cereal. It was a repeat of last night's dinner, but there was no other food in the house. My brothers devoured the bread and cereal, and I gave them each a glass of water to wash it down. I took the last piece of white bread and swallowed it.

When Mom and Dad were getting along, Dad usually fished the surrounding lakes for trout or striped bass, or he hunted in the nearby woods for rabbit. But with little money to begin with, my mother seldom shopped for food, and we children were all bony and emaciated from hunger. Hunger defined my childhood. Yet, somehow Dad always had enough to buy his drink.

One night, after work, Dad stopped by the town tavern for drinks. He mixed with his drinking friends until well into the evening, and then a dark colored car dropped him off at the house. He staggered up the concrete steps and nearly fell off the landing. Maybe at that moment, he wished he'd installed the hand railing. Dad opened the screen door, and the doorknob slipped out of his hand. He reached again for the knob and opened the door wide. He stumbled in, sat down on the sofa, adjusted himself, and burped the fetid smell of stale beer.

"Sholo! Come here, bring your sisters. Let's wrestles!" Dad commanded, slurring his words. He kneeled down on the floor, his hands steadying his body.

Wrestling was both Dad's way of playing with us, and his way of getting his back scratched. My sisters and I sat down next to him on the linoleum floor, pulling our dresses tightly between our legs. One by one, Dad tickled each of us until we could laugh no more. He grabbed our legs and twisted them around his legs, making it impossible to move or escape from him. I didn't like this game; it gave me a feeling of being shackled in a place I didn't want to be. But this was his game, and when he was high, we were expected to play. When he tired of wrestling, he turned over on his belly, and each one of us took turns scratching his back. His body flattened to the floor until he overcame his drunken stupor.

When Dad drank, I'd become crazed with fear that he would hurt Mom. His drinking often led to arguments between them. He would accuse her of having affairs, and my mother would in turn accuse Dad of seeing his old girlfriends in town. Whatever happened between them when they were alone, we didn't know; we just witnessed the consequences of their actions toward each other. But I learned early that almost always, Dad's drinking led to violence toward my mother.

One day, my parents left us children home alone. They didn't say where they were going, or when they would be back. I didn't mind when they left the house; it was quieter, and the intensity of the chaos lessened. With their absence came predictability, certain peacefulness, and a sense of order and calm throughout the house. There was no fighting. Sometimes I even wished they would stay away longer.

Outdoors, the rain subsided immediately after my parents left the house. I rummaged through the garden for vegetables, and fruit. I picked the potatoes, carrots, grapes, and peaches from our property. I washed them and sliced them to share with my brothers and sisters. With something in our bellies, I laid my brothers down for a nap. I put on an apron, and I cleaned and organized the house. I picked up dirty clothes from the floor, and I scrubbed the stained floors with a mop. When the house was clean and organized, the air felt cooler to my body.

I picked up the laundry basket with both hands. I started to go down to the dreaded basement, but then I then paused. I disliked dark and dampened places. But we needed clean clothes. I stumbled in the dark until I found the light switch. I picked up the laundry again, and I methodically took one step at a time down the shaky wooden stairs. There wasn't enough detergent for two loads, so I threw the dark and the light clothes together. I turned the machine on and went upstairs.

Several minutes later, my mom came running into the house. She was crying. She asked me to hide her upstairs in my armoire. She said Daddy would be home soon, and she was frightened. There was a sense of urgency in her tone. Something had happened between them.

I followed mom, my feet clamoring quickly up the stairway behind her. She held her pregnant belly tight in her arms. She ran to my room, she swung the armoire door open, and crawled in behind the clothes.

Fortunately, her thin body fit neatly inside. I closed the door and secured the handle in place.

"Please don't tell Daddy where I am." She whispered. "Tell the other kids not to tell."

I ran downstairs to be with my siblings, not knowing what to expect from my father when he returned home. A few minutes later, Dad arrived and swung the screen door back hard, slamming it against the exterior house wall. He was drunk again. He bent down on the floor where I was playing with Lynn.

"Have you seen mom?" he shouted in anger, as he came within a foot of my face.

We were always afraid of Dad. Mom seldom disciplined us back then; that job was left for him. Even when my parents were getting along, Mom would threaten us with Dad's reprimand as a punishment: "When your dad gets home, you are going to get it," she would say. My stomach would tense, and my nerves would tingle on edge; I could never guess how severe the punishment would be. If one sibling had been out of line, Dad would line us all up in a row, and we all would get the leather strap. But it was the waiting all day until he returned home that felt the worst. The worry lasted all day; the strapping was over in a few seconds.

The fear was the same now. I sat on the floor pretending not to notice him. I didn't want to lie; that's what I had learned in church: Do not lie. Towering over me, he bent closer towards my face, his breath swollen with alcohol. His tobacco-stained teeth glared in the light from the door; his incisors twisted at an angle from his other teeth.

"Where's your mom?" He kneeled down next to me, his face even closer to mine, and he belched loudly. His breath stunk of beer mingled with tobacco. A combination of odors always followed him. He slammed his fist on the floor.

My sisters' and brothers' faces became pasty and drawn. Roland started to cry, confused by what was happening. Lynn gave out a high-pitched wail.

"Where's your mom?" he screamed again.

"I don't know, Daddy." Lowering my head, I began to cry. Then all my brothers and sisters began to cry. Lynn and Roland came toward me. I folded my arms around them, and I turned my back to him.

"Damn you!" he cursed.

He jerked away from me. His shirt stuck to his back with sweat, and two wet rings extended from his armpits. He looked the house over, running from their bedroom back to the kitchen. He ran to the door of the stairs, wildly swinging the door open. We listened to his intense footsteps pounding up the stairs to my bedroom. There was a slight pause. A dead silence. My body trembled at the thought of the situation escalating further into violence. My heart beat louder, for I knew what would happen if he found her. *What did she do to deserve this?*

Then, the floor creaked loudly as he returned to the top of the stairs. Dad's feet pounded rapidly down the stairs. He wildly pushed the door open to the kitchen. *He didn't find her!* For a moment my breath found its rhythm.

Dad walked rapidly towards me. He paused, his eyes darting at me. I swallowed hard, and exhaling loudly, I covered my lips with both hands. His eyes looked toward the front door, and then he walked past me to the porch and slammed the screen door. He jumped into the black dusty Studebaker, and his tires squealed as he sped away.

A few minutes later, Mom tiptoed downstairs, and slowly opened the stairwell door. She was visibly shaken. My brothers and sisters ran over to her, and together we circled our arms around her. She ran to the front window, and when she saw that his car was gone, she gave a sigh of relief and walked to her bedroom. She pulled out her suitcase, and she packed her nightgown and a few items. She put out her arms and hugged us goodbye, and she left us home alone. I watched her walk down the street, her suitcase in hand and her shoulders hung low, until her body disappeared in the background.

The fog of chaos overtook me. My nerves frayed. The temperature in the house had risen. It was always hot after the fighting. I looked around the house, and again it was in disarray. My brothers' toys were scattered on the floor. Lynn's dirty diaper had fallen off, and he was urinating on the linoleum. The kitchen cabinets hung open, exposing bare shelves without food. I had to find something to feed my brothers and sisters. I had to organize the house. But instead, I collapsed on the sofa, aching for a normal and peaceful family.

A few days later, Mom returned, but my father's constant abuse was taking its toll on her spirit. She became even more withdrawn and distant, rarely attending to the needs of my young brothers. Her luminosity dimmed: She looked duller, paler, her eyes vacant. She no longer wore Hawaiian flowers in her hair, and she seldom asked my sisters and me to dance the hula anymore. Even the floral drapery across her bedroom door was fading. With no family in Indiana, no support system, and six children --- plus another one on the way --- she was a prisoner in her own home.

Most mornings, my mother stayed in bed. It was up to us to get ourselves ready for school. Usually, we went to school hungry and wearing dirty clothes. We had no choice. I was embarrassed to see the other students in their clean and pressed clothes. Once, a new student commented that I smelled bad. She hurt my feelings, but she couldn't possibly understand the neglect my brothers, sisters, and I endured.

Spring had arrived early, and with it, warmer weather. When we were too much trouble for my mother, she'd send us scattering through the screen door to the outside, and then she would lock the door to the house and would not unlock it until early evening. We ran barefoot in the yard and played tag with the neighbor kids. Without much in the way of toys, we played creatively: We collected colorful stones, found bright maple leaves and pressed them into books, and rode our bicycles—there were plenty around because of Dad's bicycle shop.

My siblings and I went about our play with hunger in our bellies; we fended for ourselves, scavenging food in the yard. Soon, I became adept at climbing trees as a way to get something to eat. My bare feet arched around the trunk of the tree, and my two hands pulled my body upward. I would hold onto a branch to steady my body with one hand, and I'd gather my skirt, creating a pocket for the fruit, with the other. While I was up in the trees, I would get close to the birds. I'd examine the myriad colors on their feathered bodies, and I'd peek into the robins' nests to admire their tiny turquoise eggs. When I'd filled my skirt full of fruit, I would descend the tree to the tiny hungry hands of my siblings. My brothers and sisters ravaged the fruit. The day looked better when our bellies were full.

Dad was working in his bike shop. I noticed for the first time that a window in his shop was broken—a crack ran through it. The shop was old, like the rest of the house. It was unkempt, with bike parts strewn about and grease stains on the linoleum. Dad must have received a couple orders for new bikes; He busied himself on the floor assembling a couple of bike frames. Dad's bikes were shiny and new, because the pieces came right off the assembly line. He didn't charge as much as a retail bike shop. On occasion, his customers provided food in exchange for a bike.

In the early evening, Dad finished his work and came into the house for dinner. Mom had fried up some trout that Dad had caught early that morning. He went into the kitchen and washed his hands beside Mom at the sink. Suddenly, an argument ensued. By their tone, I guessed the argument was a continuation of an argument from earlier in the day. They kept the matter secret; it wasn't to be shared with anyone else.

Mom called us to supper, and my brothers and sisters gathered at the table. Dad placed white bread in the middle of the table in case one of us choked on a fish bone. He went back to the refrigerator and opened a can of beer. During the meal, my mother was quiet, and she stared down at the table as she ate, and she shifted her body tensely throughout the meal. Dad finished his first beer and went back for another. When we finished supper I helped Mom clear the table and wash the dishes. She went to her bedroom still visibly upset by their argument.

Dad went out the side door to the concrete porch, drinking his third beer. I pushed the screen door open and sat beside him. I thought maybe I could calm things down between the two of them. Dad's breath reeked of beer, and his words were hard to understand. I realized he'd probably begun drinking much earlier, while he was in his shop. He said he wanted to talk to me.

"Sholo!"

I pretended not to hear.

"Sholo!" Dad repeated again.

I hated talking to him when he was in a drunken stupor because he tended to slur his words, and he would bore me to death. I shifted on the step and moved away from him without him noticing. After a few moments, I started to feel anxious about sitting next to him.

"Sholo," he started in a whisper, "I've been wanting to tell you this for a very long time."

He drew out his words, keeping his voice quiet and being careful that my mother didn't overhear our conversation. He looked behind him to see if Mom was standing there. By now he had drank two more cans of beer. He leaned forward, then backward, his head nodding in all directions as if it wasn't connected to his neck.

"What, Daddy?" I said with some curiosity, but mostly out of boredom.

He came close to my ear. "You are not my daughter!"

Thinking that he forgot who was sitting next to him, I said, "Daddy, this is Shirlee sitting next to you." I braced his upper body with my arms to try to keep him from falling backwards.

"No, Sholo. You ain't my—" His eyes were swollen, and he had tears in his eyes.

By now he had my attention, but I knew he was drunk. He always said stupid things when he was drunk.

"Daddy, what do you mean?" My voice cracked.

Dad weaved forward and backward.

"Your Mother told me the day you were born in Grandma's house here in Albion, that I was not your daddy. It hurt me real bad to know that. But I love you, and I kept you because I loved your mother. I know your mother never wanted me to tell you this, but it's the God's truth." His eyes shifted back in his head, and his head fell forward with a snap. My eyes welled up, and tears streamed down my face. *Why is he telling me this now? Why is he hurting me like this? Is it to hurt my mother? Is he trying to confuse me? He's drunk . . . it must not be true.*

Mom must have overheard what he had said because she rushed in quickly from behind us and yelled through the screen door, "You bastard! I told you to never tell!" She turned on her heel and disappeared.

I was rooted to the spot next to Dad, trying to make sense of what I had just heard. Meanwhile, Mom came back dressed up to go out on the town. She wore her shiny pearl necklace and a satin turquoise dress, her full bosom descending onto her pregnant belly. She grabbed her purse, and then approached the front door to leave.

"I'm leaving," Mom announced through the screen door.

Dad struggled to get up off the porch and walked quickly into the living room, stumbling over the frayed linoleum edge. He caught my mother just as she was walking out the front door.

"You ain't going nowhere, Bitch!" Dad yelled at her.

My mother quickly reached for the door handle, turned the knob hard and fast, and opened the door.

"You bitch!" He lunged toward her and slammed his hand on her arm, and he pushed her hard against the wall. My mother pulled her arm away from him and recoiled.

She screamed, "Don't touch me! Get away from me!" She held her belly with her arms.

My father lunged again at her, harder, with both hands. He grabbed her pretty necklace and tore it off her neck, and the white pearls scattered onto the floor.

With his right fist clenched, he pummeled her in the head and neck.

"Stop hurting me! The baby . . ."

He reached his hand again toward her neck, and he ripped her satin dress straight down the bodice. My mother dropped to the floor like a limp rag. She was silent; she had resigned. My mother's power seemed to be in her glamour, but against my father and his rage, she was powerless.

The sun shone brightly on the landscape. The sky was painted blue except for a few cirrus clouds overhead. The flowers were in full bloom; the daffodils bent their stems and danced to a gentle breeze. With such a beautiful day ahead, my parents had plans without us. So we were going to spend the weekend with Grandma.

In their excitement to see Grandma, my brothers and sisters piled into the back seat of my parents' Studebaker and fought for a seat next to the window. In the back seat, I held Lynn in my arms as I huddled close to my sisters. Roger and Roland squeezed into the front seat between my dad and my pregnant mother.

We drove to the other side of town, and the car pulled up in front of Grandma's brown-shingled house. A large window and door overlooked the porch addition to a grassy yard that lead to the edge of the railroad track. Grandma's lawn was lush green, the blades of grass freshly mowed, and ended at the large bushes next to the house. Her vegetable garden had recently been tilled and furrowed, her seeds sown in the ground waiting for growth and harvest. The green leaves were beginning to sprout, raising their heads to a welcoming sky.

Dad laid heavily on the horn to let Grandma know we had arrived. My brothers and sisters jumped out of the car and ran toward Grandma's front door. I followed behind, carrying Lynn in my arms. Hurriedly, my parents sped off down the street, kicking up dust behind the car, leaving their cares behind.

We entered the enclosed front porch through the screen door. Grandma was sitting at her Singer sewing machine. She bent her neck forward and flexed her feet as she worked the black iron pedal. She moved the cotton fabric forward with her fingertips toward the back side of the machine, and layers of fabric fell, creating mounds of folds in her lap.

Grandma was always busy making something from hand. She made all her own clothes except her long silk panties and slip. She repeatedly used the same patterns to make her printed dresses. Her slightly full, A-shaped dresses buttoned tightly to her neck and were always made with tiny floral patterns dotted in subtle pastel colors. Her matching fabric belt held tight to her wide waist with a round clear plastic fastener, and her sleeves always ran below her elbows. Her dresses were always hemmed at the ankle, so as not to expose too much skin.

Along with her sewing, Grandma made patched quilts for her neighbors in town. She collected bundles of colorful cloths for her quilts, which varied in size, length, and texture. It was her only income besides cleaning people's houses, or occasionally babysitting other parishioners' children. After Grandpa died, these sales transactions provided her the sustenance she needed to survive.

After finishing her seam run, the sewing needle came to a stop. Grandma looked up with a large grin on her face. She stood up, letting the fabric fall out of her lap and onto the floor. Her head tilted up in laughter, she turned toward us with arms stretched wide, and she embraced each one of us.

"Praise the Lord; I've been waiting for you. Let's go have something to eat," Grandma said, clapping her hands together.

Dwarfed at four foot ten, her pear-shaped body lumbered toward the kitchen in the only pair of shoes she owned—black, not too shiny, wide-heeled to steady her. Grandma went into her kitchen and opened her wooden cabinet. Her shelves contained a few canned good items that had been harvested from her vegetable garden. She removed from the cupboard two glass Kerr jars, one filled with homemade applesauce and the other of green beans.

She placed a plate on the table for each of my brothers and sisters, and she reverently scooped out a meager portion of each food and gingerly placed it on each plate. Her calloused dry hand reached for a box of crackers, and she placed one on each plate. As we gathered around the table, she bowed her head in prayer and gave thanks for our abundance. At this moment there was more than food shared at this table. Grandma's life was filled with the riches of grandchildren.

After dinner, there were plenty of hands to clean up the table and dishes. With the table wiped off, Grandma replaced the embroidered tablecloth back on top. I walked toward the open window, and a slight breeze cooled my skin. Clouds formed above us, and patters of rain began to fall.

"Grandma, why does it rain?" I asked.

"God's shedding tears."

"Why?"

"He's cleansing evil from the world."

Grandma asked if we would like to join her in the living room after she finished her work in the kitchen. She wanted to read bible stories to us. She was a Sunday school teacher. We felt luckier than the other children in her Sunday school class because we got to hear more of Grandma's bible stories at home. We were all ears.

Grandma's living room had green flowered wallpaper from a past era that tastefully accented the walls. It was simply furnished: A green couch sat along one wall, and along the other sat a dark oak and glass china cabinet with a side desk attached, a family heirloom. But my favorite piece of furniture was her high-back Hoosier rocking chair with a rose flowered seat cushion fashioned by Grandma. The rocker was a hand-crafted piece of solid oak with smooth, comfortable armrests and strong round spindles that anchored to the wooden seat and attached to a wide slat at the top.

Grandma crossed the room, sat down in her comfortable rocker, and invited me to sit on her lap. The width of her lap felt generous and soft as she wrapped her ample arms around me. She pulled me closer to her bosom. My brothers and sisters joined us in the living room, and they formed a circle at the foot of her rocking chair. Their chins rose up, and they completely focused on Grandma. It was story time.

Grandma began to tell stories with precise detail, painting a picture of the characters, their colorful garments and headdresses, and places faraway. Repeating many of the parables in the bible, she always had a moral to her story. She always had our attention.

Then, suddenly, the china cabinet began vibrating. The rattling picked up its intensity as the roar of the oncoming train neared her house. Roland raised both hands and pressed them tightly against his ears to block out the thunderous sound. All conversations and storytelling ceased as the train approached the house. The engineer sounded the whistle.

The conductors knew Grandma's house well. For the last few years, the engineers would anticipate us standing by the track, and they would throw candy pieces, which landed several feet from our shoes. Sometimes the train would pull into the station a few hundred feet from grandma's house. We would watch passengers loading and unloading, going to or from places like Chicago. People traveling to places I could only wonder about.

I jumped down from Grandma's lap and scrambled outside, stopping several feet from the railroad track. My brothers and sisters trailed behind me, their tiny feet, one in front of the other, racing to feel the power of the train. In the near distance, we could see the black engine approaching, the conductor's blue uniform shimmering in the daylight and his arm resting on the window ledge. As the train neared Grandma's house, the sounds and rhythms intensified on the track. After a while, the train made its way along, and the caboose finally made its appearance. The engine could be heard chugging into the distance, and the train's whistle sounded as it left us.

After the commotion settled down, we ran back into the house. I sat down on Grandma's lap again. She continued her storytelling. Through her gentle nature, she taught me about love, laughter, and forgiveness. Grandma was selfless, kind, and present in a way that my mother could never be. She was my anchor in a sea of torrential storms.

After storytelling, Grandma settled back in the chair, her right foot extended slightly forward, and she began rocking. The rocking chair exuded a slight rhythmic creak while it sawed back and forth. I embraced the warmth of her body close to me and the feeling of safety in her arms. We melted together in quiet solitude.

Grandma whispered in my ear, "You look tired. Are you feeling alright?" I kept my voice at a whisper, so that the others would not overhear. "I didn't sleep well last night, Grandma. There were noises downstairs that kept me up. Daddy came home late, and there was arguing."

Grandma patted my knee gently and rocked me until I fell asleep.

Grandma had once told me about her life as a young girl. She was born in Indiana in the late 1800's. Back then, many poor girls were farmed out by their own parents to help pay bills, providing labor to the townspeople. At the age of twelve, Grandma left home to clean other people's homes, launder, babysit, tend to gardens, and can fruits and vegetables. She would not be paid for her services. Money was sent home to her parents, who gave her very little pay. She was no different than an indentured servant. Often, her employers would treat her unkindly, using harsh words or demanding a heavy workload for someone beyond her years.

After Grandma married Grandpa, they set up a household in Albion. Grandpa was of German stock, was slightly built, and seemed old and bent for his age. He performed hard labor in factories when he could get work. Grandma made rugs and quilts by hand and sold them to make ends meet. They bought a home in town and lived next to the railroad tracks. Grandma bore seven children, of which only four babies survived. She remembered fondly her lost babies of many years ago. Knowing they were in heaven was her only solace. She looked forward to joining them one day.

Later, I learned that Grandpa's childhood was also harsh. His father had abandoned him and his mother on the farm when he was a young boy. Grandpa was forced into hard labor; he had to help his mother on the farm. Grandma spoke of how overworked he was at such a young age and of how he was mistreated by his mother. Every day, he wore the same charcoal grey pants with suspenders and a dark shirt. Grandpa died when I was around seven years old. Hardship may have contributed to his early death, which left Grandma alone and penniless. Though Grandma never spoke to me about how Grandfather died, the experience must have brought her closer to her faith.

Grandma's puritanical beliefs were affirmed in her faith and her family, and she passed her beliefs on to my dad and his three siblings. Yet, at the early age of eleven, my father began rebelling against the strict church doctrines. He would hide behind the shed in Grandma's backyard and smoke cigarettes. By fifteen, he was hanging out with the town's least desirable crowd, with whom he would sample hard liquor. He seemed unmanageable at such an early age. Many people never understood how my unruly dad could be the way he was with such a kind and religious mother.

At the end of the weekend, Mom and Dad came to pick us up from Grandma's. Tears pressed against the back of my eyes as I hugged Grandma goodbye. I did not want to leave. We drove back across town, and as we approached the house, my stomach felt tense, and all the good feelings I had from the weekend vaporized into the moist air. Without a word, I got out of the car, entered the house, and I rushed upstairs to my bedroom.

In my bedroom, a river of light bent its way through the branches of the maple tree and scattered shapes across my bed. As I slowly undressed, I could feel the starch from my Sunday dress against my face. I laid the dress on the bed, smoothing my hand against the embroidered train stitched neatly across the front. Trains reminded me of Grandma, and a good feeling came over me.

I realized the window was closed, so I walked toward the sill and raised it to vent the bedroom. The mother sparrow awakened in her nest, and she shrieked. A red cardinal had landed on a branch near her nest. The birds fluttered their feathers, and a squabble ensued over territorial rights. Their wings flapped, their breasts filled up, and the mother sparrow released a deafening shrill. Then the red cardinal flew away. There was a moment of calm.

Mom was very close to having her seventh baby. Her belly extended and her breasts protruded, preparing to give sustenance. She sat in the kitchen chair with her arms lowered, her hands wrapped tightly around the bottom of her belly, and her head cocked back in pain. In this condition, baby cries were ignored, children went hungry, and laundry piled up even more than usual.

One Saturday morning, I awakened to the sounds of birds fluttering outside my window. I lay in bed and listened to their melodious sounds. I stepped to the window, kneeled down, and put my elbows on the sill. It was a perfect landing spot for many birds. Some of the colorful birds flitted from limb to limb, while others settled in on the branches.

Moving back toward my bed, I decided to put on a change of clothes. I pulled open the drawer under my bed. I lifted a cotton skirt and a wrinkled short sleeve blouse from the pile of loose clothing, I slipped the blouse over my head and stepped into the band of the skirt and pulled it to my waist. Soon, the silence was interrupted again by more sounds outside the bedroom window. It was difficult to know what direction the voices were coming from. But the noise grew louder and more intense.

My sisters were asleep in their bed. We had stayed up late talking, and I was afraid they might be awakened by the noise. I moved toward the open window to close out the noise. I could hear the voices outside—they were growing louder. I stopped briefly to listen to where the sounds were coming from. A faint rustling sound persisted from my parent's bedroom window. The muscles in my body tightened. My parents were arguing. My dad's voice grew louder. My mother was shouting back.

I hurried toward the stairwell, and in my haste, my right foot slipped out from under me. I grasped the handrail attached to the wall.

At the bottom of the stairway, I opened the door quietly and slowed my pace. I tiptoed toward my parent's bedroom, carefully staying to the left of the gap in the drapery, outside their line of vision.

As I neared my parent's bedroom, I heard a rumble outside through the open front door. The air crackled with tension. The thunderous sky grew louder. Then rain pounded the concrete porch. A flash of lightning burst outside the living room windows. I locked the front door. Above the boom of thunder, I heard my mother's voice elevating. I peeked cautiously through the gap, maneuvering my body so I wouldn't be seen. I couldn't believe what I saw. I moved closer to the opening, I bent forward, and I separated the drapes a little more with my hand. I could see my parents on the bed. My father was naked, and my mother's arms and hands were extended toward him. Swiftly, Dad moved backward in anger, rolling away from my mother and landing on his back. My mother's hair was disheveled, and her arms were outstretched toward him, pushing him

27

away, begging him to stay off her. His head dropped back on his pillow, one leg rested on the mattress, and his private parts were extended. He steadied himself for a moment, and he repositioned himself on the bed, displaying more of his enhanced intimate parts. Suddenly, he retracted one leg, ready to strike like a rabid snake. He swung his leg forward quickly and kicked my pregnant mother in the stomach.

My mother let out a blood-curdling scream as she covered her belly. A second kick hammered the right side of her stomach, and my mother was forced off the edge of the bed, her body landing on the hardwood floor below. Her screams echoed throughout the house.

The thunder sounded like ocean waves magnified between the walls of our home, roaring and slamming loudly overhead. For a second, the house shook violently. A burst of heavy rain hit the rooftop. Then, Mom softened into submission. Her screams tempered. She was in shock and unable to express the sheer pain she felt. She lay on the floor, motionless. My legs turned to jelly. I felt paralyzed, but I wanted to rush to her side and help her. I didn't know what to do. We had learned to stay out of my father's way when he was angry. When my parents fought, Dad wouldn't allow us near my mother, whom I desperately wanted to protect.

My mother lay still on the floor for a few minutes. Then she began to speak, her moans rolling like a slow wind in a hurricane. Her face was slick with tears.

"Why?" she asked. "Why?"

Dad sat down on the floor next to Mom and consoled her, but he was unrepentant. He said that it wouldn't have happened if she hadn't refused him. He always blamed her. He bent down and tried to kiss her, and he told her he loved her. She reached out her limp hand to him, shedding more tears. He took this as reconciliation.

I dropped to the floor, my hands cupped over my face, my tears dampening my nightgown. "Daddy didn't mean to hurt Mommy! Daddy didn't mean to hurt Mommy!" I whispered the mantra to myself.

I quickly gained my composure and ran into the kitchen, realizing that I had left the door to the stairs open. My brothers and sisters had heard the sounds and come running downstairs. They were frightened; they had heard my mother's screams. Some of them were too small to understand, but they knew something dramatic had happened.

"Shurry, Shurry, can we play?" Roland handed me a tiny ball.

I herded the children back up the narrow flight of stairs, away from the aftermath. The world stopped around me. I tried to understand the ways in which evil overwhelms God's commands. I had witnessed a horrific act, a life-changing moment.

After half an hour, Dad realized Mom wasn't getting better. She was in her ninth month of pregnancy, and her moaning persisted. He was scared. It was time to take her to a doctor. Maybe he felt that since they had reconciled, she wouldn't tell the doctor what had actually happened. Maybe he believed the police wouldn't be called in.

Mom was still in excruciating pain. Dad bent over her and picked her up off the floor. He laid her on the bed, set her arms at her side, and lowered her nightgown over her legs. She moved her head slowly from one side to the other, stretching her neck as if waking up after a long sleep. He ran outside to the alley and opened the back door to the black Studebaker. He returned quickly and picked Mom up off the bed. He walked her to the side door, kicked open the screen, and laid her into the back seat of the waiting car.

"Sholo! Get in the backseat with mom!" he ordered. I scurried into the backseat next to her. Then he drove up the hill toward the town clinic.

The Albion Clinic was about five minutes away. Dad knew that she needed to be seen right away. As he drove, sweat beaded on his forehead, his hands shook, and he pressed down on the gas pedal. Would he get in trouble with the law?

At the medical clinic, Dad parked in the back parking lot, got Mom out of the car, and slammed through the clinic door. I followed behind.

"My wife needs to see the doctor right away! She hurt herself," Dad yelled at the nurse.

They put Mom on a gurney and took her through the back door of the clinic. The nurse placed a white sheet over her legs. The doctor greeted her along with the exam room nurse.

"Hello, Mrs. Hathaway, you look in pain," he said with some concern. "Are you ready to deliver so soon?"

The doctor noticed bruises on her arm. He nodded to the nurse as she reentered the room.

"Mr. Hathaway, would you wait in the reception room? I will get back to you later."

The nurse, dressed in her starched white cap and uniform that reached to her mid calf, motioned my father and me toward the waiting room. Then she turned to my mother and rolled her into the procedure room. Later, I learned that after the doctor had closed the door, he had stepped closer to her side and touched Mom's leg gently, so as not to alarm her.

"Mrs. Hathaway, tell me what happened."

"I fell off the bed." She turned her head away.

"Now, now," the doctor soothed. "You must tell me the truth."

After a heavy silence, Mom closed her eyes, and she reached her right hand toward her belly.

"If I tell you the truth," she said in a low voice, "he will hurt me again." She closed her eyes, but the tears escaped anyway.

The doctor slowly examined her along her belly. He noticed the red and blue swelling on her right side. He carefully placed her legs in the stirrups of the exam table, examining her vagina.

"You are going to a hospital right away, and you will stay there for a few days of observation."

Soon after, my baby brother Dallas was born.

A week later, Mom returned from the hospital. Dad had disappeared shortly after Mom went into the hospital, so he wasn't there to celebrate this blessed event. A friend brought Mom home from the hospital. She parked her old Ford Coupe along the alleyway and opened the passenger side door and helped Mom out of the car. She took Baby Dallas from Mom's arms as Mom stood up, and she then carefully handed the baby back to her.

My sisters and brothers met Mom at the door and begged to see our new brother. Mom removed the blue flannel blanket from the baby's face. As she looked down at the reddish face, tears formed in her eyes. I wondered why Mom was crying at such a happy occasion. She pressed the rest of the blanket around his tiny body form and bent her knees slightly down toward us, revealing a baby with tightly closed eyes and black hair.

"This is your new baby brother, Dallas," she announced.

Mom limped to her bedroom, with her friend holding her arm. She walked to the white bassinet next to her bed and carefully laid Dallas down. After Mom was settled in her bed, I covered her with a blanket and folded it neatly under her arms. Some color returned to her face. I went to the kitchen and made her a baloney sandwich with mayonnaise on white bread.

When I came back with the sandwich, my mother asked me to help her to the bathroom. She removed her robe and laid it on the bathtub, revealing her sheer nightgown. The bruises had darkened to a turquoise blue on the right side of her belly.

I returned to Mom's bedroom, leaned over the bassinette, bent my head over the edge, and studied Dallas closely. I touched his cheek softly with my finger. He made a face that looked like a grin, and his sweet baby happiness overtook me. His head was full of thick black hair, and his forehead was slightly flattened and misshapen. Dallas seemed thinner than most babies. His eyes were set wide apart, not close together, which looked strange to me. He looked up at me and then back up to the ceiling. His eye movements were slow, and his hands rested next to his face in tightly folded fists, as if he were protecting himself.

"He can't really see you yet," Mom said, coming up behind me.

I lowered a bottle of warm milk to his lips, and teased his mouth with the bottle nipple. He wouldn't take it. I moved the nipple gently over his lips to try to get him to latch on. Dallas began to suckle the nipple rhythmically. After a few minutes, his eyelids closed slowly, and he fell asleep. He was too young to use the blue and white rattle near his head. I removed it and placed it at the bottom of his crib. I bent over the bassinet and kissed his forehead.

There was no family celebration for Dallas's birth, like there had been for my other siblings. Dad wasn't around. We didn't see Grandma or our other relatives. It was a quiet event. I was sad that no one made a fuss over my new brother. Maybe because so many babies had been delivered in our family, the excitement of newborns had worn off.

The family didn't talk about my father's absence. If the church members knew that he was gone, they never uttered a word to me. His whereabouts was a secret that Mom kept from the children. Several weeks passed, and my father still did not come home. We had to make do with little food in the house. In our worsened poverty, both money and food became scarcer. My belly would stir with raw emptiness; it screeched inside with pain. At least when Dad was around he would occasionally go fishing or hunting and bring home something to eat.

Finally, I broke the silence surrounding his absence. "Mommy, where's Daddy?" I asked.

"He's not going to be with us for a long while," she answered.

Later that day, while I was playing on the sidewalk, the mailman handed me a letter. The envelope was thin, and I didn't recognize the return address. It was a letter from Daddy. He wrote that he couldn't get away to see us. He didn't say when he was coming home. He didn't say where he was, but he said he was going to be all right, and that he had to take care of some matters. He said he loved us, and that he missed wrestling on the floor with us. He said to say hello to Grandma for him. I folded the letter and placed it back in the envelope, and I wondered when we would see our dad again.

Fifth grade had started, and I was well into the school year. I looked forward to school. It was a respite from the problems at home. Learning was a distraction from my chaotic home life. School also meant that I would get a decent lunch provided by a government program. The predictability and orderliness of class calmed me. The excitement of seeing my friends and the newness of textbooks and fresh school supplies inspired me.

Each day, I looked forward to my classes and curiously opened each textbook, studying the print and pictures and smelling the newness of the leather covers. Often, I would slide my hand down each page, pressing it firmly as I revered the knowledge written in the words. I loved the scent of erasers and sharpened pencils, which helped me to win approval from my teachers because I endlessly practiced my cursive writing. The pictures in the geography books piqued my interest and took my imagination to interesting and peaceful places. History books reminded me that there must be a better world out there, one different from my own.

As I looked at the textbooks' photos of the past, I became curious about how other people lived their lives. I carefully studied battles and pioneer life; I examined the clothes people wore and the architecture of their buildings and interior designs. I hoped my education would make a difference in my future.

I was looking forward to open house that evening, when the teachers presented their students' progress, and the best schoolwork was displayed for parents' review. Mom and Dad had missed open house for the last three years. Dad was still gone somewhere, but I was hopeful this year that Mom would make it.

After school let out, parents arrived in droves, parking their cars wherever they could find a spot. Aunts and uncles and grandparents came to celebrate the achievements of each student. At first, everyone congregated in the gymnasium. The principal stepped up to the podium to address the students and parents. As he talked, the fluorescent ceiling light shined brightly on his bald head. He spoke of the school's vision, the teachers' efforts to inspire students, and the importance of the parents' participation. After the principal's speech, the students and parents applauded and returned to their respective classrooms.

I ran to the front entrance doors of the school to find my mom. She had promised she would come. She wasn't at the front of the school; I thought maybe she was somewhere in the audience, and I had missed her. I walked to my classroom, hoping she had gone straight there.

Parents filed into the classroom. Our teacher came in and surprised us by putting up inspirational quotes on the walls and by using colorful graphics to highlight our work. The folders on our desks were filled with our tests from various subjects. The walls exhibited the best work of the class, displaying art projects and geography tests tacked to large bulletin boards. A couple of my projects were on the wall. My cursive writing was highlighted behind the teacher as an example of the best writing in the class.

Many students proudly led their parents to their desks to share more of their classroom successes. There was excitement in the room as doting parents hovered over their children's desks, leafing through the progress folders and reviewing their work. Fathers patted their sons on the back for jobs well done. Mothers crowed over the creative work of their daughters.

I sat down at my desk and leafed through my special project folder pretending that my parents were standing above me, sharing in my successes. Occasionally, I would turn around to see if Mom had entered the room. I then distracted myself by turning to my progress notebook, hoping she would walk through the classroom door, pat me on the back, and praise me for a job well done. Suddenly, the space around me felt empty, and I felt ashamed that my parents weren't there for me. I felt alone.

After an hour, the crowd thinned out. Parents and students left the classroom. I looked at the door one more time, hoping to see my mom. But she never arrived. It was getting late. With my shoulders hunched, I picked up my folder so I wouldn't be noticed while leaving. I ran out the school door toward home, passing the town park where parents were playing with their children. The sky was a bright, fierce blue swept with pastels, as if God had taken his paintbrush and dragged it across the horizon just to brighten my day.

By the time winter arrived, Dad still hadn't come back. A few inches of snow had fallen, and all of Indiana was experiencing sub-freezing temperatures. The upstairs bedrooms were bitter cold. During the night, we could hear the wind through the windows. If the wind hit just right, snow flurries would fan onto our beds through the gaps between the walls and the windows, chilling us to the bone. I stayed in bed, securing the blanket around my legs and back. We had only a few blankets among us to keep warm. Sometimes my sisters and brothers and I would pile into the same bed, pulling our curled bodies together in warmth.

In the past, if my parents were getting along, Dad would wake up in the middle of the night to shovel coal into the iron furnace to keep the fire lit, and he would stoke it until the house warmed.

It was early morning, and my sisters and brothers were shivering from the cold. The fire in the furnace had died out. I walked downstairs to Mom's bedroom. She was asleep in her bed. I pulled the blankets back from her face.

"Mommy, it's cold upstairs."

Mom was in a deep sleep, and I couldn't wake her. These days, she sometimes stayed out late at night and came home early in the morning.

I pulled her blanket back further, exposing her back to frigid chill in the air. She sat up.

"Shirlee, go down in the basement and put coals on the fire," she snapped, and she lay back down and covered herself with her warm blankets.

Reluctantly, I walked toward the cellar door. I dreaded the trip to the basement. I opened the wood-slat door, and I reached up to turn the basement light on. Instantly, my hand felt a rill of electricity, which rushed up my elbow. My arm jolted back to my chest. I had touched the metal where the plastic switch had been missing for several years.

"I hate this switch!" I screamed at the top of my voice. Stunned from the utter shock of electricity surging up my arm, I stood there, rubbing my hands together to soothe the painful numbness in my arm. I could hear Mom laughing hysterically in her bedroom. In recent months, she not only seemed unable to sympathize with other people's pain, but also to take pleasure in it.

I stood on my tiptoes and twisted the light bulb. The dim light was just enough to see by, and I slowly stepped one foot at a time down the shaky wooden stairs into the basement. The darkness frightened me. The stairs to the basement were creaky and were not held together well. At the bottom of the stairs, the concrete basement smelled of damp mildew and mold. The coldness of the cellar chilled my body. But it had to be done: it was up to me to warm the house.

The basement was swept clean except around the coal bin where black coals were piled high. The black iron furnace was large and imposing. I circled around to the front door of the furnace. I looked through the small open vent in the door. Golden embers were scattered throughout and were dying down. I opened the furnace door and walked over to the coal bin a few feet away. With both hands, I bent over to gather up a couple pieces of the shiny black coal. A black widow spider moved slowly away from me, its red hourglass mark signaling danger. Suddenly, the spider crawled rapidly in my direction. I stepped back hurriedly and picked up a large piece of coal and hurled it in the spider's direction. My aim was off, and she slipped back into the mound of coal.

My sense of duty trumped my fear. I couldn't let her get away; she was dangerous. I grabbed the shovel nearby and quickly moved the coal aside, and her body moved again in my direction. With the tip of the shovel, I hit her with great force, splattering a red mosaic on the basement floor that contrasted with the black powdery dust.

I thought of how many times my brothers and sisters came down to the coal bin to play just after the delivery man shoveled coal through the open door to our basement. We would climb the heaping mound, blackening our bodies with chunks of coal, oblivious to the dangerous poison lurking among the coals. Now, I dreaded coming down here even more.

With my hands shaking, I leaned over and grabbed a few more chunks of coal on the opposite side of the bin. My body trembled from the damp cold as I quickly ran to the furnace door and hurled the coal onto the last of the embers and slammed the iron door closed. I peered through the vent on the furnace door, waiting for the fire to blaze, stomping my feet rhythmically up and down to keep warm. A furious blast of wind swept through the opening of the coal bin, sending more shivers up my spine. Within a few minutes, the flames began to well up, and I felt the swell of the heat. The furnace was roaring.

Outside the cellar door, daylight shone on the thermometer, it indicated the temperature was below freezing. I rushed up the steps to the kitchen. Mom was awake by now, and had finished giving my brothers a sponge bath. After she wrapped a towel around them, she tightened the robe around her waist, and then she sat on a chair next to the furnace grate. My brothers and sisters huddled around the iron grate, their arms wrapped tightly around their thin bodies, soaking in the warmth of the furnace air.

The roaring furnace was giving off an enormous blast of heat. Roland moved closer to the heat, but he fell backward onto the hot iron grate and accidentally pushed Lynn onto the grate with him. They both landed on their bare bottoms and gave out high-pitched screams. The iron grate felt like a branding iron to their butts. Their screams escalated. They were unable to get up quickly, and Lynn fell back down again with another scream.

I lunged across the kitchen floor toward both of my brothers. I grabbed Lynn and threw him away from the scorching grate, then swung fast towards Roland and threw him off the other side of the grate, burning my back.

Mom just sat there on the chair, amused at our pain. At the sight of my brothers' bare bottoms, painfully marked in a red checkerboard pattern from the fierce heat, my mother gave out a hearty laugh.

"I guess that will teach you boys to stand up!" Mom scolded.

Their cries of pain were muffled by her laughter, and the red marks immediately turned to blisters on their bottoms. My brothers became chilled and began to shiver; but they were afraid to go near the grate for warmth, their pain was so excruciating. I grabbed a bath towel and carefully covered each one of them, avoiding their checkered bottoms.

Lynn crawled across the cold floor to my mother's feet and flung himself around her ankles, begging to be picked up. She looked down at him in disgust and kicked her leg out softly, pushing him away.

"Get off me, go play."

He whimpered and crawled away; he was too young to understand. For whatever reason, Mom ignored baby Lynn most of the time, giving him little attention. His curly blond hair and delicate features had no resemblance to Dad. He had always cried infrequently and demanded little. His emaciated body suffered alone in silence.

Lynn crawled over to me, touching his bottom, complaining that it hurt. I pulled the kitchen chair away from the dinette table and laid Lynn face down across my lap, stroking his head and warming his back and arms. With the arrival of a new baby, he had begun to cry more often, as there was less milk to soothe his belly, and less of his mother's love to take away his emotional pain.

Darkness fell, and my brothers and sisters went to bed early. I helped my brothers into their bed, tucking their blankets close to their bodies. I sat at the edge of the bed, watching their empty stomachs rise and fall as they fell into soft slumber, erasing the sounds of harsh voices from their ears. The night folded around us. We all fell silently asleep, our minds slipping away from our present lives.

The next night, I was awakened by the blustery winds outside. A draft of bitter cold air slipped through the window and permeated the whole of the room. I pulled my blanket tightly around my neck for warmth, but could still feel the draft from the window. I adjusted my blanket and curled into a fetal position, trying to protect my body from the cold. I fell back asleep, but I was awakened by Dallas's cries downstairs.

It seemed like Dallas had been crying for a long time. I wondered why my mother wasn't able to stop his crying. I had to check on him, but my body resisted the cold of the night. School would start in a few hours. I needed my sleep. But the crying continued. If I ran downstairs quickly, I would find out why he was crying. There would be enough time to fall back asleep before school started. My eyes felt stuck; I was barely able to open my lids. I tumbled out of bed and descended the stairs to the living room.

I switched on the ceiling light. The bassinet was sitting in the middle of the living room. Dallas was uncovered; his blanket had fallen to the side of his body. I placed my hand on his arm to comfort him. His skin felt like cold porcelain. Goose bumps rose on his bluish skin. I tucked his blanket tightly around his body so he couldn't kick it off. His eyes were swollen from his tears. He was cold and was hungry for a bottle.

I was dressed in only a sleeveless cotton nightgown, and my body shivered from the cold. I walked a couple steps toward Mom's doorway, and I carefully folded the flowered drapery back. It was dark in her bedroom.

"Mom," I said into the darkness, "Dallas needs a bottle!"

I walked to her vanity and turned on the night-light. In the faint glow, I moved closer to the foot of her bed, and I pulled the blanket back. She wasn't in her bed. I quickly searched the rest of the house, but Mom wasn't anywhere. She wasn't home.

Dallas continued crying. My chest tightened, and I hugged myself, squeezing my arms to keep warm. *Where is Mom?* Not knowing what else to do, I went into the kitchen to get a bottle.

Too often, there wasn't enough milk in the house to feed Dallas. I grasped the handle of the refrigerator and pulled the door open to reveal bare shelves. As I feared, there was no milk for Dallas. Panic set in as Dallas's screams grew more desperate. I opened cabinet doors, looking for anything to calm his belly. A sack of sugar sat on the shelf, and I remembered that Mom gave him sugar water to satisfy his stomach when there was no milk. I grabbed the sugar bowl on the table, scooped a teaspoon of sugar into the baby bottle, and turned the tap water to warm. I filled his bottle and I replaced the top. I shook the sugary mixture well.

I walked back to the bassinette and placed the nipple in Dallas's mouth. He gave a whimper and began to suckle immediately. He calmed down. I breathed a sigh of relief.

But moments later, he stopped sucking, and he let out another desperate wail. Even he knew the difference between sugar water and sustenance. I was running out of options. What could I do for him? His body needed nourishment, he was screaming from hunger, and his belly was wretched from the emptiness.

I held the top of the bassinet with my hands, moving it slowly back and forth. His cries deepened, and my hands tensed. I began to shake the bassinet harder. I began to cry and scream at the same time.

"Please don't cry Dallas!" I pleaded. "Please don't cry."

I removed his diaper, which was soaking wet and soiled. His bottom was red, raw, and infected from having lain in the same diaper for hours. There were sores on his bottom the size of a dime. He wasn't just hungry; he was in pain. I looked through Mom's dresser for a clean diaper, but I found none. So I carefully washed his bottom, and I left him without a diaper in hopes it might help to heal his severe rash. I doubled the blanket and covered him tightly, but I left his bottom exposed to the cold air.

By the time Dallas's cries lost strength, and he had fallen asleep from hunger and exhaustion, it was four in the morning. But almost as soon as Dallas had quieted down, baby Lynn began to cry with hunger. I ran upstairs and lifted Lynn from the bed where he lay in the middle between Roger and Roland, who were both sound asleep. I sat down on the wooden floor and rocked him back and forth, warming his body until he fell asleep in my arms. I placed Lynn back between my two brothers to stay warm.

Taking the blanket from my bed, I went downstairs and curled up on the velvet sofa next to Dallas's bassinet. I watched the darkness around me; everything looked scary and unfamiliar. The slightest sound was frightening, the dark foreboding. The quiet of the night magnified every sound echoing from within the walls; I could feel the creaks and bends of the house in the cores of my bones.

Feeling alone and abandoned by my parents, I would wake at the slightest sound with my stomach tensed in fear. My skin felt as though there were a vapor of ice hovering over my body, and I pulled the blanket over my arms to keep the cold of the night away. I finally fell asleep when the blackness of the night was at its deepest. Too soon, it was broken by the flicker of daylight.

"Get up! Get up!" Mom yelled, roughly nudging me. Her voice was edged with disgust that I had overslept for school. She didn't mention where she had been all night, leaving us home alone.

"Get the other kids up and get to school!"

I ran upstairs and woke my sisters and brothers.

"Please get up, we're late for school!" I cried, pulling the blankets down to the end of the beds.

We rummaged for anything we could find to wear, and we left for school without anything to eat.

That day, our teacher announced that school would end early; the school staff had business to take care of. I left the school grounds and walked down Main Street past the city park. Families gathered around tables and wicker baskets of food, and the smell of barbeques filled the air.

After another short block, I approached my home. I could see a white car parked in front of my house. A grey-haired woman opened the car door and walked up the concrete steps to the front screen door. She was dressed in crisp blue linen clothes and wore a matching belt tight at her waist, and she clasped a black briefcase tightly in one hand. She knocked boldly on the screen door, and my mother, dressed in a robe, answered the door. Mom held her robe tight to her neck with one hand, and was holding Roland on her hip with the other. I picked up my pace and ran to the house.

"Mrs. Hathaway, I am Mrs. Fhiant from the Noble County Welfare Department," the woman said. "May I come in?"

My mother ushered Mrs. Fhiant into the house, and I trailed behind her. My brothers and sisters were playing with a colorful top, spinning it in circles on the linoleum floor. Their hair was disheveled, their clothes wrinkled. Baby Dallas lay on the sofa without a diaper. His bottom was chafed red, the skin infected from a lack of diaper changes, from a lack of diapers period. By the doctor's instructions, a white medicine was to be applied to Dallas's sores when his diapers were removed. He was crying.

He was always crying.

I ran to the sofa and tried to calm him, wishing I could take his pain away and soothe the hunger in his belly.

Mrs. Fhiant sat down at the dinette table.

"I have read the report from the physician regarding Dallas's condition. Could you tell me exactly what happened? "

My mother walked to the end of the sofa, which perpetually stank of urine and sour milk. She sat down at the opposite end from the baby.

"He kicked me in my pregnant stomach really hard." Mom bowed her head, as if she was ashamed that this was her life. "He went into a rage because I refused him."

Mrs. Fhiant looked around the room, stared at the blue velvet sofa, stained and faded. She observed the lower halves of the walls that were colored with crayons and children's sketches of a life that would never be. She looked sympathetically at my mother, at Dallas, at all of us.

"Mrs. Hathaway, you can't stay here with him. It's been six months; he will be coming back soon. The children can't stay here. You are unable to support them. We will need to take custody of the children."

My mother lowered her head even more and said, "I understand."

Custody was a word I didn't understand, nevertheless I knew our lives were going to change.

The following week, the air was humid and thick. When I returned from school, the house was unusually quiet. I couldn't hear Dallas crying in the living room. I walked to the bassinet to check on him, but he wasn't there. My mother wasn't home, and I didn't know where she was. Suddenly, Dad came out of the bedroom zipping up his pants; he moved in slow motion, drunk. He tucked his shirt into his pants.

I wasn't expecting to see him. "Daddy, Daddy, where have you been?" I said in a rush. "Where's Dallas?"

"Find your other brothers and sisters and get them in the car." His voice sounded urgent. He walked to the front window and glanced out to Hazel Street, as if expecting someone.

My belly was drum-tight from hunger, but I knew there wasn't anything to eat. Following Dad's orders, I ran upstairs to get my brothers and sisters. My brothers had just lain down for a nap, and I gently roused them awake. I found a clean diaper on the dresser, and I quickly changed Lynn. I pulled him up to my waist for one moment.

"Get down here and get in the car!" Dad yelled up the stairs.

Together my other brothers sat up and rubbed their eyes. They crawled out of bed, putting on anything they could find, whether clean or dirty.

"Sissy and Diane! Downstairs!" I screamed through the door to our bedroom.

I looked for Dallas again. He wasn't in his crib. I reached for his baby blanket and pulled it close to my nose. It smelled of his sweet baby scent.

"Get in the car, it's in the alley. Do it now!" Dad's voice was still urgent.
I swung the rusty screen door outward, and I stepped onto the hot cement porch. With Lynn in my arms, I headed straight for our black Studebaker. I sat in the front seat with Lynn on my lap. The hot vinyl stung as it stuck to my skin. My brothers and sisters crawled into the back of the car. Though I could barely see over the dashboard, I noticed a woman across the street looking at us. Then my father came rushing through the screen door. He climbed into the driver's seat, lit a cigarette, and stared ahead to Hazel Street. He seemed nervous and distracted. He blew smoke out of his nose, and he flicked ashes out the car window. He began clenching and unclenching his jaw. Suddenly, his eyes welled up.

At the end of the alley across Hazel Street, a woman came into view. She was dressed conservatively, with a short hairdo and black oxford shoes. She looked official in her uniform, and was looking intently in our direction.

I saw a shadow move slowly to the woman's left. A person stepped sideways and into the sun toward the woman. It was my mother! She was dressed in a grey dress and was wearing a shiny necklace. I could see her red lipstick clearly from a distance. Tears moistened her black eye-makeup, causing it to smudge. Her eyelashes rested like fringed half-moons on her cheeks. Teardrops darkened the fabric of her dress in charcoal beads. She tilted her head back and looked to the sky for a brief moment, and then she clasped her hands to her chin. She began shaking uncontrollably. The woman standing beside her reached over and held her arm. Mom was standing next to a suitcase. Her arms extended in our direction, she reached her hands toward us, and she mouthed, "I love you, I love you."

My brothers and sisters strained their necks to see over the seat.

"Daddy, Daddy! Where's mommy going?" I cried.

The fear of abandonment deepened the anxiety in my stomach. I closed my eyes and took a deep breath, sobbing so hard that I choked from the mucous in my throat.

41

Mom waved with her full hand, but then her hands retracted and covered her mouth. The uniformed lady placed her arm gently on my mother and pulled her away. Mom slipped back into the shadow and moved away, into the distance.

"Daddy, where is Mommy going? Daddy, where are we going?" I asked.

"Nowhere! Get back in the house, now!"

We were terrified and confused about what was happening, but we knew better than to question Dad. His eyes were fixed straight ahead where my mother had stood a moment ago. He didn't look at us. My brothers and sisters exited the car, and they all stood next to me on the concrete porch. Lynn was still in my arms. Then, Dad sped off, turning up Hazel Street toward downtown, and left us in the dust-filled alley.

Two weeks later, spring hung in the air and held promise for a mild summer. I looked out the side screen door toward the garden and to the cloudy sky. It was beginning to sprinkle. Across the street, the neighbors pulled out of their driveways and headed for work.

My mother had been gone for two weeks, and it was hard to concentrate at school. I really missed her, and worried for her safety. Dad left home a lot, leaving me with the children. Dallas was still gone from his crib. No one would tell me where he was. Together, Sissy and I helped with the diaper changing, bottles feeding, bathing and dressing of my brothers. The responsibilities felt overwhelming for our young ages.

Suddenly, there was a knock on the front door.

"Hello, I'm Mrs. Fhiant, Director of the Welfare Department. May I speak to your father?"

"Mrs. Fhiant is here to see you, Daddy!" I called over my shoulder.

"Let her in. Tell her I'll be right out," he shouted.

I opened the door, and Mrs. Fhiant walked to the center of the living room. A man in a dark uniform followed behind her and stepped aside to the corner of the room. Mrs. Fhiant walked passed the wicker bassinet and glimpsed down at the empty mattress where Dallas had been missing for two weeks. She stood there momentarily and then proceeded toward the sofa.

My brother's were seated on the sofa, their eyes focused on the strangers in our home. My sisters came down the stairs and sat at the far end of the sofa. They held hands.

Dad joined us and stood at the edge of the living room. He gave a quick nod of respect to the man in uniform, and then he shifted his eyes downward. Mrs. Fhiant adjusted her posture, and struck a confident pose. She inhaled, and stood up tall as if to say, *I'm in charge now.*

"Children, I have talked to your mother, and she won't be coming back right now. Dallas is safe and staying with another family," she paused for a moment. "Your father is unable to care for you, but we are going to provide places for you to stay."

Since I was the oldest, Mrs. Fhiant's eyes were fixed on me. Her lips continued to mouth words I could no longer hear. My mind had shifted to another dimension. My thoughts escaped me. But I was forced to bring my focus back to the moment. Mrs. Fhiant was speaking about a new family. *Did I hear her correctly? A new family?* My stomach tightened, and I felt anxious. My nails dug into my palms, and my arms dropped to my sides. I tried not to show my fear. I started to speak, but instead I inhaled quickly, and closed my mouth and swallowed hard.

My brothers sat dutifully on the sofa with their hands folded on their laps. Their expressionless faces showed that they did not completely comprehend what was about to happen.

"Shirlee, you and your sisters will be staying with Pastor Kenny and his wife. The boys will go to other homes, and that decision will be settled this afternoon."

Dad stood there, his hands shifting and clenching. He looked sober for the first time in a long time.

"When will we be with Mommy and Daddy?" I asked. "Will we be a family again? Please, will all of my brothers and sisters be together again?"

My eyes reddened, and I bowed my head. My hands covered my eyes to try to keep the tears from falling. My chin trembled, and my words stuck in the back of my throat.

"Your life will change for a while, but we hope that you can be a family again, if things work out," Mrs. Fhiant assured me.

The rain began to pound on the rooftop, and a fog descended over me. Our world was collapsing around us. My head fought the dizziness. From observing the world around me, I had caught glimpses of other families'

43

lives; from my early years I knew that the way we were living was not the way God meant our lives to be.

Mrs. Fhiant tried to explain to my brothers that they would be moving, but their faces still showed little understanding of their future. After a moment, Roger, the oldest brother, began to understand the change that was about to happen. Tears formed in his eyes, and he leaned forward and lowered his head toward his lap. His tiny hands covered his face. A tear slipped through his slightly parted legs and dripped onto the worn flowered linoleum below.

I looked up to the ceiling to keep back my tears. My breathing was shallow, my palms were damp, and my stomach was tense from the unplanned separation. The pain in my heart flowed in and out like waves. My head spun like a toy top with blurred colors.

"Girls, say good-bye to your brothers," Mrs. Fhiant ordered me and my sisters.

I walked toward Roger. His hands were cupped over his face, fighting the tears. I gently removed his hands and looked into his swollen eyes.

"We will be together again, you'll see," I said in an unconvincing voice.

The lump in my throat swelled. Our world was careening down the highway at full speed, without a map or even a clear sense of where the journey would take us, and everything I knew blurred around me. All the things I loved were disappearing. Mommy was gone, and Daddy wouldn't see us for a while. My brothers were going to a home, but we didn't know where. When would I see them again?

I leaned over and kissed Roger's cheek, then knelt down in front of him. I saw his fallen tear on the floor beside my knee. I touched his tear gently with my index finger, folded it in my hand, and placed my hand on my heart. I reached my arms around his tiny body and held him.

Still kneeling, I moved to the right and looked into Roland and Lynn's eyes, and I told them how much I loved them. I knew I needed them in my life. I pulled them close to me and reached my arms around them both, hugging them hard. But my arms weren't big enough or strong enough to hold onto them forever.

I stood quickly, turning my body firmly towards Mrs. Fhiant.

"Where is Dallas, Mrs. Fhiant?" I asked.

"He will be taken care of," she said, "don't you worry."

This wasn't the answer I wanted to hear. I wanted more information, specific information. Where was Dallas? Where were my brothers going? There was so much uncertainty about the process of separating us, and how it would be handled. I needed more information and time to process what our future held.

By now, Dad was in tears, and his body heaved back and forth.

"Kids, I'm so sorry," Dad cried.

The room felt airless, despite the sounds of breathing for our situation. Our family had fallen into palpable disarray. We were in search of something to hold on to, but the gauzy grey sky outside and the suffocating air made us feel even more dislocated. I didn't know if I would ever recover from the hopelessness of my family.

Mrs. Fhiant gave each of us a small fabric bag to pack our personal items in. I ran upstairs to the armoire and pulled out my baby dress that my mother had crocheted. I pulled the drawer open and removed a photo of myself as a baby.

Dad called us to his side, and he hugged us hard. He said he didn't know where he would be in the future, but that he would be back for us some day soon.

Outside, the rain had subsided. We left our home, my feet slowly stepping down each concrete step, as I tried not to slip and fall. I paused for a second, and I gave the last step a deliberate stomp. Mrs. Fhiant called for my sisters, and we got into her Government Issued car. She drove us to Pastor Kenney's parsonage.

My sisters and I were fond of Pastor Kenny and his wife. Mrs. Fhiant told us that we'd be living in their home temporarily until we were placed permanently in a foster home. That way, we could still go to our church, still see Grandma on Sundays, and still attend the same grammar school. Our friends would be close by. In the meantime, Mommy and Daddy could get better. Maybe Dad would stop drinking and they would stop fighting. Maybe, in the future, we could be a family again.

When we arrived at the parsonage, some ladies from the church were there to help Pastor Kenney's wife clean us and set up our sleeping arrangements. They scrubbed our hair well, gave us soapy baths, and dried us with crisp fresh-smelling towels. They dressed us in different clothing, and it felt like a new beginning.

CHAPTER TWO
No New Beginnings

And for a while, it was a new beginning. In Pastor Kenney's home, they always spoke kind words and there was never any fighting. There was plenty of food, and we always ate meals on time. Church members would stop by to visit with Pastor Kenney and see if they could help out with the three new live-ins.

Pastor Kenney negotiated with the church families who were interested in taking in my sisters and me on a more permanent basis. We were considered well-behaved and well-mannered, and we were loved by many church members. The family who took us in would be compensated for our care.

I stepped out onto the front porch, and sat on the wooden swing. I watched the traffic pass on Main Street. Occasionally, church members drove past the parsonage and honked their horn. I relaxed back into a gentle swing, and the motion calmed me and the wooden arms embraced me. In these surroundings, the fog of chaos was beginning to lift.

We stayed with Pastor Kenny and his wife for three months, never knowing where my parents were living, nor where my brothers were staying. At the end of our stay, he informed us that a home had been found with one of the church members. He said Mrs. Fhiant would be arriving soon to the parsonage, and that we would be moving to another foster home.

We sat near the front door waiting for Mrs. Fhiant, our suitcases ready. Questions about our new home swirled in my head. Who were these people? Would they genuinely care about us? Would they treat us kindly? How long would we be there?

A few moments later, Mrs. Fhiant knocked on the door. She was alone this time. She instructed us to get in her car, which was parked in front of the parsonage. Pastor Kenney and his wife followed behind us and packed our suitcases in the trunk.

We thanked Pastor Kenney and his wife for taking care of us. They had shown us what a real home felt like, and how it felt to have parents that care about your wellbeing and who create a calm and predictable environment that doesn't distract you from learning.

Mrs. Fhiant drove several miles outside of town. I lowered the car window, and the cool wind streamed through my hair and pressed the cotton fabric against my body. The smell of steamy earth wafted in the air. Soon, she turned off the paved road onto the main country road.

The recent rain turned the dirt roads into a mixture of mud and dirt. Mrs. Fhiant's car picked up speed. The dirt kicked up against the bottom of her car, stones rhythmically smashing loudly on the undercarriage. Dust rolled up behind the car, blocking my view of anything behind us. I observed the Indiana countryside, with its endless fields that stretched to the horizon. We drove past saltbox houses and scattered farm implements and unpainted weathered barns punctuated with tall silos. Clusters of wooded areas and shiny ponds with floating lily pads broke up the farmland.

Farm animals dotted the landscape; sheep grazed while little lambs hid under their mothers' bellies. A calf leaned close to its mother, suckling its daily nourishment. Barbed wire fences lined the sweet pastures. Horses stood with their tails swishing, keeping their heads steadfastly low. Through the car window, I watched the telephone poles pass by quickly, one after another at a dizzying speed, as if they were being sucked up by the dust and fury of our driving. Suddenly, the wind slapped some strands of hair over my face, blurring my view. I quickly brushed back the hair from my face, and I rolled the window back up.

On the drive to our new foster home, Mrs. Fhiant explained that the foster parents were long-time members of our church. At my mother's request, the welfare department had made an effort to keep my sisters and me together.

Meanwhile, the rest of my family was scattered somewhere in the world. We didn't know where my mother had disappeared to, nor where my dad was living. I wondered where my brothers were living, but Mrs. Fhiant hadn't mentioned them. The emptiness of life without them felt like sitting in the scorching sun without shade; it burnt through the surface of my skin to the depths of my heart. *Where are my brothers? Are they being fed? Does Dallas have a dry diaper on? Is someone holding him so he doesn't cry anymore?*

Mrs. Fhiant slowed the car down. The smashing sound of stones hitting the undercarriage began to subside. My sisters sat upright in the back seat, straining their necks with curiosity. They looked over the front seat at the white saltbox house situated up the narrow lane. Cows and sheep dotted the pasture next to the road. Horses swished their tails to remove flies as a light breeze brushed their backs.

The sun was low across the fields, and its amber light set fire to the land. The field colors ran rich with seams of honey and gold. The property was surrounded by barbed wire fencing and aged wooden posts to keep the animals in. A steel mailbox painted with letters and anchored to a wooden post on the road identified their house. I rolled down my window to the scent of straw permeating the air.

Trees lined each side of the lane and tall, uncut grass grew along the fence. We turned left onto the dirt lane and drove over the untamed grass growing up the center. At the top of the lane sat a large windmill that slowly wound its paddles in the subtle breeze. A weathered red barn sat surrounded by cow pies and red roosters and hens scurrying about the barnyard and scratching into the brown soil. The red barn was two stories. At ground level, a large sliding door exposed cow stalls in an orderly line that were used at milking time. Attached to the barn was a smaller building that held shiny large aluminum milk cans submerged in ice water, awaiting pickup from the dairy vendor.

Mrs. Fhiant parked the car next to the spinning windmill. The rhythmic sounds of the windmill echoed in our ears. A chicken coop with cracked and dirty windows sat next to the driveway. There were other sheds around the house; one housed the pigs, who took advantage of the mud to cool. A pungent barnyard odor wrapped around us.

The many sounds in the barnyard created a certain peacefulness: The clucking of chickens, the occasional shriek of an unseen bird, the lambs bleating softly in the field. Next to one of the sheds, I could hear muffled grunts from the pigs rooting busily in the muddy mire. An occasional whinny from the horses added to the soft symphony of sounds.

At eleven years old, I was excited to see so many animals on the farm. I imagined we could feed the pigs, get close to the ewes, and milk the cows. I turned to my sisters, who looked frightened of moving to a new home. I placed my hands on their hands to reassure them.

49

"Just remember everything is temporary, until Mom and Dad can get back together," I whispered to my sisters. "We have each other until then."

Perched on a slight hill above the car was a saltbox clapboard house with a dilapidated, unusable porch facing the main road. The house was painted a dull white, and the paint was peeling off in places. The main entrance to the house was the back door that faced the garden. There was no sidewalk to the rotting front porch. Thick green grass surrounded the house, and two very large maple trees shaded the lawn. While seated in the car, Mrs. Fhiant turned to us.

"This is where you will be living," she said with certainty in her voice, but she didn't say for how long.

I turned to my reticent sisters; I felt hopeful for the future.

"Shall we go in and meet your foster parents?" Mrs. Fhiant asked us.

I stayed in the car, hesitating. The yard was fenced in to protect the home's privacy. I sat for a moment looking to Mrs. Fhiant for a nod of approval. She exited the car and motioned to me with her hand. With my stomach churning, I slowly grasped the car door handle and stepped out onto the dirt driveway, turning around to look at my surroundings. I watched the roosters milling about the barnyard and crowing with discontent, and I saw the pigs locked in pens, rolling in mud and grunting. And the grunts and the crowing combined to create a festive atmosphere.

"Let's go!" I whispered to my sisters.

Mrs. Fhiant walked toward the gate and gestured to me to enter first. My younger sisters grasped my hands and followed behind me. I reached for the handle of the steel gate. Attached to the steel chain was a rusty padlock that swung between two steel posts. As I entered the gate, my arm brushed against the padlock, and it felt cold to the touch, impenetrable and razor sharp at the edges. We walked up the concrete sidewalk, which lead to the main entrance of the house. A large vegetable garden dominated the right side of the sidewalk. Parts of the garden were still uprooted—it was being prepared for sowing.

We came to the screened door, which was hanging at an angle and didn't fit the doorway. A lady came running to the door.

"We've been expecting you!" she said with excitement.

Our new foster mother was dressed in blue jeans and a plaid western-style blouse. She had tanned leather skin that was wrinkled beyond her forty-something years. Her high cheekbones were hollow, and she had a very sharp nose and chin. Her gray hair was cut shorter than what was allowed at the church, and she wore it with a slight flip at the ends. I recognized her from church, but I did not remember ever speaking to her.

Her husband stood next to her. He was tall and lean with a stern face, and his skin was shiny from scrubbing his face too hard with soap. His fingers were worn, blunt with farm work and years of digging in the soil. They had four children of their own. Our foster mother smiled warmly as Mrs. Fhiant introduced each of us.

We stepped into the family room with its polished checkered brown and white floor tiles. An irregular stone fireplace with a deer head perched over the mantel dominated the room. Last winter's ashes sat heaped in the fireplace grate. A green ping-pong table with a net was centered in the family room, and there were paddles and balls on the table in the ready–to-play position.

In the far corner was an upright Steinway piano that was missing its ivory keys at one end of the keyboard, and music sheets were folded neatly on the sheet holder. A large picture window opposite the piano wall showed a view of the barn.

Our foster mother asked if we would like to go to our room, and told us it was upstairs. One of her daughters showed us the way. My sisters and I firmly gripped our bags that held our meager belongings. We straightened our spines and thrust our shoulders back, walking forward with a spirit of hope. At the bottom of the staircase, I turned to Mrs. Fhiant and thanked her. She said to let her know if I needed anything

We entered the narrow brown stairway that wound upward and around a corner and sharply ascended to the top. The room smelled freshly painted. It was one of three bedrooms on the second floor. Two sides of the room had casement windows, allowing ample air circulation and light into the space. An iron bed with a single mattress would sleep all three of us.

One window had a westerly view of the main country road on one side and a view of the woods and pasture on the other. Three horses were grazing in the field, and a brown stallion dashed forward and kicked up his legs. I raised the windows, and removed the wooden screens to air out the room. I leaned out the window, smelling the fresh farm air.

I laid our suitcases on the chair, and I carefully removed my only valuable possessions: the hand-made pink crocheted baby dress from my mother, and a color photograph of me as a baby in the same crocheted dress. Between two walls was a closed cabinet with four doors and an exposed wooden pole that would serve as our closet.

I hung my baby dress and gently unfolded the gathers, pressing out any wrinkles. I felt sad, and I missed my mother. My sisters and I finished unpacking our suitcases. We giggled for a moment, feeling nervous and hopeful, and we ran downstairs to meet our new family.

For the last six months, our foster parents' oldest daughter had been away at licensed vocational nurse training in nearby Marion, a small city about sixty miles away. But she was back home for the summer to help out with the new arrivals. She was my favorite of the two sisters. She was plump, not thin like the younger one. She engaged with us girls the most. She taught us how to bake and cook for the family. She enjoyed teasing us and making us laugh. But she wasn't in our life long before she went back to nurses' training. I didn't understand why she had to be the sister to go away. Occasionally, she would return home to visit at the holidays, but small-town farm life was not in her future.

The second-oldest daughter was attractive and had shoulder length brown hair that dropped into a flip. She was thin and firmly built, and she wore no makeup except Vaseline to make her lips shine. Her teeth were perfect, and she had a nice smile. Her eyelashes were naturally long and thick. She could sew well, and she made many of her own clothes.

My younger foster sister relished being popular and well liked, but she was really second in popularity to another high school senior, a popular " sweater girl", as she was called by her classmates, who dressed in colorful fitted angora sweaters with beaded trim at the collar. The sweater girl had the preacher's son's interest.

My foster sister could sing well, and she was part of the school chorus. She made excellent grades in school and dated occasionally. But at times she could be mean, even violent. If I didn't do what she wanted when she wanted it, she would bend my small finger back until it was so painful that I fell to my knees and begged for her to stop. Over time, the pressure left a slight bend in my small finger.

Their only son was a couple years younger than me. He wore his crew-cut hair waxed upwards, and the ridge of his nose had a slight bump that could only be seen from his side profile. He had a volatile temper and showed his arrogant bull headedness when it came to a compromise in sports or getting his way. He would often get physical when he was angry with me. We would get into wrestling matches over trivial things. When he would go into a tirade, I would usually come out sweaty with rumpled and torn clothes, red skin, and bruises.

My foster brother and I played basketball in the barn and climbed hay bales and swung on thick ropes from one side of the barn to the other. When we tired of that, we would form tunnels in the hay. If the neighbor's kids stopped by to borrow a farm tool, we would play baseball with them out in one of the mowed fields.

The fourth child, a small baby girl, spent most of the time with my foster mother. Sometimes Diane would watch the baby while my foster mother worked at her desk, and we did our chores.

A few months after settling into the foster home, I stood by the open window and breathed the fresh air deeply through my nostrils and exhaled long and hard. Grasshoppers and crickets chirped throughout the early evening in rhythmic a cappella, but a sound in the distance created a break in their music. The crickets fell into a profound silence. I noticed the quiet of the fields. I realized that this is what freedom feels like, freedom from chaos. My sisters seemed less worried about food and were more relaxed without my parents fighting. My thoughts turned to where my parents were living, and I wondered if they had forgotten us. I wondered if we would see my brothers soon. The last of the sun hit my body, relaxing every muscle. Unexpectedly, a gentle breeze swept over my back, cooling me.

Every day, farmers took their tractors and machinery over the dirt roads to the fields, and when they finished plowing, they would leave them sitting in the field. When I heard the Ford tractor engine idling and rattling near the barn, I ran quickly to see if I could ride along. Riding on the fender of the old Ford tractor was the highlight of my day. At times, I was scared I would fall off the tractor. But the apprehension tightened my grip. I soaked in the sounds of spring's new birth: sheep bleating, hiding under their mothers' udders; birds chirping overhead, landing on trees swaying in the breeze.

The farm had three horses. Midnight, my favorite, was shiny black, with a deeply arched back and large hoofs. I learned to approach her from the front, because she was known to kick out her back legs in a spirited moment. I had watched my foster brother mount her bareback and ride her across the field, and one afternoon I decided to try to do the same.

When Midnight saw me, her tail swished wildly, as if tempting me to ride her. I brought her a carrot and hid it behind my back. I rubbed her nose and gave her the carrot, and I held it in my hand until she finished. I patted her nose and carefully put her reins over her head, gently moving my hand along her neck to her shoulder. I led her to a nearby weathered bench and mounted her bareback from the side. I settled in the arch of her back, my legs tightened around her belly, and she galloped off. I yanked her reins back, slowing her down. She walked at a gentle pace around the field.

All at once, Midnight took off with a surge of speed, dangerously thrusting my body backward. As her speed picked up, I bounced from one side of her back to the other. I bounced upward, and I tightened my legs harder, and landed to the side of her back. I had lost control of her speed, and I only had a bridal bit and reins to control her direction, so I cued her in from left to right, trying desperately to slow her down. Then, as suddenly as she took off, she came to a stop, propelling me forward hard against the back of her neck. I pulled her reins, and I dismounted from her back. Shaken by her betrayal, I looked her in the eye and scolded her telling her never to do that again.

The farm animals were the best part of living in the foster home. The sheep, goats, chickens, rabbits, and pigs each had their own fenced-in area with a shed for shelter against the weather. Cows grazed in the fields until milking time in the evening, and then they were brought into the barn for their own protection against weather and predators. Work on the farm was never ending.

For the first few months, I assisted my foster mother with the food preparation, watching as she cooked, baked, and fried food. My foster sister used to help, but soon she was distracted with her school activities and dating, leaving the heavy work to us. It became my job to prepare dinner each evening for eight people and to clean the house once a week with my sisters, iron the clothing, and to tend to the garden in the summer. Sundays were reserved for church worship both in the morning and evening. No farm work, except feeding the animals, was performed. Rest on the Sabbath was tightly observed.

The farm provided all the sustenance we needed to survive. Saturdays were "bake days." We prepared food on Saturday to last throughout the week. We mixed large bowls of pie dough, and rolled it out into several pie tins. We used fruits picked from nearby bushes and trees to make blueberry and cherry pies. And my favorite dessert, a moist chocolate cake, was baked and served with a dollop of whipping cream, whipped to perfection from fresh cream brought up daily from the barn in shiny aluminum pails.

Another responsibility of mine was to collect chicken eggs. With my wicker basket filled with yellow straw, I went outdoors to the chicken coop. The chickens laid their eggs in aluminum cubbies. If I timed it right, I could catch the chicken laying her eggs. I enjoyed squeezing the back of a chicken and helping her expel the soft shell of the egg, forcing it out onto the bed of straw, though I don't know if they appreciated my assistance. But I enjoyed being part of the delivery, handling the egg gently, and feeling the soft white shell hardening in my hands. After collecting several eggs, I would carefully place the eggs in the wicker basket for breakfast that morning.

We labored in the garden until sunset, pulling weeds. That was the hardest job, particularly on the hot and humid days of summer. The sun would beat down on my back, and my body would sweat and burn from the heat. My bare hands pulled and tore weeds from the soil, clearing away any unwanted growth. Occasionally, a spider would crawl onto my clothing, which would ignite my fear of black widows. I didn't have gloves, and my hands would get torn up from the razor-sharp weeds slicing my skin as I uprooted them. Squatting and bending down for hours was uncomfortable. My ankles felt strained, and it was very painful. I realized soon that my slender ankles were not built to hold even my tiny body for long.

My foster father held down two jobs. He was often tired. In the early morning, after he milked the cows and fed the animals, he would head out to his day job at the lumberyard, and he would return at the end of his day to more farm work. On weekends he drove the John Deere tractor, pulling disks and plows to prepare the fields. I liked it when he went to his day job because sometimes he was cold and grouchy toward my sisters and me.

The years passed, and I turned 13, officially becoming a teenager. By then, my sisters and I had been living in our foster home for two years. Shopping was a once-a-year event for "The Girls," and on this trip we each would be getting a new dress and a pair of shoes for church. We drove to Kendallville, about 20 miles from Albion. I looked forward to shopping; the clean, crisp feeling of new clothes made me happy. They had a different scent than the hand-me-down welfare clothes I used to wear. The inventory at the store was sparse, but we always found something to buy. I slipped on different dresses, and the rustle of starched petticoats and the feel of silky or satiny underwear lifted my spirit and made me feel special. After shopping, we carried our bags down Main Street, and I observed the displays of fashions for young children and teenagers in the windows of the merchant shops, flaunting expensive dresses and accessories that I could only dream about.

Out of the blue, my foster mother said that my brother Dallas lived just a couple blocks off of Main Street. She had arranged a visit. It had been two years since we had last seen him. Would he know who I was? My sisters and I skipped along, our legs in unison, excited to see Dallas. Tall trees lined both sides of the street for blocks. We finally arrived at a grey, two-story home, the exterior neatly painted. A large maple tree shaded the front of the house. We scrambled ahead of my foster mother and climbed up the steps of the front wooden porch. When she caught up to us, my foster mother took our shopping bags and slipped them over her left shoulder. She knocked on the front door.

A modestly dressed salt-and-pepper–haired lady answered the door and introduced herself as Mrs. Holler. She was short and rather portly, and she wore an embroidered apron around her bodice and waist. She invited us into her foyer. Her voice was soft. She smiled and led us into her living room. My foster mother and the lady spoke quietly with each other, and I edged closer to them so I could hear their conversation.

"Dallas was examined by a physician and was declared mentally retarded," Mrs. Holler whispered. "He will be a slow learner," she leaned closer to my foster mother, "because of an injury before his birth. When Dallas was removed from the home, he was diagnosed with rickets, a vitamin D deficiency from a lack of milk."

"That's quite unheard of these days," my foster mother responded.

"Yes, it is," Mrs. Holler said, then turned toward us. "Would you girls like to see Dallas?" she asked.

There was a rush of excitement among us. My sisters and I grabbed each other's hands and followed Mrs. Holler upstairs.

At the top landing, we were led into a room that faced the street. The room was painted white and was bare of furnishings except for a crib and a changing table. There were no pictures on the walls; there were no baby toys to stimulate him; there were no photos of Dallas. A maple tree stood outside the window. At least Dallas could look through the window and watch the cars pass below.

I caught a glimpse of a small face on a misshapen dome of a head between the bars of the crib. I moved closer. Dallas was sitting up in his bed. His face appeared flatter than I remembered, and his forehead more prominent. His eyes showed no expression, and his arms rested at his sides. His black hair was thick, and his powder blue outfit was pressed crisply with starch. He didn't move much.

Seeing Dallas, I wanted to hold him, but instead I just stood there. It had been so long since I had seen my baby brother that he almost felt like a stranger to me, not like my brother. The moment felt very formal, almost surreal. I took a few more steps toward his crib. The walls echoed as my feet shuffled on the hardwood floor. I slipped my hand gently through the bars of the crib, toward him, and I touched his hand. He didn't respond.

My frustration and despair mounted. Didn't these people know that we were once a family? There wasn't anywhere to sit in the room. Couldn't they have helped us reconnect with our brother by creating a place to hold him so I could tell him I was sorry? I was sorry that we couldn't be there for him. I was sorry that I couldn't keep him warm at night or feed him real milk in his bottle. Were we just siblings, scattered like seeds between two towns that would never grow together or unite again? I wanted to hold Dallas and bring the whole family back together; I wanted to bring Dallas home. The visit felt rushed, awkward, and we were soon out the door. But I knew I would come back for Dallas, one day.

Relations with our foster parents became strained over the years. My foster mother started to wear her hair rolled in a twist like a paper wasps' nest, and her age was catching up with her. Maybe the responsibility of taking in three foster children was becoming too difficult. More and more often, she'd say we didn't perform our chores to her satisfaction. She walked the path between the laundry room and the living room, griping at us the whole time, her shoulders bent, her voice growing ever more shrill. We were beginning to feel like indentured servants. Wasn't she being paid to care for us? We wanted to do our share, but our contribution to the chores seemed to be out of proportion to our ages. Her own children's contributions were minimal at best. The criticisms from my foster mother were becoming unbearable for my sisters and me.

How does a foster child describe to the world the feeling of being verbally assaulted for just being yourself, for trying to do your best. My sisters and I never fit in with our foster family, and we were always made to feel different. Feelings of loneliness consumed me, living in someone else's home without my brothers. I missed being in my own home. Even though things were difficult when we lived with our parents, I thought that I'd rather go hungry with all my siblings, together, than be fed by strangers.

I went outside to get some fresh air and to get away from my foster mother's constant reprimands. The horses were grazing in the field. The pigs were basking in the sunlight, feeling the freedom after a cold winter. Muffled grunts came from the barnyard as the pigs busily rooted in their muddy mire. In the fields, the cows mooed in unison, and the new calves huddled next to their mothers, suckling life-giving nutrients.

Quietly, I walked to the back of the house so no one would notice my absence. I stood behind the trunk of a cherry tree, finding sanctuary there. Above me, birds roosted on the tree branches, and they flew up and passed noisily over my head. I placed my hand upon a low-lying limb, and I raised myself up into the tree, stepping on the tree's nodules, ascending to a secure limb.

A weathered birdhouse hung precariously from a branch. I chose not to disturb its contents and instead sat on the opposite side of the trunk. I perched myself high on a branch, studying the birdhouse, and I looked down to the world below me. Sitting there in silence, I felt more secure.

But still, I felt timid, like a sparrow, helpless in changing my sisters' and my situation. I thought that if I were a bird, I would not live here. I would launch myself from this tree and soar into the sky, way above the piercing place below. I would keep flying to see what other places were out there, places I had only seen in pictures. I imagined large cities, vast oceans, blue lakes, and tall mountains. My wings would carry me until I found a happy place, and then I would return for my sisters and brothers, and bring them all home with me.

Except for school or church, we were kept isolated on the farm. We attended church three times a week, but the parishioners didn't know how our foster family treated us. We didn't know how to tell about our mistreatment, or that we were made to feel like outsiders in their home. At fourteen years old, I was cooking, cleaning, and ironing; I was performing onerous household and farm tasks. I was a very hard worker, and I always tried to please my foster parents but my foster mother's dissatisfaction grew.

At times, my foster mother's increasingly harsh words felt verbally abusive, causing my body to shake, my stomach to tighten, and my nerves to fray. Her harsh words reminded me of my father's verbal abuse towards my mother. The old fears started to creep in again. My foster mother's endless rebukes made me feel separated and alone, just like when my parents would leave me home alone, and I did not know what would happen to me. When my foster mother criticized my cooking, I was reminded of the abundance of food at their house in contrast to the scarcity of food and milk before. But a child needs more than food and shelter to feel happy and secure. Without the acceptance and unconditional love we craved, my sisters and I felt like we were simply occupying rented space in someone's home. And unlike physical abuse, the emotional and psychological scars were not visible.

My sisters and I did as we were told. We never talked back. We couldn't defend ourselves. Nevertheless, our foster parents found reasons to pick on us. When my foster mother was having a really bad day, we would get the brunt of her anger. It made us feel unwanted and different. Our foster family began referring to us as the "The Girls" more and more frequently. And "we girls" started to become regular targets, which made us feel anxious and afraid. We would often go to our room and cry on the bed together. What did we do to deserve these criticisms? Of course, my foster siblings didn't mind when my foster parents were upset with us: It kept them out of battle.

Sometimes, on the rare occasion when my foster mother was in a good mood, she permitted me to spend a few hours at my best friend Carole's house. She would drive me in her pink and black Desoto and drop me off at Carole's home.

Carole's parents owned a chicken farm close by. I loved visiting Carole's house because I got to see how other people lived. Carole had many interests, outside of my daily life; she showed me there was a whole other world out there.

Carole was the most attractive girl in my class. She had chestnut brown hair with gold streaks throughout, and when she twirled around, a faint scent of perfume wafted in the air. Her lips were full and were the color of pomegranate, and her breath had a sweet fragrance. And when she smiled, she lit up the room, and when she laughed, the sound was contagious.

Carole was also one of the smartest students in my class. She and I both sought good grades and practiced good penmanship. Her friendship inspired my love of school. We shared our homework assignments in study hall, dividing up the work between us. In the evenings, we would call each other on the telephone, and we would review our homework answers with one another. It was a great way to finish our schoolwork quickly, and to talk about things that only teenaged girls find important.

In study hall, we often traded notes hidden inside a pen. We talked about our crushes on certain boys, which changed as often as the weather. We wrote the notes in pig Latin in case a teacher found the pen and discovered its contents. Carole would lend me her lipstick during class, and it made me feel almost as beautiful as she was. Since wearing lipstick was forbidden in my religion, I wore it in defiance of my foster mother. I rubbed it off before my foster mother could see it on my lips. I didn't die of cancer from wearing the lipstick, as my foster mother said I would.

We studied for the school spelling bee competition together. Spelling was easy for me; I won second place to the county. It was a big deal; I made it in the town paper. I missed the word fugitive by spelling it: f-u-d-g-i-t-i-v-e. That extra D got my photo onto the front page of the Albion paper, with me holding up a sign that read: f-u-g-i-t-i-v-e. It brought me lots of unwanted attention.

I acted like a comedian most of the time to help reduce the stress of my home life, and Carole was my best audience. We shared many laughs, and she doubled my joy. She had a caring quality, and she would inspire me without criticizing me. She expanded my world beyond what I thought possible, and I felt honored to have her as my best friend. Without Carole's friendship, my grandmother, and the church as my foundation, I don't know if I would have survived my childhood. Carole didn't judge me by my family life. Not only was she someone I respected and emulated, but she was a great listener. Her personality was always upbeat, and together we tried to find humor in my darkened world.

I was fascinated by Carole's collection of glossy photos of movie stars. She would send letters to the Hollywood stars and would request a photo, and they would send her a black-and-white autographed photo in return. Carole had a stack of glamorous photos of women with beautifully applied makeup that accentuated their features. When I looked at them, I realized that my Mom could have been a movie star. Carole had photos of male stars, too, who had handsome good looks and wore stylish suits. They looked well kept, like they really liked their lives. I wanted to be different. I wanted to be like them.

I truly felt I had a friend in Carole. And when I was able to visit her, I saw how a happy family lived. I didn't understand why my foster mother wouldn't allow more visits with her. It didn't occur to me to invite Carole over to my house, probably because the idea wasn't encouraged. The foster home never felt like my own home, and the idea of inviting her over just never came to mind. We seldom discussed my issues with the foster home, but Carole suspected my unhappiness.

In the four and half years since we had moved to our foster home, we rarely had contact with our parents or brothers. Recently, Grandma hadn't been coming to church, and we also hadn't heard from her, making us wonder if she had moved. Although our brother Roger rode the same school bus, we rarely connected with him, and when we did, it was only for a few seconds. On the crowded school bus, he sat at the very back, and we were the last to be picked up on the bus route. By the time we got to school, the class bell would be about to ring, and we had to rush our separate ways to our classrooms.

One Saturday, after my chores were done for the day, I lay on the lawn looking up at the blue sky. White cirrus clouds swirled in their feathery forms. Suddenly, the silence was broken by a dog's barking, which meant a visitor was coming up the lane. I ran out to the steel front gate, and peered down the driveway. From a distance, I could see a young boy. He had been dropped off by a car that was kicking up dust as it drove into the distance. As he walked up the lane, his brown hair blew in the wind, and sunlight and shadows danced upon his light olive skin. He raised his head, sweeping his hair off his forehead to reveal his dark brown eyes. Then he picked up his pace and started running toward me with his arms outstretched.

It was Roger!

"Sisters, come over here!" I screamed at the top of my lungs, and I ran to meet Roger halfway up the lane.

My sisters followed on my heels, and with our arms outstretched, we all collided with our brother. We embraced in one big huddle, dancing up and down for joy. We walked together back up the lane toward the windmill and through the shiny steel gate. We sat on the lawn under the maple tree in a circle, our knees touching, and we held hands. We had so much to talk about.

Roger lived down the road about a half mile. He was living with Mrs. Fhiant's son and his wife. He said he was very happy living there, and he told us about all the fun places he had visited and about the freedom he had to visit his friends. They treated him well. We asked if he knew where Roland and Lynn were living. He told us they were just down the road too, about a quarter mile away, even closer to us than his house was. He said he had visited with them, and that Roland confided to him that he and Lynn were not happy with their foster parents.

After an hour of visiting with Roger, my foster brother came out to join us on the lawn and asked if we would like to play tag. We'd play tag when there were four or more kids to play with. We enjoyed the competition of running away from each other and seeing who was the fastest runner.

It wasn't long before it was my foster brother's turn to be the tagger. He roughly tagged one of my sisters. Then he ran after me. After a couple laps around the backyard, he tagged me, hitting me hard on the back and pushing me down.

Roger had always been a pretty fast runner, and he started sprinting before my foster brother could get going after he'd pushed me. The chase was on, but it wasn't long before my foster brother got his momentum. Roger ran around the house once with my foster brother following behind. The second time around, my foster brother reached out his arm to tag Roger, but he was still not close enough. Roger veered to the left, and my foster brother reached out his arm again. This time he tagged Roger hard, throwing him facedown on the grass, where he tumbled on to his back. Then my foster brother jumped on top of Roger, raising his fists and swinging at Roger's face and torso.

It didn't take much to make my foster brother angry. His face had turned red, and he began hitting Roger viciously. Roger hadn't even provoked him, but my foster brother didn't want that kind of competition around the farm, not even from our brother Roger.

"Stop! Stop! Get off of Roger!" I ran at full speed and knocked him off of my brother.

Roger bent forward, and jumped off the ground as soon as he could, shaking grass and dirt off of his head. Roger looked at my foster brother, trying to make sense of what had just happened to him. He lowered his

61

head to his shirt, brushed off the grass, straightened his belt, and looked at me.

"I'd better go home," Roger said, wiping the blood from his lip. And that was the last time Roger visited us at our foster home.

We never heard from our other brothers, Roland and Lynn, and it wasn't until much later that we learned more about their unhappiness in their foster home. When my family separated, Roland and Lynn were sent to a foster home together. Their foster parents were older, and they had no children of their own. Children were bothersome to them, but the welfare check that arrived monthly was too enticing to give up; it was the couple's major source of income.

The couple spent their days watching television. When one went out to go shopping, the other would stay home to make sure the boys remained in their room. When my brothers arrived home each day after school with their books under their arms, they'd march dutifully to their room and stay there all evening. They did as they were told.

At suppertime they were allowed out of their room for half an hour to eat their meager meal of baloney and white bread, the household staple for the two boys. When their meal was finished, they washed their own dishes and returned to their bedroom. If they dawdled, the foster mother would herd them into their room and turn off the lights. She would close the door and tell them to stay there for the rest of the night.

Roland told me of one memory from one of his first Christmases with his foster family when he was seven years old. He remembered that the landscape was blanketed in white, and clumps of snow piled heavily on bare branches. It was a Christmas tradition, when snowfalls were plentiful, that we'd watch for Santa Claus on his sleigh as he passed by people's homes. We could hear the jingle of sleigh bells in the distance, and the horses rhythmically prancing on the packed snow as the sleigh neared. A generous townsman gave his time to bring joy to the Albion children during the holidays, bringing his sleigh through the town and over country roads.

When Roland and Lynn, then five years old, heard the sleigh bells, they ran out of their bedroom to the front living room, and leaned into the large window, pressing their noses hard against the glass to catch a glimpse of the sleigh. They raised their hands and they cupped their ears in the direction of the festive jingling. The sleigh bells grew louder. The thumping of horse's hoofs came closer to the house.

Roland and Lynn looked excitedly out over the snow-covered road. Suddenly, the horses slowed down from a brisk gallop, and the sleigh appeared, and they saw Santa donned in his bright red suit and red cap trimmed in white fur. Santa pulled gently on the reins as the horses whinnied into the gentle silence. His large knotted white bag hung securely over his shoulder. His cheeks were red from the bitter cold, and he waved at the little boys standing in the window. My brothers' noses pressed tightly against the window, their eyes lit up with imagination and hope, and their tiny hands waved with exuberance. But it was all over in a couple of minutes.

"Ok, boys, get back to your room," their foster father said.

"Will Santa be back soon?" they asked.

"No. Not for a long time."

The sleigh bells jingled one last time, and the sleigh moved further down the road and faded into the background. But the boys were hopeful. Hope was all they had.

My younger foster sister was going to graduate from high school that year, and she would be going to college in the fall. Supper conversation had been centered on her moving away to college. There also had been discussion about my foster brother attending college in the future. One evening, when everyone was seated at the table, the discussion about college came up yet again.

"I want to go to college, too!" I piped in enthusiastically.

"*You* want to go to college?" my foster mother responded sarcastically. "And how do you think that's going to happen?

"My spirit was dampened by the question, and my eyes lowered. My body sunk down in the chair.

"I don't know yet," my voice had lowered to a whisper.

"You girls will only cook and clean houses," my foster mother said. "Yes, that's what you will do."

The meal ended, and together my sisters and I cleared the table of dishes. I piled the dishes in the sink, added soap, and scrubbed furiously. My sisters felt the same assault. They had dreams, too. But cleaning someone else's house for the rest of our lives was not a part of our dreams. No, we didn't yet have a plan about how to pay for college. No, no one had come forth in our lives and offered to help us make a plan for college. We only knew that we wanted better and more empowered lives for ourselves. In that moment, I felt my resolve crawl up my legs and through my body.

"I will go to college! I'll show them!" I said under my breath.

A delivery truck drove up the dirt lane toward the house. Our foster parents had ordered their first television set, and it had just arrived. A man in a blue uniform carried the box into the living room, and he placed it on the round walnut table in the corner. The man hooked up the television and adjusted it. A fuzzy picture appeared on the screen, and it gradually became clearer. He began flipping through a handful of channels and checking the volume control. The sound blasted through the speakers, and he lowered it to a listenable level.

"Here," the installer said, "are a couple of family programs you might enjoy watching: *The Donna Reed Show* and *The Adventures of Ozzie & Harriet.*"

He gathered up the boxes, loaded them in the truck, and drove down the lane.

Television had finally made its way to Albion. It was a novelty in town, and it created a lot of curiosity. Owning a television was worldly, and at first it was considered sinful in the eyes of most church members. But slowly, television was beginning to be accepted by the more liberal church members.

Everyone took turns flipping the channels, looking around the back to see where the picture was coming from, sliding their hands over the glass screen, and rubbing the smooth wood finish. We explored what programming was available. My foster father turned the channel to *The Donna Reed Show.* We all sat on the sectional, and passed around a bowl of popcorn.

Donna Reed was the mother and was the star of the show. She was married to a doctor, and they had a couple of children. Donna wore a starched apron that symbolized the perfect homemaker. She represented the scent of homemade bread and proper meals. Her eyes twinkled when she spoke to her children, her voice was soft and polite, and her smile was radiant, as if an unkind word never left her lips.

Her duty was to care for her family by cooking meals and setting a table adorned with colorful flower centerpieces. Her children's clothing was pressed, and the house was neat and tidy. The family spoke gently about what everyone did during the day. She seemed to care about what her children did at school and what friendships they enjoyed. When her children arrived home, she greeted them with joy, helped them out of their jackets, and served them milk and cookies. She loved her husband and children. When her husband got home from his office, she greeted him with a warm smile. They spoke kindly to one another. They never fought. They handled their disagreements with civility. This was the idyllic family that I wanted in my life. I watched that television show every day, and studied every word of it. I wanted that life for my brothers and sisters. I wanted that life for me.

I walked to the television screen and placed my hand on Donna's face. I thought a child could feel safe inside that box. When the program was over, I flipped to *Ozzie & Harriet*. I was coming of age and I had been noticing boys around me. There was David Nelson, the oldest son, but I had my eyes on the younger son, Ricky—my first Hollywood crush. He wore his dark hair swept back, with a one lock dangling over his forehead. He had dark eyes and a sweet smile. His nose was the perfect shape. When he picked up his guitar to sing, his voice and smile took my breath away. Why didn't we have boys in town that looked like him? I wondered how I could become so infatuated through the television screen. Temporarily, television transported me out of my world, and gave me hope that my future life could be better.

"Girls! Get down here and do your chores!" our foster mother yelled.

Lately, we found our foster home unbearable with all the outbursts of yelling and criticism from people who seemed to not care about our hearts or our futures. We had lived there for four years. My sisters and I still shared the same lumpy mattress. I was not ungrateful to them. At least we had shelter over our heads, and we weren't starving. There was always food, and plenty of it. Once a year we received a new set of new clothes, and someone was always at home for us.

We were appreciative that they took us in. They weren't bad people, they were just people committed to hard work and holding onto their farm. While the welfare check they received each month helped to keep the farm financially afloat, I'm sure the challenges of taking on three more children were significant. They were unable to understand our emotional and psychological needs. We needed to not be criticized and to not feel separate from their family as if we were foreign or different. We had a profound need to feel appreciated and loved unconditionally.

After a day of chores—weeding the garden, doing laundry, ironing, and preparing meals—my tired body melted into the chair. My thoughts reflected on my past life, the scenes of my father's violence etched on the insides of my eyelids. In our foster home, we were no longer witnesses to Dad's violence. My Mother's abuse had distracted her from being a caring and nurturing mother. We missed her, not because she was a good mother, but because every child wants a mother.

As a teenager, it was becoming harder to tolerate the injustices of our life. My foster mother's criticisms were harsher than ever. My foster father got meaner at the supper table expecting food to be on the table when he walked in for the evening. At the end of the day, we never knew when he would finish his barn chores. I would pace the window facing the barn anticipating, calculating and stressing when the barn lights would turn out. If dinner was undercooked or overcooked, he would dole out harsh criticisms. We felt like outsiders, as if we had leprosy or some disease. We were always good kids. We were polite and well behaved, and we worked hard. It didn't seem right.

It was late into the night, the quiet time halfway between sunset and the sunrise. The night animals and insects were quiet from their hunt during the night. I wasn't asleep, and I rose from my bed and walked to the window to view the deep black sky and contemplate my life. The longer I stared at the dark sky, the more bright stars appeared in the depths of the universe.

My sisters were asleep in the bed, and I crawled in quietly next to them. Sometimes we felt like the forgotten kids—no one really knew how difficult it was to be a foster child. I woke up each day in a bed I shouldn't be sleeping in, and I ate with someone else's family. I cried violently into my pillow until the cold wetness prompted me to turn it over to the other side. I found sleep an escape from my problems.

Two months before my eighth grade graduation, we received a call from my mother. My parents seldom called us—maybe once or twice a year. But when they telephoned, my foster mother would make us feel like we were bad children from a sinful lot, just by association with my parents.

On this call, we learned that my mother had moved to Chicago, and she asked my foster mother if we could come visit her. It seemed strange that my mother should have to ask permission to see her daughters. My foster mother listened for a couple of minutes then exhaled deeply. Without a goodbye, my foster mother hung up the phone.

My foster mother immediately reacted with anger, going into a tirade. She gritted her teeth. She said my mother was unable to take care of us. My dad was the town drunk, and he couldn't take care of us either. She said my mother's life was sinful because she abandoned her children and caroused with other men. And we were of the same bloodline. If we visited her, we would be exposed to her sinful life.

"If you go to Chicago, you girls can never come back here!" she threatened. "If you come back, you will be put in a juvenile home for bad kids."

"Bad kids? We aren't bad kids!" I said under my breath. Receiving a phone call from my mother shouldn't have been a fraught moment placed on our shoulders. It should have been celebrated.

If our foster parents didn't take us back, where would we go? I was determined to change our lives, so I had to find a way to get us out of there. I went upstairs to my bedroom, and lay in bed, enveloped in the salty steam of the air. My eyes burned. Sweat soaked my sheet. My tongue was dry, and I was thirsty. The open window let in flies that crawled on my skin, taking advantage of the moisture. I closed my eyes, blocking the world out, and fell asleep.

The next day, I quietly rose early from my bed. I ran outside where I could find comfort. The sunlight painted the landscape with bright colors. I ran across the driveway to the barnyard. My body shook, and I cried uncontrollably. The barn stank with the smell of cow dung, horse urine, old dusty chicken droppings, and sour milk thrown aside. I walked up to the weathered gate twice my height and stepped onto the first rail. I wasn't high enough to see over the top, so I stepped up one more rail and leaned my arms on the top of the gate, resting my chin on my arms.

The sun was beating across the undulating fields. It gave me solace to look at the quiet calm of the fields, to see the cattle and sheep grazing, to hear the sounds of a calf suckling its mother with contentment and a full belly of milk. The pasture was lush green with tufts of grass rising out of it, and the landscape was sprinkled with flowers. For a moment, the scenery calmed me. A fence surrounded the acreage, keeping the animals from escaping to the outside. I wondered, if I opened the gate to free them, would the animals make it on their own?

Out of the shadow of a distant tree, Midnight's shiny black coat glistened in the sun. She came gently toward me. As she approached me, her head lifted up and dropped down, and she gave a whinny and moved closer to me. I reached out my hand toward her, pretending I had something for her to eat. I patted her nose and I could smell her warm breath and smell of grazing. When she discovered that my hand was empty, she jerked her head to the side and walked away. I was going to miss Midnight. I was going to miss all the animals. But I knew what I had to do.

Outside, menacing clouds formed overhead in heavy, dense columns rising up to considerable heights. The clouds were mountainous, their topmost portions spreading out in anvil shapes; it was a sure sign of severe weather.

Lunch recess would start in fifteen minutes. It had been difficult to focus at school that day. My math teacher scolded me a couple of times for fidgeting and for not being able to answer the questions. My chest was pounding during class, and my stomach was tense and in pain. My anxiety level was over the top.

The school bell rang, and the sound reverberated through my body. Students walked to the cafeteria, I sat at my desk until everyone left the classroom. Then I quickly gathered my schoolbooks and exited into the empty hallway. I ran quietly down the stairwell to the front door of the school. I held the door handle tightly and paused one last time. I exited through the doors.

I felt a fierce urgency, and I began moving quickly toward the street. My feet felt guided by an external force. The school grounds were empty. I felt nervous and frightfully alone. I saw my childhood race before me at breakneck speed, and I wondered if we could ever be happy like other children. I begged for my fear to go away, and for my courage to not leave me. What I was about to do could leave my sisters and me without a place to live. Our future was uncertain.

I was breaking school policy by leaving the school grounds—something I had never done before. It was in my nature to always follow the rules. But I was on a mission. This is what I needed to do for my sisters, who were as unhappy as I was living in the foster home.

My thoughts about our future accelerated, and my fears did not stop me as I headed for the street that led downtown. *I can get in big trouble for this,* I thought, but my body just kept moving forward, as if it had shifted into fifth gear. I quickened my pace, and I crossed the street and walked off the school grounds.

So lost in my thoughts, I didn't see the car coming out of the driveway to my right. The driver honked loudly to get my attention, and I jumped at the sound, dropping my books on the paved street. The driver waited while I picked them up and secured them under my arm. My legs were weak, my body trembled, and I held tightly onto my books. I hastened my walk toward downtown. It was several blocks away, but it felt like it was at the edge of the horizon.

I didn't know where Mrs. Fhiant's office was located, but all Noble County government offices were located in Albion at the courthouse building. I reasoned that the Noble County Welfare Office must be located there. The courthouse was about four blocks away from school in the cobblestone town square.

The courthouse was familiar to me; when Mom and Dad had business to take care of downtown, they would drop us outside the courthouse, and we would play on the lawn. If we needed a restroom, we would use the one just inside the courthouse doors. We explored the courthouse halls. History was recorded in its walls. We peeked into the glass doors where government business was conducted. The heightened doorways and windows from a past era seemed intimidating. The hallowed halls echoed the sounds of the heavy doors opening and closing and of leather shoes pounding the hard floors. Oak file drawers filled with documents opened and closed. Someone in an official uniform would come out and ask us where our parents were and would remove us from the building. I had not been there since I was little.

I finally reached the town square. I crossed the cobblestone street to the courthouse. I tilted my head toward the sky, and the skies cleared as rapidly as they had darkened. I hastily crossed the lush green lawn with one deliberate step after another. I moved steadily toward the courthouse. Then the clouds changed again, holding back the rain, and the sky turned greyer and darker, and the clouds were building up with a fierce speed. My breath was heavy, and the muscles in my hands felt sore from my tight grip on my books. My feet carried me forward; I was driven by the sheer will to survive and change our lives to something better.

Mrs. Fhiant, please be there. Please be there!

As I walked up to the tall brick building, I glanced at its rising cupola. I gently grabbed the door handle, and then I dropped my hand. I looked down for a moment in desperation, my palms sweating, my face beaded with moisture from the long walk. I firmly grabbed the handle again and swung open the heavy glass door. I turned my back to the next set of doors, still holding onto my books, and I used my back to push through those doors to the main lobby. My heart pounded even louder. I went into the restroom, pushing the oak door with the frosted glass aside, and it felt familiar.

Which door is Mrs. Fhiant behind? How do I explain to her how unhappy we are? What if she turns me away? What if she won't help us?

I walked slowly up to a red-haired lady sitting behind a wide wooden counter.

"I'm looking for Mrs. Fhiant?" My voice was barely audible, cracking nervously.

"Please wait here." She went into the back office.

The wait seemed like an eternity. My thoughts swirled in my head as I tried to find the right words to describe why I was there.

"Please come in. Mrs. Fhiant will see you."

The red-haired lady led me past the counter and to the back office. Mrs. Fhiant stood up and greeted me with a friendly smile.

"Why, Shirlee, shouldn't you be in school?"

"Yes I should be, Mrs. Fhiant. But I need to talk to you.

"Please have a seat, and tell me what's on your mind." She pulled a chair from the corner and placed it to the side of her desk, and she sat down facing me. I was suddenly comforted by her position.

"Mrs. Fhiant," I hesitated, and I bowed my head and clasped my hands together.

"Mrs. Fhiant . . ." I paused again, and I looked up at her and then lowered my eyes to my lap.

"My sisters and I are very unhappy."

I was dizzy with exhaustion, and my nerves felt as though they were beaten rapidly like a drum. I started to cry uncontrollably.

"Now, now," she consoled. "Please tell me. You're safe with me."

"Our foster parents have been treating us mean." Very mean! They have threatened to put us in the reform school for bad kids. We aren't bad kids!

Mrs. Fhiant tried to be consoling, but the tears continued to stream down my face. She handed me her handkerchief, and I wiped away my tears.

"This all started because my mother wants to see us." They called her names and said we were just like her. They said if we visit my mother we can't come back and we won't have a place to live. Reform school is where we would go. You know, where bad girls go. We aren't bad.

"Now, now," she said as she gently put her hand on my hands.

"Mrs. Fhiant, I am so afraid for my sisters! I pray every night and day that we can move somewhere happy. My sisters and I cry every night together. We have no contact with our brothers or see our parents.

"She leaned towards me, her voice kind and understanding. "Let me look into this.

"But I'm afraid to go back to the farm after talking to you," I said.

"Don't worry, everything will be fine. Let me drive you back."

I got into the front seat of Mrs. Fhiant's government car. The tires rumbled over the cobblestones, leaving the town square behind. We passed the church on Main Street and drove up the highway a few miles before turning onto the country road.

Soon after, we were driving up the lane to the house. It was about the same time that the school bus dropped us off each day. My stomach tensed, and I was in pain. But I knew I had to trust Mrs. Fhiant with our fate. My foster mother was there to greet us at the door. Someone must have called to tell her that we were coming. My foster mother was friendly to Mrs. Fhiant, and she changed the tone of her voice when she spoke to me.

"Well, hello, Shirlee!" She said, as if nothing had happened.

"Shirlee, I would like to speak privately to your foster mother. Would you mind going to the other room?" Mrs. Fhiant asked.

I removed my books from the table, and I went upstairs to my bedroom. My sisters weren't back from school yet. Spring was nearly over, and the temperature had risen to 95 degrees, and the humidity was high. Our room was suffocating because of the heat from the western sun and the lack of curtains over the casement windows. But this was where I felt safe.

Ten minutes passed, and I heard Mrs. Fhiant leave the back door.

I could hear the school bus open its doors down the lane. I went to the window and saw my sisters walking up the lane. As the school bus traveled down the road, Mrs. Fhiant's car turned right at the lane, driving away slowly so as not to kick up dust behind her car. I watched her taillights move down the road and then speed up. The dust formed a large rolling cloud behind her, and she disappeared into the afternoon.

Mrs. Fhiant was involved now, and she would keep a close eye on our situation. Over the next couple of weeks, Mrs. Fhiant visited us on the farm at a moment's notice. Since I was the oldest sister, she would ask that I talk to her in the car, out of the hearing range of my foster family. We talked about how my sisters and I were being treated and how we felt, and I asked her questions about Mom and Dad.

The intensity in the foster home was palpable. Our foster parents continued to call us "The Girls," and we walked around with our heads low, filled with uncertainty about our future. We diligently performed our chores as always, but my foster mother no longer constantly griped at us. She was careful what she said to us. She was cool and distant toward us. My foster sister and brother ignored us. Supper conversations were uncomfortable because we ate in complete silence. I felt like I rather would have starved than sit through another silent supper.

The following week, Mrs. Fhiant called. She asked if my sisters and I would like to visit with our mother for two weeks in Chicago. My foster mother stood next to me, so I was careful not to exude any joy.

"Yes, we would," I said in a faint voice, because I knew what would happen if I expressed too much joy at wanting to see my mother.

I didn't dare get my hopes up, but Mrs. Fhiant confirmed that we were going to Chicago to spend a couple weeks with my mother. She asked that we pack our things and be ready for our trip. Our mother would pick us up. I placed the phone gently on the receiver, and my feet carried me hastily up the stairs. I felt as though I was floating. I closed the door behind me, and I woke my sisters. "Wake up! Wake up! We're going to see Mom!"

On the day of our departure to Chicago, my sisters and I hopped out of bed and held hands while we jumped up and down. But our excitement was immediately dampened because we realized that Mrs. Fhiant hadn't mentioned where we would live when we returned from our visit. We decided not to dwell on that just yet.

The air felt clean and fresh, and I stepped to the window. Midnight was grazing in the field.

"Take care of yourself," I said to her as I breathed deeply and filled my lungs.

I started to pack my small bag, and I walked toward the closet pole. I didn't want to leave my favorite baby dress behind. I flipped through our dresses, but it wasn't there. I had seen it hanging there the night before. I did another pass through my sisters' dresses and separated each item of clothing to make sure that I hadn't missed it. I checked the dresser drawers in the corner, and it wasn't there either. What could have happened to my baby dress?

My sisters looked through their items, but they had not packed it either. I pushed my stepping stool to the closet area, and I looked on the shelf above my clothes. I couldn't find my baby dress. This was the only treasured item I owned from my mother, besides my baby picture in my crocheted dress. I couldn't ask my foster mother if she knew why my dress was removed from my closet because the tension in the house made it difficult to communicate.

I carefully wrapped my photo with a piece of plain white paper, held it against my heart, and slipped it in the pocket of my suitcase, patting it gently.

I closed my suitcase, grabbed the leather handle, and held on tight. I took a deep breath, exhaling hard. I walked toward the bedroom door and turned around one last time to look at our bedroom, glancing once more at the closet from which my beloved baby dress had disappeared. *I hope we never come back!*

Outside the bedroom window, the sky overhead displayed all the brilliant hues of the spectrum, as if Mother Nature had painted glowing brush strokes and dancing bands of light across the sky. In the distance, cars passed our house, and rolls of dust followed behind them on the dirt road.

The dogs were barking. At the end of the dirt lane, a white Cadillac with a glinting chrome grill appeared. It drove up the lane, did a circle in the barnyard, and parked below the spinning windmill. Three blue jays perched on the windmill struts, softly warbling, and they stretched their wings and soared off northward.

A tall, dark-haired man stepped out of the car, and an auburn-haired woman followed behind him. It was my mother, coming to take us to Chicago. Mom didn't have a car, so she had brought her boyfriend to drive us there. He opened the gate for my mother and gently took her hand as they walked up the sidewalk. I ran downstairs swinging the back door wildly open. Mom picked up her pace and walked quickly toward us, her arms outstretched. We dropped our suitcases and piled into her arms.

My mother's hair was swept up in a tight French twist, which was not often seen in this area. Her chiseled features stood out against her ruby red lipstick. She looked happier and more radiant than I had ever seen her.

Mom introduced her new boyfriend to my foster parents, and then she introduced my sisters and me. Mom appeared uncomfortable in front of our foster parents. They knew too much about her life, and she knew they would judge her. Mom was in a hurry to get back to Chicago, and she suggested that we leave immediately. Without hesitation, I grabbed the leather handle of my suitcase, wishing I could walk away from this part of my life just as I walked through the steel gate to the car.

The orange sunset settled in behind the tall trees, as the new darkness brought uncertainty about our future. I relaxed in the back seat of the car with my sisters sitting quietly on either side of me. I wondered about the city of Chicago. What would a large city look like, smell like, and feel like? As we drove the highway to Chicago, a train sped along the track next to us, and the engineer sounded the whistle; it brought back memories of Grandma.

The air conditioning felt cool against my skin, and the leather seats embraced my weary body. Mom's boyfriend stopped at the first Dairy Queen we passed. He ordered three ice cream cones for my sisters and me. The taste of vanilla ice cream agreed with my palate as I licked and twisted the cone. Shortly after we finished, I fell asleep on Sissy's shoulder, and Diane fell asleep on my lap.

"Wake up! Wake up!" Mom called out some time later.

In the dark of the night, we arrived at Mom's apartment in Chicago. It was a large one-room apartment attached to the back of the owner's house. This was all my mother could afford with her wages as a waitress. The landlord was an elderly lady who kept out of my mother's business, and Mom liked it that way. Mom had arrived in Chicago without any marketable job skills. She was taken in by a married Greek couple who owned a restaurant, and they taught her how to serve their customers and collect the money at the cash register.

Since Mom didn't own a car, we sat in her apartment for most of our visit. Together we laughed and talked about a few happy memories. It was the first time we had bonded with our mother in several years. But we didn't have many good memories to talk about, so Mom turned on the television, and we watched the late-night television shows.

Occasionally, Mom's boyfriend would pick us up in his car, and he'd take us to a fun park or to dinner. We stopped by a bar restaurant to meet her close friends. Mom never drank or smoked. She never liked the taste of alcohol. But because she came to Chicago without a support system, these people became her friends. The bar reminded me of my dad, who had always spent a lot of time drinking in bars. I was uncomfortable being there, with the stench of alcohol permeating the air. I sat outside on a patch of lawn watching cars speed by, wondering where the drivers were going and what their family lives were like. My mother asked if something was wrong. I guess the stench of alcohol had left her memory.

The two-week visit with my mother went by quickly. We still didn't know where we would live when we returned. Mom was unable to care for us. A couple days before we were supposed to leave Chicago, Mrs. Fhiant called mom. They had a brief conversation, and Mom hung up the phone.

"Shirlee, Mrs. Fhiant says she hasn't found another place for you and your sisters to live. She's still to work on it. For now, all of you will be going back to the foster home."

At that moment, I wish I had a magic wand to change our lives.

On our last day at our foster home, the heat rose into our second-floor bedroom, and the sweltering humidity was unbearable. The tension in the house was palpable. It had been decided that my sisters and I would go to live with my dad in Marion, and he was coming to pick us up. I wondered if he had changed his ways. Had he stopped drinking and managed his anger issues? I sat silently on the edge of the small bed huddled together with my sisters. For five years, its lumpy mattress and steel springs held our tiny bodies, and we hid there in its warmth and protection from an unkind world. We had just been marking time, always hopeful of reuniting with our parents.

A week before, my sisters and I had returned from visiting our mother in Chicago. But upon our return, we were clearly unwanted by the foster family. We were tainted by our mother's past, and we were being punished for visiting her, for having a natural desire to want to visit our mother.

With no other foster placement available at such short notice, Mrs. Fhiant determined that my sisters and I would live with my dad. Our stay would be temporary. Our future was still uncertain.

While packing my belongings for our move to Dad's, I saved my best school projects to show him, along with a potholder I made with grandma, and a beaded ankle bracelet placed on me at the time of birth. I discovered that some of my personal belongings had been tossed into a trash can. I bent down and retrieved the items and placed them in my bag. Someday I would have control over my life.

I stopped and stared at my baby picture cupped in my hand. The happy smile on my baby face was filled with innocence, unaware of what my future would hold. I wrapped it in paper and carefully placed it in a book. I looked outside and tried to forget my confused life. The window overlooked the green field and the dirt road. A gust of wind spreads leaves around the yard. I studied the length of the dirt road, and I wished I could know what the future held and what the end of the road would bring. In the distance, the road came to a T, and I knew I would have to always choose the right road to take me where I wanted to go.

I wondered how my brothers were doing. I missed them. I'd spent four and half years living apart from my brothers, the four of them in three different foster homes, and I never knew what their lives were like. The adults in charge of us never understood how our brothers' absence affected our lives, and they seldom arranged visits among us. I was always wondering, questioning, and seeking answers about their lives.

My thoughts returned to the field. Midnight stood in the tall grass and swished her tail while drinking from a large, rusty barrel. I was going to miss her. I was going to miss all the animals. My relationship with them had taught me about unconditional love. Suddenly in the distance clouds of rolling dust kicked up. A car sped quickly toward the house, and I soon recognized Dad's lime green van. He slowed down at the entrance to the lane, stopped momentarily, and then accelerated to the top of the lane.

"Girls, your dad is here to pick you up. Get down here right away!" my foster mother barked from the bottom of the stairwell.

Dad knocked on the back door. We opened the door and stepped outside, holding our suitcases.

"Get to the van now, get in!" he whispered in my ear before we had a chance to say good-bye to my foster parents. We followed him to the van, and he quickly packed our belongings in the back.

My foster parents stepped outside, walked toward the steel gate, and stopped. I turned toward them to say good-bye. Grandma had taught me about forgiveness, and at this moment, I didn't want to remember the miserable times in the foster home, but to reflect on the positive moments. But Dad's hand lightly shoved my back towards the open van door.

I was happy to be leaving the foster home. As a foster child, it feels unnatural to live in someone else's home, to live somewhere other than your own home without your parents, even bad parents. Criticism from foster parents feels more punitive than your own parents' criticisms.

"Get in!" Dad repeated sternly. He seemed to be in even more of a hurry to leave their property than my mom had been. Maybe he could sense their discontent about his lifestyle of drinking and carousing. Dad lowered his head and walked back to the front gate. He shook hands with my foster parents.

My foster parents stood silently on the other side of the gate. My foster father placed his hands around my foster mother's shoulder. She had tears in her eyes. We were good kids. We weren't any trouble to them. We worked hard to do the right thing.

Dad returned quickly to the van, and started the engine. I stared out the car window at my foster parents, and waved my hand at them. Dad drove fast down the lane, making a sharp right turn. He pressed the gas pedal hard to the floor. He followed the road for a couple miles, and then he turned onto the paved highway leading to Main Street. After a couple miles, he slowed the van down as he reached the city-limit sign. I breathed in deeply and exhaled loudly.

Dad drove through Albion on the way to his home in Marion, about sixty miles away. We passed our church. I noted for the last time its red-brick exterior and white steeple and carved white doors. Memories of Grandma and Pastor Kenny's kindness were what anchored my tumultuous life. I was going to miss the church. I was going to miss Grandma.

"Daddy, please drive by our house on Hazel Street!" I begged.

Just a block after the church, Dad turned left onto Hazel Street. Our home looked the same as I remembered. But strangely, it didn't register as our home. Home meant something different to me now. Dad turned again at the next corner, passing the park where I played, and we drove across Main Street to Albion Jefferson School. I stared across the playground, and I fixed my eyes on the entrance to the red-brick school.

Thank you, Albion Jefferson, for teaching me my love of learning. Thank you for choosing such excellent teachers that inspired me to reach for greater knowledge. And thank you, Carole, for being the best friend anyone could ask for. Hopefully, my education and discipline will serve me sometime in the future.

The van tires rumbled over the cobblestone street. Dad was circling the courthouse square. It was the pulse of the town. I studied the courthouse for the last time. It stood erect, proud. I closed my eyes and remembered the day I walked to Mrs. Fhiant's office, and how that had felt like the longest journey of my life as I desperately sought a path to her office door, desperately sought a happier life. I had been afraid and tired, but I knew that she could help my sisters and me. *Thank you, Mrs. Fhiant, for caring about us.*

Dad turned the corner, and glanced toward the bar where he spent so many evenings getting drunk before coming home. He slowed the van and peered inside the open bar door. *Please Daddy, don't stop!* Then he pressed the gas pedal hard, and the van sped forward.

The drive around town was important to me; it was a way to remember the good memories and the bad memories. I felt a profound gratitude for the good people of Albion who helped shape my values and encouraged my strength.

Along the drive to Marion, Dad mentioned that Roland and Lynn lived with him. Some time ago, Dad took custody of them. With this news, I felt overwhelmingly excited to see my brothers.

"Will Dallas be at your house? Will Roger be there?" I asked.

"No. Dallas and Roger are living elsewhere." His voice weakened, and his chin quivered.

An hour later, we arrived in Marion. Dad pulled into the dirt driveway. He lived in the poorer side of town. His home was a small white single-story house with a thick concrete porch attached to the front. There was no roof over the porch to block the sun or the rain.

Dad turned off the car and warned us to stay away from the grey house next door, and to never talk to anyone at the house. According to Dad, the neighbors had a questionable reputation. On weekends, they held noisy parties. Several cars with Illinois license plates drove on and off the property at random.

The glass front doors of the house swung wildly open, and two small boys leapt off the porch --- Lynn and Roland. They were six and nine years old, they were both towheads, and they were diminutive figures for their age.

Dad showed us around his two-bedroom house. The bunk beds in one room held my two small brothers. My sisters and I would share that same room with them. Dad had the other bedroom. The only bathroom was in disrepair, and the plumbing was rusted. The freestanding porcelain tub was often backed up with black gunk, making it impossible to bathe. Sponge baths were the norm in the household, if you could find a clean washrag. Dad's house wasn't very clean, partly because it was old and decrepit, and partly because he had never given it a thorough cleaning.

The house held in the swelter of the summer heat; the narrow windows only let in a little draft. There were no fans to circulate the air. On days with heavy rain, leaks from the ceiling wetted the kitchen floor.

Over the next few months, we were crowded in the house together, but we were united. I enjoyed hearing the sounds of my brothers playing ball and running through the house. The patter of their feet saddened me sometimes, because I remembered the empty spaces in my life when they were not there. Their voices reminded me of the void in my past that couldn't be filled. We'd spent five years of our lives apart from one another. It made me realize how we had been forced to accept our broken family, and how incomplete our family life was. Dallas and Roger were still somewhere out there. No one thought it was important to help connect us.

It was early in the evening, and Dad left the house without notice. He was gone for most of the evening. I busied myself like I had on Hazel Street, cleaning and putting things in order. My brothers were dirty from playing all day. I washed them with a wet cloth and put them to bed. The air in the bedroom felt stuffy, even claustrophobic, from the recent rain. There was only one window in the bedroom. A large crack ran through the glass, but clear plastic had been nailed to the frame to keep the rain out. I removed the plastic, rolling it up and securing it in place, and raised the window as high as it would go. Years of warping and chipped paint stopped the window about half way. I tied the tattered drapery to the side of the bunk bed to allow more air into the room. A slight breeze swept through the house. The evening air began to cool off. I turned off the lights.

As I was preparing for bed, I heard my Dad come in the back door. He tripped over the kitchen chair and knocked it to the floor, and his body fell hard on the linoleum. I ran to see if he was hurt. As I reached for his arm, the smell of alcohol invaded the air. My heart sank. Dad was drunk. His eyelids drooped like a flag at half-mast honoring the dead. He stood up and wobbled outside to the back concrete porch, his arms flapping like broken chicken wings, his knees lifting, one after the other, to balance himself, and his hands feebly slapping his moving knees.

"Come here, Sholo!"

I moved in his direction, but he suddenly collapsed into a heap on the top step.

"You know, I still love your mother."

"I know Dad, you still love mom," I gently affirmed what he said.

"You, knoooow," he said, slurring his words. "You ain't my daughter. But I still loooove you."

"Oh!" I said, knowing it was the alcohol talking, and remembering the past.

"No, hear me. You ain't my daughter, Sholo. You have a different dad." His voice was barely audible.

"Your mother was dating someone else before I met her. She told me the day you were born, you ain't my child."

"Dad, are you sure?" I asked, not knowing what to believe.

"Yes, as the night is dark!" He stood up with wobbling legs, trying to keep his balance. He bent backwards, and he cried like a hooting owl, unaware that his sadness permeated the air. I held his arm tight as he sat down. He lay back on the cool concrete, and he fell asleep there for the rest of the night. I lay next to Dad and looked to the heavens for answers. There was a moment of silence and welcomed calm between the dark of night and the light of daybreak. I fell asleep next to him.

CHAPTER THREE

The Long Winter

everal months later, I turned sixteen. The day passed without fanfare, as if my birth wasn't important. I decided to sleep until noon. When I got out of bed, I pushed aside the thin curtains, and I looked through the crooked window frame. Snow blanketed the ground, and the temperature had risen from the overnight high of 20 degrees to 30 degrees. The pure white snow reminded me of Christmas on Hazel Street, when Santa would pass by in his sleigh, his horses prancing and bells jingling, creating a festive air in the town. A gust of cold wind blew through a crack in the window, tossing my bangs to the side of my forehead. I grasped my nightgown and pulled it tightly against my neck.

Dad pushed the bedroom door open.

"Sholo! Your mom will be here soon to take your sisters and you to Chicago!"

Six months earlier, Mom had promised she would be back for us. But over the last five years, she had always promised things and never delivered, so I had not really expected it to happen. Now, as usual, my sisters and I were the last to know about changes in our lives, as if our opinions didn't matter. Adults would shift our lives suddenly, leaving us no time to process the changes or make preparations emotionally. We had been living with Dad for seven months and moving again meant leaving my brothers behind. Once again, my siblings and I would be split apart. I struggled to hold back the tears.

I was in the middle of the ninth grade at Marion High School, and I would miss my high school chorus. It gave me joy to sing and be a part of a group. For the most part, I was too embarrassed to bring a friend home. Dad was drinking heavily and food was scarce in the house. I avoided making close friends because I lived in an undesirable neighborhood, and we lived differently than other families. It's hard to fit in when you know you are different. I lived poor. I didn't want to be poor. Poverty to me meant a lack of education that might lead to alcoholism, abuse, and neglect. From childhood, poverty manifested itself in me physically, psychologically, and emotionally. I withdrew because I felt inferior; I was cautious around wealthier students so they would not judge me. So here in Marion, I avoided deep friendships. I missed my friend Carole because we had a history together, and she never judged me based on my home life. She was a secure rock in a rush of pebbles constantly moving downstream. I desperately wanted to call Carole, but Dad didn't have a telephone so I couldn't.

My sisters and I would move to Chicago to live with Mom and her new husband, Lee. She met him a few months ago, and they were recently married. After her marriage, Mom was eager to bring us to live with her. But neither of our parents was prepared to take Dallas and deal with his special needs. I looked forward to seeing my mother.

That afternoon, the sound of rolling tires crunched over the frozen snow, and the brakes skidded to a sudden stop, and the engine turned off. The polished car with sleek fins design sat quietly in Dad's driveway.

"That must be Mom and her new husband!" I said.

I ran to the bedroom and grabbed my bag filled with my personal items. I threw my dress over my slip, and I ran to the living room window and swept back the torn drapery, looking again at the sleek shiny car. My mother and my new stepfather were seated in a shadow in the front seat. My stepfather, Lee, sat staring ahead, resting his elbow on the steering wheel, and then he turned to my mother. For a few minutes, there seemed to be some heated conversation between them. Soon after, my stepfather stepped out of the car and turned again toward my mother. He bent his head down toward the driver window and paused. He looked at my mother, and she shook her head strongly from side to side. Mom wanted no contact with my dad.

Lee was dressed in a short-sleeve shirt, ignoring the bitter cold. He stepped up on the porch and stomped snow from his feet, looking down at his shoes, which were polished to a high sheen—a leftover habit from his military service during World War II. He walked to the front of the house and knocked lightly on the glass door. He stood tall, and I couldn't tell if he was young or old. He wore his thick dark hair parted neatly to the side. In his starched shirt pocket he carried a shiny gold pen. His freshly pressed pants were made of fine smooth fabric.

Dad turned off the boxing match, hesitated, and then laid his beer can on the floor next to his feet. His blond hair was dull and uncombed, and his belly protruded below his bare chest. He quickly zipped up his belt-less pants and walked to the front door and opened it. Lee introduced himself to my father and extended his hand. Dad wiped both hands on his pants and shook Lee's hands cordially. Dad motioned for Lee to enter the living room.

"Would you care for a beer?" Dad offered.

"I'm sorry, it's getting late, with a couple stops along the way, and we have dinner planned this evening. We need to head back to Chicago," Lee said.

Before he closed the glass door, Dad's eyes darted towards the salmon colored car, and then he looked back toward Lee.

"Sholo!" Dad yelled from across the room. "Your mother is here to pick you up," he said with a slight crack in his voice. He swallowed hard.

The bag that held my personal belongings was packed and sitting near the front door. It contained all of my very few life possessions—a mix of new and second hand clothes and a tattered pair of shoes. I looked around the house for anything I may have left behind. I reached for my children's bible sitting on the corner table and packed it in my paper bag.

My eyes glanced around the house at the decrepit linoleum floors, the dirty, peeling wallpaper stained from years of use. I sat down on the couch next to where Lynn was standing, and I exhaled quietly. Lynn moved his body close to me; his sweet, innocent fragrance still remained, his angelic face, pale from his asthma, struggled as he breathed. I leaned over and lifted him on my lap. My hand caressed his ear, because I knew he suffered from allergies and ear infections. My hand gently brushed the side of his face, and I wished our lives could be different. We had lived separate lives for five years in foster homes, and we'd just reunited a few months ago, and now we had to move away from one another again. I was overcome with sadness.

Roland walked passed me. He didn't know I would be leaving. I grabbed his arm and pulled him close to Lynn and me. I leaned forward, and I placed my head on his shoulder. He turned and put his arms gently around my neck, his tiny body pressing close to me. He saw my suitcase sitting by the front door, and his face looked confused.

Still standing outside on the porch, Lee shivered from the cold, and he announced that we should be leaving. I walked toward my possessions, feeling both reluctant and eager simultaneously, and I picked up my bag.

"Diane, Sissy, bring your bags. Your mom is here!" Dad called out.

I stepped outside the front door and waved to my mother. Dad followed behind me, lighting a cigarette, and then he staggered toward me, his eyes red and tearful. He placed his arms heavily on my shoulder, and his cigarette dangled from his left hand. I could smell the burning cigarette and the alcohol on his breath. He glanced at the car again and then abruptly walked back into the house, slamming the screen door hard behind him.

Lee placed his hand on my shoulder and led me toward the car. He put our bags inside the trunk, and I jumped in the back seat. *I was going to live with my mom.* She was glad to see me, and she turned her shoulders and reached her hands toward me, smiling with affection.

As my sisters settled in the car next to me, Lee turned the key in the ignition, and the car rolled forward. I looked back at the house; my brother's noses were pressed up against the glass door, and their tiny hands were waving. I turned in my seat, facing the window, and I placed the palm of my hand flat against the glass, capturing the last seconds of our good-bye. Tears filled my eyes as I yearned for more time with them, and as the car drove forward, my brothers' images faded in the distance.

A few miles down the road, we reached the main boulevard that lead out of town. I adjusted myself into the leather seat, and I rested my hand on the arm panel. The Buick smelled like a new car, and the heater felt warm to my skin. Lee drove with his elbow resting on the leather door panel and his hand idly on the wheel, though he turned corners adeptly with the skill of a racecar driver. He spun the wheel in a full circle, and we turned onto the highway to Chicago.

Lee's cigarette hung loosely from his fingers, and jets of smoke swirled outside the crack in the window. I could see Lee's eyes clearly in the rear view mirror. He explained that he was an only child and that he loved the idea of surrounding himself with a large family. He was supportive of Mom bringing us to Chicago. Together they promised to eventually bring my brothers to live in Chicago with them too.

"When will my brothers move to Chicago?" I asked.

"In due time," Lee said.

Settling back in his seat, confident in his driving, Lee selected a music station and turned up the volume of the radio.

"Turn that radio down!" Mother excoriated. Lee explained that his ears were damaged from his line of work—he was a welder at the steel mill. There was little conversation in the car after that.

The sun sank in the west, and swollen clouds cast purple and rose streaks across the sky. I enjoyed the ride through the northern Indiana landscape with its undulating hills and rolling two-lane highways that stretched for miles. I leaned back in my seat and exhaled gently. The warmth of the sun touched my shoulders, relaxing me.

"Are you comfortable?" Mom asked. What she really meant was, *Do you like our new car?*

"Thanks Mom, very comfortable!"

Mom turned toward Lee and discussed school and future plans for us. I studied Mom's exquisite profile; she belonged in a cameo—the proud lines of her face and her lustrous thick auburn hair suggested an imperial beauty.

With a final wink, the sun set as a red ball, sinking behind the horizon. Dusk set in. The landscape dimmed before us as far as the eye could see. We passed snow banks that lined the highway and fading into the darkness. Lee held the wheel as the radio played "Strangers in the Night." My eyes felt the heaviness of the day, but I forced them open, not wanting to miss the scenery.

The night came on black and clear. The road seemed long as we drove into the darkness, and I closed my eyes, and I felt the great plain of darkness stretch out before me, and I let the dark of the night relax me into complete sleep.

"Wake up! Wake up! We're near Chicago!" Mom said excitedly as we crossed the Illinois state line. I had fallen asleep on the drive during my first visit to Chicago, and my mother wanted to make sure I didn't miss seeing the city again.

The road was still dark and was edged with silhouetted trees. Brilliant scattered lights hung close in the darkness. Gradually, we drove to the top of a slight grade, and we could see neon signs written on the blackness of the sky. I squinted my eyes, ready to take in the new sights.

As we approached the Chicago Skyway, the landscape became dotted with street lamps that stood shining and erect. My eyes were overwhelmed; they weren't used to the spectacle of city lights. Then I saw thousands of sparkling colored lights that filled both sides of the skyway. Signs of all shapes and sizes grew larger as we approached them.

Lake Michigan was to the east, and its foaming white waves splashed against the night sky, and commercial docks lined the shore, filled with ships and boats. A faint glow streamed from behind the distant buildings, the reflection of thousands of unknown lights. The electric breath of Chicago filled the sky.

Proud to show off his city, Lee sounded like a tour guide, and pointed his finger at the buildings of the steel industry where he worked. Far in the distance, we saw tall clouds of industrial smoke billowing toward a gauzy dark sky. Beyond the Chicago Skyway, the cityscape was glowing like hot coals in the dark. Lake Michigan shone with broken reflections of high-rises flickering on the black water; the iridescence of the moonlight caught on the water's surface as well. Low-wattage streetlights radiated for blocks. Streaks of car headlights moved quickly in all directions.

Chicago had a powerful personality. Moving to the city from a small town shocked my system. The city had an energy that I had never felt before. It felt like being born again. I was eager to feel, smell, and absorb the city. Since I would be living there, I wanted it to be my city, too.

"Mom, are we close to your home?" I asked. I wanted to get a sense of time and distance.

"We'll be home soon!" Mom bellowed.

I rolled down the back window, inhaled deeply, and laid my chin on the windowsill, the cold wind smashing against my hair, blowing my past away. We exited the Skyway onto the main boulevard. I observed the tree-lined streets filled with houses and apartment buildings closely lined up and down each side. Cement walkways dissected the minuscule lawns of each dwelling, and concrete steps led to glass-enclosed front porches. The landscape was so different from my small town and countryside.

Lee parallel parked in front of a two-story apartment building. He turned the radio off, and for a few seconds, I could hear my heart beat with excitement. But suddenly, my stomach tightened with a fear of the unknown resonating through my body.

Mom and Lee had settled into an area of Chicago called South Shore. Our apartment was several blocks from Rainbow Beach, a popular sandy beach along Lake Michigan. The neighborhood was neatly tended and was filled with brown single-family brick homes and two-story apartments. It was the nicest neighborhood within driving distance to the steel mill where my stepfather worked as a welder. My parents chose this location so we could be near a good school. Even though my mom had a limited education herself, she had learned through experience the importance of education.

Lee handed my belongings to me and then walked up the steps of the apartment building and unlocked the beveled glass entry door. He motioned to us to enter the hallway foyer. The entry was also used by two other neighbors who lived on the first and second floor.

My parents' one-bedroom apartment was located in the basement of the building. Mom referred to it as a "garden apartment," which made it sound less dark and damp, and less poor. Mom proudly invited us in. The apartment had recently been renovated with highly polished tile floors, and freshly painted walls. Mom had furnished the apartment with early American furnishings: spinning wheel lamps, cushions and pillows made of colonial-style fabrics in, and a cuckoo clock that went off every hour on the hour. The kitchen and the bathroom could only be accessed through my parents' bedroom. My sister and I had to be sure to empty our bladders before bedtime, since we had to walk through my parent's bedroom to get to the bathroom.

My sisters and I would sleep in the living room on the foldout divan. The ground-level living room window faced the street and had a view of the mowed grass and the front sidewalk. At night, if Mom didn't close the drapes, it felt like the whole world could see us watching television, playing games, and reading books.

South Shore High School was located out our back door just past our neighbor's gate, so our walk to school was short and convenient. Semester had officially started two weeks before. We registered for school immediately.

In the halls, the school had an air of academic achievement. It had scored high in the state. The students were driven to achieve academically and to go on to higher learning. My parents just wanted me to graduate and get a job.

Most of the students were wholesome and preppy. I felt inferior to them, with their city lifestyles and wealth. I didn't have their money or their taste in clothes. I didn't dress as fashionably as the other students, and, at 16, I desperately wanted to fit in. To make it worse, I had a bad case of acne. My hairstyle made my head feel misshapen—the blunt-cut ends looked uneven. How would I ever make friends? I decided that dressing differently might help me fit in.

On the weekend, I removed one of my dresses from my drawer, and I displayed it for my mother's approval. I was proud of my handmade dress that I had designed from a paper pattern. I had skillfully trimmed the arms and hem in a white bric-a-brac, and I'd stitched it straight, with attention to detail. It was a ninth-grade home economics class project. I proudly laid the dress on her bed. I pressed out the wrinkles and smoothed the fabric to the edges. I called out for my mother to look at my handiwork.

"Mom, what do you think of me wearing this to school?" I was seeking her approval of my tailoring, even if she didn't think I should wear it.

"Nah, you don't want to wear this to school here." She laughed. "It's old fashioned. The students will make fun of you!"

My pride was diminished, so I carefully folded my dress and placed it back in my drawer, forgetting any hope of approval.

A few hours later, my parents returned from a shopping trip, and they revealed new clothes in different colors and styles.

"Shirlee, these are for you!" Mom said excitedly.

"Wow, brand new clothes!" I exclaimed in disbelief. My eyes grew wide.

I quickly rustled through the shopping bags, pulling out the stylish new clothes. I picked out a turquoise dress that fit slimly through the waist and bodice. I slipped it over my head and down my thin body, the scent of its newness filling me with excitement.

"Very nice!" Mom said.

"Turn around, Shirlee." My stepfather asked, as he placed a shiny rhinestone necklace around my neck.

Mom took me to the mirror so I could see my new look. Then my stepfather handed me a pair of low heels to match the dress. The fabric felt comfortable on my body.

"You can wear that to school," Mom said.

"Shirlee, we want to take you to dinner, but it's cold out, baby!" Lee sang, slightly out of tune.

Lee wrapped a black knee-length cashmere coat with a faux mink collar around my shoulders. Mom opened the closet door and pulled out her evening dress, and she slipped it on. Together, we stood in the mirror admiring my new look, each of us sparkling. *Is this what bonding with your mother feels like? Is this what other girls feel when they share a moment with their mother?* I felt elated.

Lee made reservations for a dinner theater. He dressed in a dark pinstriped suit with a matching tie and polished black shoes. Upon first appearance, you wouldn't know that Lee was a welder by day because he was such a fashionable gentleman in the evening. Often, Mom told strangers that he was a movie producer because a couple years earlier, Lee signed up for classes in editing eight-millimeter home movies. This was his hobby, and he was passionate about it. But in Mom's mind, the lie elevated her status in life.

Lee wasn't college educated, but he made interesting conversation, and he tried to raise the standard of our lives. Entertainment was Lee's biggest expenditure. After the dinner theater, Lee drove us to go ballroom dancing at the infamous Aragon ballroom in downtown Chicago. We danced the night away in front of television cameras.

A few weeks into the school semester, I had still not made a single friend. But in history class, a quiet and unassuming girl sat behind me. She had long, thin blond hair, and she wore glasses that tilted slightly on her small rabbit-like nose. She expressed little confidence. One day, while we were taking an exam, I felt a warm breath near the back of my head. I turned and found her peeking over my shoulder. She shrugged at me with a look of helplessness. She hadn't studied for the test, and she looked desperate for the answers. I looked to make sure the teacher's attention was elsewhere, and moved my shoulder slightly to reveal my answers. I felt okay with helping her.

After the exam, I introduced myself. Her name was Sharyn. Although I felt guilty about cheating, I was happy I had made a friend. Sharing my answers with her was a bonding moment. We soon became good friends, and I started spending time at her home after school and on weekends, where we'd look through fashion magazines until I understood the latest fashions. I helped Sharyn with her self-esteem, and she helped me to dress more like the school crowd. Sharyn's suggestions about styling my hair and how to wear makeup and what clothes to wear helped tone down my misfit look. My acne cleared up, and I felt more confident in myself. Soon after, I began to fit into the Chicago scene.

My church taught me that wearing makeup and jewelry was a sin. But I felt no guilt in wearing lipstick. I enjoyed the color and shine on my lips, and I felt more grown up and feminine. My new, fitted clothes enhanced my thin shape, reminding me that my body was not something to hide or be ashamed of. I had never understood how one dressed defined who you were under God's eyes. It was important for me to observe the dress standards of the Chicago scene, just as I did at my church.

Because of Sharyn's gentle nature and selfless manner, she was able to cope with my abundance of energy and my chronic anxiety brought on by the unpredictable events and changes in my life. In the summer, we'd take trips to Rainbow Beach. Sharyn and I spent hours talking, laying on beach towels, and digging our feet in the sand. She helped me pick out my first bathing suit when I was seventeen. My religion had never allowed me to wear a bathing suit—only dresses were allowed in the water so we never exposed too much skin. My new bathing suit led to my first severe sunburn, and I suffered from the burn on my legs and arms for days, unable to walk.

Sharyn's home life was idyllic. Her parents were kind, and soft-spoken. They calmly discussed family ideas. Her parents must have thought of me as an anomaly from her other well-to-do Jewish friends. Meanwhile, Sharyn's home life and my home life were taking different paths.

A few months into my parents' marriage, it was becoming obvious that problems were surfacing between my mother and stepfather. Mom took on two different personalities; sometimes displaying moments of spirited affection toward Lee, and then her good moods would wither like daffodils.

Mom's need for control and attention became desperate. She irritated Lee by baiting him, playfully waltzing in front of him, using her feminine wiles to get his attention, and then begging him to hit her, trying to get a reaction. It was as though she wanted to relive our childhood over again when Dad abused her. Lee never threatened my mother or abused her. Soon, my stepfather began to lose the twinkle in his eye, the glow of the honeymoon. The tension between them grew. In her new marriage, this became Mom's idea about how to live. She had an unusual way of being in this world.

It was a warm and humid evening. The outside air felt dead with quiet. Then suddenly, I heard voices arguing at a fever pitch. At first, I thought it might be the neighbors. I walked down the hallway toward the kitchen window. My muscles began to tighten as I realized the arguments were coming from the kitchen. My parents were arguing loudly.

My stepfather was seated at the dinette table, and a cigarette dangled from his fingers, its ashes scattered on the table from a breeze through the window. Lee looked startled by Mom's yelling. Suddenly, Mom reached toward the kitchen counter and picked up a coffee cup, and she threw hot coffee on Lee's head. Lee was face stunned. He hesitated for a moment, looking down at his crisp white shirt, dripping with warm brown liquid. Then he moved his chair back, his tall body rose, and he walked quickly out of the kitchen past my mother, dripping brown liquid along the floor as he went. My mother stood there with her chin up and her shoulders back, satisfied that she had won the argument.

Later that evening, I found Lee sitting at the kitchen table dressed in a clean shirt, looking pale and drawn, one hand supporting his head. His other hand held on a cigarette, the ash leaning off the end. He was too defeated to knock it into the ashtray. He chained smoked into the evening, sprinkling more ashes carelessly on the table and overflowing the ashtray with cigarette butts as he tried to make sense of my mother's changing moods. I sat next to him, and I removed the cigarette from his hand and placed it into the ashtray. I distracted him with questions about his work and family. He talked. I listened.

At one point, I asked my stepfather if taking in three new daughters was straining their marriage. But Lee reassured me that he genuinely enjoyed having us around. He enjoyed surprising us with gifts and taking us out to restaurants, museums, and the theater.

While seated in his chair, Lee bent down and removed his shoes and socks. I noticed a large scar on his leg.

"What happened to your leg?"

"It's a war injury from World War II," he answered, then paused. "I would rather not talk about it. It was a dark period in my life."

"What did you learn from being in a war?" I asked.

"I never wanted to go hungry again."

Later, I asked my mother about his war years. She opened their dresser drawer, and hidden at the bottom was Lee's Purple Heart, with a silhouette of George Washington on the face. She seemed less interested in this part of Lee's life, but she mentioned that he earned his Purple Heart for his bravery in Normandy, France. It seemed like an object of this importance should be displayed on the wall. I thought he deserved another award for tolerating my Mother's moods.

Snow had fallen, and the white powder that covered the Chicago landscape was pure and untouched. Trees clumped like icicle palaces stood erected, buses lumbered along the streets spewing out smoke from their tail pipes, and passengers hopped on and off the buses. Automobiles sped past me in all directions, and snow and ice tumbled off car roofs. The movement of the city had an air of gaiety. The energy of the city made me feel alive.

After school, I shopped at the local market and walked along the main boulevard balancing grocery bags, switching the weight of the bags from one hand to another. I entered the foyer of our apartment and stamped the

91

snow flurries from my shoes, dulling their leather finish. I placed the key in the door. The apartment was quiet, so I guessed my parents were away.

Usually, our evenings were filled with Lee's favorite television programming, the volume loudly turned up due to his hearing problem. While studying, I learned to block the sound out. But I was excited to take advantage of this quiet opportunity to study.

After putting away the groceries, I sat on the divan, arranged the flowered pillow for comfort, and flipped through the pages of my homework, concentrating on my studies. But soon, I found the calmness unsettling; I was so used to the sounds of the television and constant bickering. My body felt restless, and I was unable to concentrate. I closed my eyes, relaxed my muscles, and fell asleep.

An hour later, my parents arrived home from shopping. Mom had picked up White Castle hamburgers for dinner, and she laid them on the dinette table. I sat down at the table with my sister, giggling over the bite-sized burgers, a Chicago experience. I scarfed down four of the mini burgers. When my mom finished cleaning up, she left the kitchen to watch television. My stepfather sat down and joined me at the table. He unfolded the Sun Times newspaper, and he laid it flat on the table. As he read the paper, he jokingly called out some job possibilities for me from the classified section. He read out ridiculous jobs for my inexperienced seventeen years. Belly dancer wanted, Doctor needed at a clinic, sewer, cleaner. We both laughed riotously. Nevertheless, his joking gave me an idea.

"May I read the newspaper when you are finished?" I asked, and Lee immediately handed me the classifieds, discarding the remaining pages in the garbage can.

I grabbed a pen from the kitchen drawer, and I folded the newspaper tightly, placing it under my arm. Slipping quietly through the basement door, I walked up the back stairs to the backyard. The orange sun was sinking in the west, and the temperature was in the mid-thirties, but there was enough light to look through the jobs section. I brushed the snow aside and sat down on the lounge chair, and combed every line of the jobs section, circling every job possibility. When I finished, I folded the paper and cupped it in my hand, disposing of the extra pages in the large waste can next to the alley.

After school the next day, I picked up the phone and called the classified prospects. I set up my first interview with the local bank. It was a small and friendly neighborhood bank situated on a busy boulevard at the crossing of three major intersections. It was six blocks from my home. If I accepted the job, I would get experience in banking, and I'd have a job to include on my resume for the future.

The job was in the operations department on the second floor above the main lobby of the bank. The position required filing and reconciling bank checks. The manager was willing to work with my high school hours. The pay was low, but I'd save my money so I could move out of the house, away from the bickering. I accepted the job willingly, and would start work the following week.

To get to the bank operations area, I had to enter through a locked exterior door. I worked in a large room with four grey file cabinets that housed customers' checks. On one side of the room, two large bookkeeping machines were installed for processing checks. A long table sat in the center of the room and was shared by several people sorting checks and verifying books and documents. The controller's office was a separate office adjacent to the bank operations room.

Once a month, we prepared bank statements for delivery to the customers. My job was to verify that the customers' signatures on their checks matched their bank statements in order to avoid fraudulent withdrawals, and then I'd file checks alphabetically by name into the folders. Bookkeepers worked very late hours, and they often stayed caffeinated late into the day just to stay through the day's work. The odor of coffee and cigarette smoke hung in the air all day. My bosses and co-workers were fun to be around, and they taught me a lot about banking. I looked forward to coming in each day.

Two weeks later, my boss handed me my first paycheck. He congratulated me, and he said I was performing my job well. I held the paycheck in both hands, staring at my meager hard-earned wages. After folding the check in half, I slipped it in the side pocket of my purse, patted it with my hand, and zipped the purse tightly. I held off depositing the check in the bank because I wanted to open it again and look at it over and over. The printed piece of paper meant freedom: freedom to move out of my parents' apartment and away from the arguing. I felt a sense of achievement, and that my efforts were appreciated, and it empowered me for the future. I knew I could do anything I wanted.

This paycheck meant that in a couple months I could have my own apartment. My sisters could join me if they wanted to live with me. Maybe my brothers would want to live with me too. Maybe we would be a family again. I jotted down my plans on a torn piece of paper. Maybe one day I would make enough money to pay for college. I kicked up my heels and breathed a sigh of relief, and I felt like celebrating.

I raced home, excited to share the news of my first check with my mom. She was seated in the kitchen with a cup of coffee, and I pulled my check from my purse and laid it on the table in front of her. She gazed down on the check and studied the amount. I waited for her approval and her acknowledgement of a job well done.

"Shirlee, this will pay for your share of the rent," Mom said firmly.

"But, Mom . . ." I pleaded. "Please let me keep my hard- earned money." I choked up and swallowed hard. When I reached for the check, my mom's hand swept it away.

"Money is tight, and this will help. Period!"

In one moment, my hopes for the future were dashed.

Snow had been falling all day. Several inches of snow blanketed the ground, and it blocked out the basement window from the street outside. I had spent a restless couple of hours in bed. The cuckoo clock indicated that it was before midnight. I felt a chill go up my spine. I pulled the blankets close to my neck, and I tucked the bottom blanket under my feet and along my legs. Diane was asleep on the floor next to me. I reached down and tucked her blanket tight against her back.

Suddenly, my sisters were awakened by noises in the other room. My stepfather and mother were quarreling. I couldn't hear what they were saying, but I could hear their voices escalating and the sounds growing more intense. I needed to get some sleep; school would start in a few hours. I placed my hands over my ears to block out the rising voices, and I tightly closed my eyes. Abruptly, the bedroom door swung open, and the living room ceiling light snapped on. The light blinded my eyes like sun on a glaring hot day. I covered my eyes with the blanket.

Lee furiously walked across the room carrying a large hammer in his hand, and he approached the two living room windows located at ground level. Snow was stacked solid against the exterior glass. With both hands, Lee reached toward the curtain rod and sharply spread the drapery aside. Next came the sound of metal smashing down on the windowsill. I sat up, pulling the blanket tightly against my neck and shoulders.

Just as swiftly as he had slammed one window open, he immediately reached for the other window, and slammed it up as well. Lee picked up the hammer, and removed a nail from his pocket. He pounded the nail into the wooden frame. He took another nail from his pocket and pounded hard against the windows, sealing both open windows in place, and exposing the room to the cold outdoors

My mother entered the living room, speechless.

"There!" he yelled at my mother, who stood in shock behind him. "See if I care!"

They walked back into the bedroom, slamming the door behind them. Frost penetrated the air. I threw aside the blankets, and I stepped onto the cold tiled floors, shivering in my cotton nightgown. I had to close the windows, or we would freeze. I moved the wooden stool against the wall. I put on my bathrobe and tightened it around me, and I climbed up the stool toward the open window. I grabbed the top of the frame and pulled down hard, trying desperately to close it. It wouldn't budge. I locked my fingers to the top of the frame and kicked the wooden stool away from the wall, hanging my full weight on the window frame, stretching my body in the air. The window was locked in place. The strength in my fingers gave out, and I let go, falling hard on the polished floor below. Defeated and shivering, I returned to the divan.

We shivered through the night. Diane crawled onto the narrow divan next to me, her body precariously hanging on the edge of the shared bed. The temperature outside dipped to the low twenties. We wrapped the blankets tightly around our thin bodies, doubling our warmth. Sudden gusts of light snow flurries misted the room, coating my eyelashes. I swept them away and fell into a deep, exhausted sleep

A couple months later, Mom announced she was pregnant. The baby was due in six months. This would be Lee's first child, and Mom's eighth. There was joy in the anticipation of the baby's arrival. Mom loved having babies, but mainly she loved the pregnancy glow. She felt more beautiful. She received attention.

The front door to the apartment opened, and I heard bumping and crashing sounds. Mom and my stepfather entered the apartment with bags and boxes of brand new clothing for the arriving baby. Lee rolled in a pretty white bassinette with yellow flowered sheets and yellow blankets with "baby" embroidered on them. Stacks of diapers sat on a hamper. Stuffed animals, baby books, and toys spilled out of a bag. Mom unwrapped baby outfits small enough to fit a medium doll. My stepfather surprised my mother with his new 8 mm movie camera. He wanted to capture the baby's first moments.

Mom was happily focused on the details of the new arrival. I questioned the wisdom of Mom bringing another baby into our world of chaos when she had failed so miserably as a mother, abandoning my four brothers and my two sisters and me, unable to take care of herself against my father's violence. She had no physical or emotional ability to take care of us. Why was she bringing a new baby into this world, into this house?

Wrought with pangs of jealousy, I watched mom enjoy the new baby clothes. As children, we had worn second-hand, ill-fitting clothes that she rarely laundered, and sometimes we had no clothes at all. Where was the camera to capture the insane moments of our life, to document our history, when the basic necessities of life were neglected?

My thoughts were conflicted, shifting from joy to envy. I felt overwrought with intense emotions about our childhood, and my feelings erupted about feeding yet another mouth when we had starved. We still had no contact with my brothers. We had no plan to see them. We didn't talk about Dallas.

Seared in my memory was an image of Dallas in his foster home, alone, upstairs and out of the way. Were his cries heard? Was he being fed? Did someone love him like my sisters and I loved him? When we were separated he was only a few months old, and he didn't know who we were or that he had brothers and sisters who loved him. But it was too sad to wonder about his life when we were just trying to get through our lives.

For the next few months, my mom and stepfather continued to celebrate the joy and anticipation of a baby. But my mother continued her game of manipulating and ignoring my stepfather for days, using this blessed event to control her relationship with him. Often, their arguments lasted for days. Then suddenly, a calm came over the home. My mom was feeling the birthing pains. She called Lee at the steel mill. Lee came home early, gathered mom's packed suitcase, and took mom to the hospital. I understood that she had had a hysterectomy, which delayed her recovery. She was gone for several days.

On the day Mom was finally discharged from the hospital, I paced at the front window, looking over the lawn, in anticipation of Mom and the baby coming home. I stopped for a moment and rested my chin on the windowsill, overlooking the street.

My stepfather's car pulled up in front of the apartment. He got out of the car, and he enthusiastically ran around the back of the car to the passenger door. He opened the door and reached out his hand to help my mother from the car. In her arms, she held a pink bundle of tightly wrapped cloth.

"The baby's here!" I screamed excitedly.

They walked up the sidewalk through the front entry doors. I could hear their footsteps on the stairs to our apartment. I rushed to the front door and swung it open. Mom and Lee stepped into the apartment, their faces beaming with joy. Mom bent forward, leaning the pink bundle down toward me, and removing the blanket from the baby's head. She revealed a sweet-smelling baby with a wide forehead, like my stepfathers, and tufts of dark hair on her head.

"This is your baby sister, Jeanine," my mom announced.

The baby's eyes were tightly closed. Then Baby Jeanine suddenly flinched, and she gave a whimper. Mom sat down on the divan in the living room.

"Do you want to hold her?" Mom asked, as she placed her in my arms.

Jeanine was radiant and beautiful. Her baby scent reminded me of her sweet innocence. All my negative feelings melted from me. I felt guilty for thinking that I didn't want a new baby in our life. I couldn't believe that I'd thought there was a possibility of a different life without her, a different life for us. I held her tight.

It was Sunday morning at the end of May, and the house was unusually quiet. Lee was busy reading the Sunday newspaper, and Mom was still in bed. I needed to get away for a while. With Mom's permission, I took Jeanine for a stroller ride through the neighborhood. The sun brightened the green lawns and the bushes planted throughout the neighborhood. I stopped frequently to fuss over the baby, adjusting her blanket and keeping the sun from burning her eyes.

I came to the corner of Jeffrey Boulevard. Overhead, the bus sign indicated that a bus was heading to downtown Chicago. I checked my pocket for money, and the Jeffrey bus pulled up in front of me. I maneuvered toward the door. The driver gestured and stepped down to help me. He lifted the folded stroller and placed it between the seats. I followed behind him and sat down next to the stroller with Jeanine in my arms.

After a few stops, the bus turned onto Lake Shore Drive and rolled along Lake Michigan Boulevard toward downtown Chicago. I secured Jeanine's blanket safely around her, tilting her tiny face and shiny eyes towards the bus window. *There is a vast and wonderful world awaiting you. Don't be hindered in life by anything.*

The bus sputtered along, soothing Jeanine to sleep. I relaxed back in the seat, watching the world outside, intrigued by the rhythm and movement of the city. Stretched in the distance was a long line of boxcars spaced evenly, resembling a spinal cord; they slowed uniformly to red signal lights. Our bus route passed neighborhoods of flat rooftops that sent columns of heat shimmering into the air. Beggars stood on corners, looking for handouts from passing pedestrians. One older man in a tattered grey coat lay in the street in a drunken stupor. Another drunken man urinated in a gutter near the tracks. Out of nowhere, a thought came to my mind: *Could one of those beggars be my birthfather?*

I remembered again the shock I had felt when I heard my dad, in a drunken stupor, say he was not my father. It had disappeared from my mind until now. I reflected on the day my dad told me I was born in my grandmother's house, and how he had learned I was not his daughter. Could this be why he drank? Could this moment have changed who he was meant to be? Did that betrayal create his rage? Could that be why he abused my mother? Did Dad wonder if Dallas was his baby and that's why he kicked her in the stomach? Could Mom's guilt be the reason she stayed in an abusive relationship? If my mother was seeing two men, how could she be sure of my birthfather? I shook my head, overwhelmed. I didn't want to think about it now. I resisted all those thoughts.

The bus completed the loop downtown, and returned back again to South Shore. When we arrived back home, my stepfather was waiting. He had gone shopping and brought more baby gifts in colorfully wrapped boxes and bags. He doted over Jeanine, and he showered her with attention. He pulled out his eight millimeter camera and filmed her every move. Lee's attention toward the baby sent Mom into a fit; she demanded my stepfather stay away from the baby.

Winter arrived early my last year of high school. A ferocious snowstorm had paralyzed Chicago. The overnight temperature dipped to the low twenties. I glanced out the window of the bank. The bitter-cold air shimmered around the moon, casting a glow on the white landscape; orange halos glimmered around the tall black street lamps.

The bank books had balanced without reconciling. I locked up the check file drawers, and I cleared my desk. My date was waiting in the parking lot. The snow had blanketed his car, and he started the windshield wipers. I motioned through the window that I would be out soon. We wanted to celebrate my eighteenth birthday by dining at a nice restaurant, but by the time we closed down bank operations, I had only an hour to grab a bite to eat. Mom wanted me home by midnight.

Lately, Mom's mood had been more erratic, and her actions were unpredictable. Living with Mom felt like living in two different hemispheres, one lucid and one insane. I wanted to love her, but she made it difficult.

Since there was not enough time for a nice dinner, we ordered burgers and fries at the local McDonald's. After talking for a while, I noticed that the clock on the wall indicated a quarter to twelve. The manager said his clock was accurate. Outside, the snow was falling faster and had accumulated a few more inches on the ground.

"I must be back home by midnight," I reminded my date.

We hurried to the car, and even more snow covered the windshield. My date scraped the snow off the windshield, and we jumped back in the car and rolled out onto the snow-covered streets. The streets were quiet except for the sound of rubber tires lumbering over the snow. The window wipers swept the windshield as each new flock of snowflakes pasted against the glass. We continued down Seventy-Ninth Street, still a few minutes from my house.

My date pulled onto my street, and he looked for an open parking spot. Most of our neighbors had settled into their apartments for the evening, so all the parking spaces were filled. He drove down the block and circled around, and he headed back to our apartment again. Still, there were no parking spots available. My watch showed a couple minutes before midnight. Assuming not too many cars would be coming down the street at this hour of the night, my date parked the car in the middle of the street in front of our apartment. He walked to the passenger side, opened the car door, and held out his hand; I got out and he gently took my elbow and led me through the snow in my high heels. Our eyes met, we hesitated, and I thanked him for spending time with me on my birthday.

My hand pulled my jacket cuff away from my wrist. My watch showed midnight. *I'm just on time.* I opened our entry door, and I walked down the stairs, placing my key in the lock. I turned it slowly, so as not to wake my parents. I opened the door, and my mother stood there in front of me. She was in one of her moods. In her arms, she held a bundle of my clothes, some of them still on the wire hangers from the closet. She charged past me and tossed my clothes out onto the hallway floor.

"Get out!" she yelled. "I told you to be home at midnight!"

"But I'm home on time!" I explained, pointing to my wristwatch to show her the time.

"Get out!" She screamed.

Embarrassed that the neighbors above our apartment would hear her screaming, I ran past my mother into my parents' bedroom, and I opened the closet door. I quickly grabbed my small suitcase and hurried back into the hallway. My legs felt wobbly from the sudden assault, but I bent down quickly and gathered my strewn clothes, dusting them off and shoving them into the bag. I zipped my suitcase, grabbed the handle, and ran up the stairs.

"Get out!" she yelled again. "And don't come back!"

"It's freezing out there, what are you doing?" Lee had joined Mom in the doorway and faced Mom with a cold look.

"Let her go!" Mom yelled at Lee.

While they argued, I continued up the stairs, pounding my heels against the steps.

"Shirlee, Shirlee, please don't leave!" Lee called after me as he followed me up the stairs.

I reached the top landing, and my free hand pulled the lobby door open. Lee appeared behind me and grabbed my arm holding the suitcase, and he yanked me hard toward him, preventing me from leaving. I was caught off guard, and my high heels slipped backward onto the top step of the stairway, and gravity pulled me down the stairs. I held out my hand to grab the rail, but my fingers missed, and I tumbled down the stairs and hit the hard floor below. My body landed hard on the cold tile surface.

Assuming that I would eventually follow him, Lee stamped back down the stairs with my suitcase in hand, and he went into the apartment, slamming the door behind him. My mother could be heard through the door.

"She deserved it!" she screamed, and they continued to argue.

I composed myself and staggered toward the front entry door. Fortunately, my purse had flown into the corner of the foyer during my fall. I quickly grabbed it, and I swung open the front door and stepped carefully onto the snow-covered steps.

"What will I do? Where will I go?" I whispered to myself.

Fear took hold of my body. I pressed both hands hard against my mouth. I had no cash, only my checkbook. It was in the middle of the night. I couldn't call Sharyn. I couldn't call my date. I was embarrassed about my life. I was exhausted, and I couldn't think. My world seemed fuzzy and out of focus. It didn't make sense. I pressed harder against my mouth in desperation. *What will happen to me?*

The north winds blew harshly against my body. It was fearfully cold, and the snowstorm was becoming more severe. I buttoned my long coat with the fur collar, and I wrapped my white scarf tightly around my neck, tucking it solidly inside my coat. I checked my pockets for my gloves, but I had left them in my date's car. I walked forward in my four-inch high heels, slipping and sliding my way down the snow-covered walkway. It was a terrible night to be without boots.

Overhead, a gust of wind stirred the tree branches, dusting snow on my coat, and I brushed it off with my bare hands. After a few more steps, it began to sleet and snow, and the ice hit my head and pelted my face. The strong winds whipped my hair to and fro and pushed my hair back off my forehead, and wet drops of sleet melted on my icy fingers.

I couldn't think of any other place to go at that hour, so I continued walking north on Jeffrey Boulevard, the compass within me wavering at every corner trying to decide which of the three different directions would lead me to warmth and safety. It felt strange to feel my feet slipping in many directions, precariously holding my balance. I walked slowly so I wouldn't fall down.

Apartments lined both sides of the boulevard. The white snowflakes contrasted the dark evening and fell heavily on the hoods of cars, blanketing everything in sight. The brilliant frozen raindrops on telephone wires were backlit, and they looked like a sparkling necklace draped over a dark dress. There were no businesses on either side of the street, no place I could stay for the night. I could not remember any hotels or motels in the area. I would need to walk many blocks to Seventy-First Street where the Illinois Central train rail crossed over. I was cold and confused, and I didn't know which direction I should take my chances with.

I was confronted with the terrors of the night. The difficult night's walk became marked by my tears, my cold hands and feet, numb from the snow and ice, and my down-to-the-bone exhaustion. I looked up at a street light on the corner. It was a glove of light, a beacon of hope, guiding my way. Without the light, I would be lost. I saw an empty stretch of space across the boulevard—an abandoned park—so I moved quickly to the next block. In the distance, I saw a closed shop with an electric bulb that kept blinking on and off, as if winking at me with evil intent. Up ahead in an alley, a shadow moved quickly into the recesses between the buildings, alarming my senses and sending chills up my spine. I stepped into an icy snow bank up to my calves, out onto the icy boulevard away from any danger, and I turned my head side to side, looking back, and looking sideways. My eyes glanced around until the chills disappeared.

The cold deepened, as if rising from the frozen earth. I walked endlessly, hoping I would find a place to stay for the night. I found Chicago shocking and bizarre and beautiful in its venality, but meeting it head on in this way was frightening.

At one in the morning, the cold increased in intensity with the bleakness that usually precedes another severe snowstorm. I feared there was no more hope for warmth, as the Seventy-First Street shops were darkened, and the storefronts were closed except for a couple bars. A door to one bar was left open. As I passed by, the smell of alcohol wreaked the night air. The sounds of music and debauchery filtered out the door. The empty, dim-lit windows enhanced my feeling of being alone. I just wanted to wave my arms and scream out loud, "I'm out here alone, helpless and cold, God please help me! I will let this moment belong to you, to right it and make it whole."

Up ahead, snow glistened under the street lamps, lighting my way. Snow fell off my hair, powdering my eyelashes heavily. I wiped my cold and numb fingers against my eyes and slid the icy mush to the side of my face. I turned my body around at the slightest sound, shrinking in dread of the bent, snow-covered human figures moving to and fro.

I moved in a zigzag motion, avoiding alleyways and entrances. What frightened me was the night, the fear of the unknown; I was afraid that daylight would not return. What would my fate hold? I'd been thrown out like a piece of garbage in the middle of a cold night by the mother sent by God to protect me. There is evil in the world, and it's closer than I want to believe.

I realized that all I'd ever wanted in life to find happiness, love, and stability. It seemed like it had been a never-ending journey, an unattainable goal. But I would live with the hope that the blustery snowstorms would turn to glorious days. I knew there was goodness in the world, and I would live my life in the sun.

After six more blocks of walking, I crossed over the train track and spotted the faint lights of an eight-story building in the distance. A mesh of sleet whirled around the entrance, making it difficult to see inside. I raced forward with difficulty against the gusts of powerful winds, my feet feeling like they were detached from my body. By the time I reached the building my toes were frozen stumps. I looked down at my feet, only to discover I had broken the heel of my pump somewhere in the last block, during the blank span of time I'd been running for warmth.

I arrived at the front entrance to the building. Chills coursed up and down my arms and legs. Standing at the interior entrance, a grey-haired gentleman slipped on his hat, adjusted his coat, and opened the outside door. I quickly raced toward him.

"Sir, Sir! Please hold the door!" I yelled.

This was my only opportunity to thaw my feet from the cold. I walked further into the lobby, and the warmth made me realize just how cold I had been outside in the freezing temperatures. My body's cold tissues had been tempered only by fear; the sheer intensity of it numbed my extremities from the cold, and I found enjoyment in the warm lobby reviving my arteries.

The scent of housekeeping chemicals permeated the air. A mop and bucket was sitting in the corner of the lobby. A shadow moved in the back room. I slowly walked toward the high wooden counter, rubbing my hands and blowing warm air from my mouth onto my fingertips. I realized I was in a hotel. I rang the bell.

A short, middle-aged man rushed to the counter. His thinning hair stuck to his head like tufts of grass clinging to soil. I gave a deep sigh of relief.

"I need a room," I said timidly, my legs shaky from the walk, my shoes painted with white salt, my feet frozen from the ice. I adjusted my broken heel to stand level with the counter.

"Tonight, or for the month?" he inquired.

I couldn't think beyond the next minute. I lowered my head, placed my elbows on the high counter, and clasped my ice-cold hands over my forehead. For sure, I wasn't going home soon. I had no money in my checking account, but I would be paid at the bank the next day, and the amount would cover a half month's rent. I wrote the check. The manager handed me the key.

"The elevator is to your right," the manager directed me.

I opened the elevator door and pressed open the iron sliding door, and I pushed the button to the eighth floor. I leaned back and exhaled deeply. I survived the night and the long walk. My energy saved me. It will always save me until God runs it out.

The long hallway had an unidentifiable scent. I walked quietly down it to the last numbered door, and I turned the key slowly. The studio apartment was furnished with a table and two chairs, a four-drawer cherry dresser, a green textured sofa, and a Murphy bed located in the wall. After examining the room, I returned to the front door, my hand bolting the lock hard.

A few minutes passed, and I wanted to find my orientation in the neighborhood. I walked to the window overlooking the boulevard and I spread the drapes apart. The snow had subsided. The hotel was across the street from the prestigious South Shore Country club. The front entrance of the club was softly lit in the night. Well-dressed couples exited the grand lobby after dining in luxury, their bellies full, getting in expensive warm cars to go home. In the distance, a dark glassy view of Lake Michigan illuminated with reflections on the water. I closed the drapes tightly. With the little strength left in my body, I pulled the Murphy bed down to the floor, turned off the ceiling light, lay down on the white crisp sheets too exhausted to move, and fell soundly asleep.

The next morning, I was awakened by the garbage truck, the sound of metal banging against metal. My nerves were frayed, and my muscles were weakened from last night's event. I needed a couple of days to recover. I didn't have the strength to walk the ten blocks to school and work. The front desk allowed me to use their telephone. I called into the office, taking the day off.

I hadn't eaten since my date the night before. I had no cash. I used the phone again, arranging a dinner date with Tom for the early evening. He made dinner reservations at a nearby restaurant. We sat in the corner booth, and the leather felt warm to my skin. I moved closer to him, explaining my situation with my parents. He understood, and he asked how he could help me. I asked if he would drive me to my parents' apartment.

We parked down the street. At Mom's apartment, the living room draperies were wide open, our world on display. Mom's early-American spinning wheel lamps lit the room. I couldn't find Lee's car parked anywhere. My parents weren't sitting in the living room. I walked to the side of the apartment. Their bedroom light was out. They were either in the kitchen or they had gone shopping. But Diane was at home watching television.

I went up to the window and kneeled down to the side, tapping lightly. Diane cautiously moved towards the window. I called her name softly again so as not to frighten her. Then, I slowly moved my face close to the window so she could see me in the light of the street lamp. Her face lit up, and she smiled. She lifted the window.

"Shirlee, are you okay? I've been worried about you. Stay here, I'll check on mom and Lee."

She quickly tiptoed towards their bedroom, pushing the door slightly open, and she looked down the hallway to the kitchen, and she closed the door again. At the end of the hallway, she saw mom seated at the dinette table. She ran back to the living room window.

"They're back from shopping, they're in the kitchen! We'll have to be quick. Do you need some food?" Her sweet voice was punctuated with concern. She pulled out a bag hidden behind the divan. "I was saving this for you. It contains money and snacks."

"Thanks, Di! You're the best. Stay near the window at nights; I will tap lightly for you. Miss you."

Driving back to my apartment, I held my date's hand tightly. I wished I had the safety and security of a happy home life. I wished I had the warmth and love of caring parents.

Monday through Friday, in changeable weather, I walked the ten blocks to school. I dealt with hunger constantly. My stomach churned in pain from lack of food, half starved; I never knew where my next meal would come from. Living alone at eighteen years old added stress and anxiety to my life. Between work and school, I was barely surviving my circumstances. Fortunately, I was blessed with an abundance of energy, driven by sheer anxiety. It would help me survive.

I faced unexpected events each day. After school, I walked several blocks to the bank. One day, a man grabbed me from behind. I ran away from him, but I was always worried about my safety. My work kept me at the bank into the late hours of the night, leaving me with no choice but to walk many blocks in the dark back to my apartment.

My financial situation was dire; since my total rent equaled my monthly salary, I had nothing left for any other needs. But I was grateful for the additional help from my sister, who kept me supplied with snacks and bare necessities. On occasion, my date would give me a ride back to the apartment.

No one but my date knew about my living situation, not even my best friend Sharyn. I didn't want her to worry about me. I didn't tell my co-workers because I was too ashamed to share the difficulties of my life, the humiliation of my abnormal childhood. I was afraid my mother's issues would reflect on my capabilities. I didn't want sympathy; I only wanted recognition for my merits. No matter my hunger, my worry about paying rent, or my hurt feet from long walks to school and work, I sucked it up out of sheer pride.

The bank job was going well. I was learning about teamwork, individual responsibility, and work ethic. I formed relationships that kept my balance against so much personal adversity. My boss, Barry, was of even temperament, and he found ways to cheer me up after a long day of school and work. If I misfiled checks, he would tease me and encourage me to do better. My coworkers celebrated birthdays and holidays with cakes and homemade dishes. I felt secure at the bank. They became my family.

One evening, there was a knock on my apartment door. I was hesitant to open it. Because I lived in a building with questionable characters, I'd occasionally hear my door handle turn slowly and quietly in the middle of the night, and it would send chills up my spine. I always made a point to secure my locks when I closed the door behind me.

Moving cautiously, I held the chain lock to my door, and I hesitated. I opened the door slowly, and I looked through the gap down the hall. There appeared to be no one out in the hallway. I slid the chain and removed it, slowly opened the door, and glanced again both ways down the hallway. At the side of my door were two bags of groceries filled with food. I quickly rustled through the bags. Between a couple food items was a loose twenty dollar bill.

"Who could have left this for me?" I wondered. "I won't starve now!" I weighed a thin ninety-five pounds, so I embraced the bags of food as if they were my lifeblood, and they were. Closing the door, I gently carried them to the kitchen and stacked a couple items in the cabinet and refrigerator, parceling out several days worth of meals.

Saturdays were our busiest days at the bank. I would work a half-day, increasing my pace at checking signatures and filing checks away. I was bent over the table checking signatures and preparing them for the file drawers, when the door to the operations department opened, and my stepfather walked in. How did he get into operations? Security always locked the back door to the operations department.

It had been several months since I had last spoken to my parents. Lee glanced in my direction, but he didn't acknowledge me. He quickly turned the corner and entered the controller's office, closing the door. He must have arranged a meeting to have access to this department. But why would he meet with the controller? His account was at a different bank. My curiosity burned like fire, and my eyes glanced curiously at the controller's solid door, watching it for any movement.

Ten minutes passed, and the door to the controller's office swung open. Lee raced out of the office, his face drawn. He swiftly approached the exit. The controller followed at Lee's heels, his lips pursed in disgust, his finger pointing aggressively toward the door downstairs.

The controller calmly walked toward me and asked quietly to speak with me. My muscles tightened, and I took a deep breath. Was Lee here to discuss opening an account, or had I missed a fraudulent signature? I followed him into his office. He turned and waved his hand toward the chair in front of his desk.

"Please have a seat, Shirlee."

I sat down. The leather seat was still warm where my stepfather had sat. After I settled into the chair, the controller gently tapped the back of my chair with the palm of his hand, hesitated, and walked around the front of his desk. Resting on his mahogany desk were folders surrounded by ledgers, open black binders, various calculators and scattered papers of policy agreements. He sat down and closed a file folder marked "Confidential."

The controller was a man of impeccable taste with shiny black hair; he wore a matching black suit tailored perfectly to his body. Sitting down in his black leather chair, he adjusted himself comfortably in his seat. Then he leaned forward, pushed his dark framed glasses up with his index finger, and clasped his hands.

"Your stepfather, if you can call him that, walked in here and asked if I would fire you," he said.

I gasped, not knowing what to say. Why would Lee have done that? I needed this job, or I couldn't survive. I would have nowhere to go if I lost my job. I would have no money. What did I do to deserve this?

The controller cleared his throat in uneasiness and proceeded to explain.

"I listened to your stepfather's story for a few minutes, but it didn't fit with my truth about you. I told him you were a good worker, an honest and valuable asset to the bank, and . . . and . . . and that he should get the hell out of here, and never step foot in here again."

Tears streamed down my face. I felt that my life had been exposed and that I had almost lost my job as a result. The controller pulled a pressed white handkerchief from his suit jacket and handed it to me. His voice filled with compassion.

"Shirlee, you have nothing to worry about, you are not losing your job, and I'm sorry for what is happening to you."

"Oh, thank you, thank you so much!" I dabbed my eyes with his handkerchief. "I will work even harder than I have, I'm so grateful."

"Please, there is nothing more for you to do that you aren't already doing," he reassured me.

The controller rose from his desk and walked to my chair, patting my shoulder. Then he walked behind my chair and pulled it back. As I rose from the chair, he shook my hand, and I left his office.

My co-workers knew that something had upset me, and they tried to cheer me up. They brought out a chocolate cake that one of them had baked. Someone served me a thin slice and placed it on the table next to me.

"I want you to know how much you are appreciated!" the head bookkeeper exclaimed.

"You don't know how much you all mean to me," I said, looking around the room. Another tear formed in my eye.

I walked back to my apartment and took the elevator to my floor. I unlocked my door and walked to the window overlooking the South Shore

Country Club. *I wonder if those people understand my world. I wonder if they ever had family difficulties like mine.* I fantasized about the Donna Reed Show. I admired the closeness of that family, the nurturing mother, and the stable home life. My parents had pushed me out of their home when I was eighteen, and then they tried to get me fired from my job, the only sustenance I had. Where did my parents think I would live if I had no place to go? How would I get anything to eat? There had to be an ending to all this insanity. I was determined to survive in this battleground of sheer chaos. I just wanted to walk into my future and claim it.

Winter ended early and the snow finally changed to slush, sending water trickling down the storm drains. I opened the window near the sink and poked my head out, enjoying the view from my eighth-floor apartment. Below my window, a white ash tree sprouted dark green leaves, and its upright branches swayed in the light breeze. The breeze tickled the surrounding plants, letting them know they were surrounded by nature's awakening. I studied the tree. Proud. Strong. Standing erect. Weathering the winter storms.

A stream of warm light broke through a cloud, and the bright rays hit my shoulders and warmed my body. I lifted the window higher, and I poked my head out again and inhaled the fresh air. Ah! Fresh air and warmth: God's natural ingredients. An orchestra of melodious bird sounds echoed through the trees. It calmed my spirit. I walked to the other side of the room and lifted the other window. I looked down over Jeffrey Boulevard at the stream of cars and imagined a more perfect world somewhere out there.

Over the green lawn next to the boulevard, a uniformed man was raking dried hackberry leaves and clearing the weeds from the dead plants. A grey-haired lady walked her dog. She stopped on the sidewalk, bent down, affectionately petted her dog and adjusted its collar, and gently walked away.

Across the street, I studied a wealthy neighborhood of large homes and mansions, their soft lights dimmed in their large picture windows accented by rich velvet and brocade draperies hanging from carved wooden rods, emanating a lifestyle the antithesis of my own, where money meant security, good taste, and freedom. The thought gave me pleasure, if only for a fleeting moment. How I wish my life could be different. I felt very alone at times.

I was determined to survive. I had to move forward. I had to organize myself in protest of my life. I quickly busied myself by cleaning and organizing my apartment, sterilizing my history. I cleaned the surfaces of my counters and bare cupboards. I alphabetized the spices. I cleaned the door handles, and I bleached the bathroom floor. I folded the clothes in my closet, and I placed them neatly in the drawer next to my bible. My clothes reminded me of my sister, who cared enough to slip my clothes out the window to me, risking her place at home.

I touched the bible with my hand, and it reminded me of Grandma. It had been a while since I had visited her. Memories of her laughter tickled my spirit. She laughed so easily. I walked to the dresser and lifted Grandma's photo and placed it close to my heart. I remembered when I had taken her picture, and it felt as if she were here now.

Grandma had moved from Albion to Marion to be near my Dad. The last time I had seen her was after a snowstorm had hit Marion, leaving a couple of feet of snow on the landscape. After the snowstorm subsided, I had shown up on her doorstep. Her excitement at seeing me was contagious.

"Grandma, I would like to take you to lunch!" I said when she opened the door. The winter snow was still deep, and Grandma put on black oversized boots. They were half her height when she was sitting on a chair, and she extended her legs in mid air, and laid her head back on the chair, cackling as her loose dentures clicked. We laughed together at how silly she looked.

I set her photo back on the table, and I raised my forefinger to my lips and planted a kiss on Grandma's face. I didn't have a way of visiting her now, but I desperately wanted to see her. I wanted to see my brothers. Where was Dallas? Where was Roger? With our lives so disjointed, when would we be together again?

That spring, I graduated from high school. With graduation behind me, I put all my efforts into my job at the bank. One day in late fall, as the tree shadows lengthened on the sidewalk, a car pulled up alongside me, frightening me. I jumped back from the curb. It was my stepfather. His passenger side window rolled down.

"Shirlee, I'd like to talk to you," he said. "Please get in the car."

My tired feet welcomed the relief from walking the many blocks to the bank. I accepted the ride. He drove me to the bank parking lot. Lee placed his hand on my shoulder and apologized for my mother kicking me out.

"I left you the bags of groceries. I hope that made up for some of the wrong doings," he said. He sighed. "You know how your mother can be at times. Hopefully she will be better in the future."

"Thank you. I hope so," I said, my hands folded neatly in my lap.

"We'd like you to move back home," he continued. "We're moving into a new three-bedroom apartment on Jeffrey Boulevard. It will be closer to your bank. Your mom and I want to bring your brothers from Indiana to Chicago. You could have your own bedroom, and your own bathroom. If you paid us rent, that will really help us out."

"Will Dallas come, too?" I asked.

"Yes, later, after we settle into the apartment."

"But what about the fighting?"

"You know how your mother gets at times," Lee said. "She's sorry afterward. Your mother just gets in these moods, you know."

"But will you promise there will be no fighting?" I looked him in the eye.

"She said things would be different." Lee sounded convinced by her words.

Lee always apologized for Mom's behavior. He apologized for the arguments. He worked hard to make our family work, and he tried to make us happy. But she wouldn't let him. Why wouldn't she apologize and promise not to hurt me again? I could trust Lee, but could I trust my mother? Would Mom finally change?

I listened hard. Very hard.

"Wait, I have something for you." He reached in his pocket and gave me a twenty-dollar bill—enough money to buy food for the week and bus fare back to my apartment.

"Oh, thank you," I said, tucking the bill into my purse. "This really helps!" Promising Lee I would think about his offer to move back home, I exited the car, and I walked toward the operations door. Before entering, I looked down at my feet, hesitating for a moment. There was so much to think about. Although I was starving most of the time, things were settling down for me in my apartment. My life was peaceful. Was it the right decision to move back home?

I wanted a mother who would be kind to the family. I enjoyed spending time with Lee. Lee was reasonable until Mom pushed him to the breaking point. I wanted to be with my brothers and sisters. We could be a family again.

My parents promised to stop fighting, and I reluctantly agreed to move back home. It meant that my brothers would be moving there soon. I wanted our family to reunite. I wanted a rhythm to my life like nature's rhythms—harmonious and predictable like the seasons. Maybe this would mark a new beginning.

That evening, I sat at the table and composed a long letter, dense with dark ink. It listed everything I wished for my life and for my family. I was going to carve out a niche for myself, and I would help my brothers and sisters. I folded the paper into a tiny airplane, and I walked to my open window and cast my hopes to the heavens.

The phone rang. It was my parents. They were on their way over to my apartment with boxes to help me move. It was the first of the month, and I would give Mom my salary check for my rent. It seemed like a lot to pay in rent; it left no money for me. But if it meant being with my brothers and sisters and helping my family, it would be worth it. And mom's new apartment would be a closer walk to the bank.

My stepfather picked me up at my apartment, and drove me to their new home. Mom met me at the door; she was happy to see me. She pointed to the large living room, highlighted by a large picture window with a view of the passing traffic and buses that can take you anywhere in Chicago. Mom walked me to my bedroom, proud that I had an adjacent bathroom. She had bought brand new bedroom furniture for me. She personally decorated the bed beautifully with a matching comforter and draperies. The back bedroom had a corner window that overlooked the flat, grassy yard surrounded by a steel fence. There were no trees and or bushes. A large aluminum garbage can sat conveniently in the corner near the garage, so it was easy to empty out the garbage.

Mom seemed happy. She was most happy when she was designing a new home. Decorating brought out the creative side of her, and she was easy to be around. Lee supported her desires to make the home beautiful and enjoyed watching her in these moments.

Along with the newness of the apartment, there was an air of joy in our home. We would begin again as a family; when Mom was happy, everyone was happy.

Our lives were still scattered in different locations. Roger and Dallas would join us sometime soon. We seldom talked about Dallas, or our memories of how Dallas came to be in the world because his absence from our life was too painful to discuss. My mind rewound to my last visit at his foster home: Dallas left alone in his sterile room, completely isolated from the action downstairs, his crib lacking toys or stimulation.

But at least he had nourishment to recover from rickets as a baby. He didn't have to cry from wet diapers and diaper rash anymore.

Alone in my new bedroom, I prepared for my date that evening. Suddenly, I heard a gaggle of voices in the kitchen, happy voices. I walked into the kitchen to get a drink of water. My mom and sisters congregated in a huddle around a little boy. My sisters' voices elevated in excitement.

Mom stepped away from the huddle, revealing Dallas leaning shyly against the kitchen wall. Smiling, he seemed amused by all the attention. At nine years old, he was diminutive for his age, and he was dressed in a pair of blue jeans and a red and blue plaid shirt. His eyes, set wide apart, gleamed like uncut brown gems, and they were accentuated by his long black eyelashes. He had dark hair—lots of it. His face resembled my dad's, with a larger nose and protruding front teeth. He was quiet. But he would respond in little grunts when we spoke to him. He knew no words. He couldn't talk.

Conversations with Dallas were one-way. He made little effort to engage verbally. His needs were few. If he wanted something from you, he would point his finger or grunt. If he liked what you said, he smiled.

"Mom, why don't you teach Dallas to talk, send him to school?" I asked.

"No, I don't need to teach him to talk. He will learn on his own."

After the excitement settled down, I wanted to make a connection with Dallas. I gently took his hand and sat him down on the sofa. I explained that I was his oldest sister and that when he was a baby I fed him his bottle and changed his diaper. But he just stared up at me inquisitively. I led him to my room and showed him a photograph of himself as a baby when we were still a family. He studied the photograph, and with little expression, he walked away, disinterested. We were strangers to Dallas. He couldn't make the connection that we were his family, the same family charged to take care of him and protect him. It would take time.

Later, Mom confirmed that Dallas was deemed mentally retarded by the professionals. He would be slow in learning. Suddenly, the memory of Dallas's birth came back fast and hard. I shivered as I replayed the scene in my head; I had seen how Dallas was damaged at birth, how his life on earth was forever changed by one simple, unforgivable act. Now, here he was back in our life nine years later, a stranger to his own family.

My stepfather was genuinely interested in Dallas, and he spent a lot of time with him. I would always hear Lee and Dallas laughing in the kitchen. Lee joked and cajoled with Dallas, and they played games. Games seemed to be a way to reach Dallas.

Lee played simple magic games with Dallas. He did the quarter-behind-the-ear trick, and the money-in-the-scarf trick. Dallas was amused by every move. He quickly realized that money had value. Lee always let Dallas keep his winnings, and then Lee would take Dallas shopping.

Soon, Dallas wanted to be like his new daddy. Dallas particularly liked Lee's shiny gold pen that he wore attached to his pocket—it would always go missing from Lee's dresser. With Dallas's winnings Lee bought Dallas a set of his own pens. Pens were his rewards. And after a while, Dallas had a collection of many pens.

Lee soon discovered that he had a buddy in Dallas. We'd find Lee in the backyard of the apartment, attempting to teach Dallas how to play ball or badminton. Lee brought out Dallas's laughter, and together they laughed a lot. Dallas was even making an effort to say one or two words. Dallas was a way to get out of the house when Mom was in one of her moods. Dallas and Lee would go anywhere together—they'd drive in the car, go shopping, and eat out at restaurants. Lee enjoyed amusement parks. He would take Dallas on carnival rides, and Lee would act like a kid all over again.

When Dallas and Lee's relationship became even closer, Mom began to feel neglected by my stepfather just as she had after Jeanine was born. When Dallas and Lee were having fun, my mother would interrupt their joy. She felt left out of their relationship, and she'd often mope on the couch, criticizing Lee for spending too much time with Dallas and not enough with her. Caring for baby Jeanine wasn't enough. My mother needed Lee's full attention.

Shopping at the mall became a Saturday ritual. Mom prioritized dressing well; she'd apply her makeup with care, and she'd always wear her auburn hair in a stylish bouffant. She was proud of her new life, her new car, and the nice neighborhood she lived in. And she liked buying clothes for the family.

One Saturday, Mom dressed Dallas in a winter coat. After she buttoned his coat, I realized it was too big for him. It was too long and too wide, and the cuffs fell well below his hands.

"Mom, we're going to the store anyway, shouldn't we return the coat for an appropriate size?" I asked.

"Never mind, he'll grow into it!" Her tone meant that the conversation would end there.

My parents drove us to the nearest Community Discount Store, where prices were lower, and where the merchandise was mediocre. The store had a large selection of clothes and household items. My parents and

113

Jeanine went in one different direction with Dallas, while my sisters and I split off to the teenage section to look for the latest styles.

"We'll be back!" Lee hollered. With his hand on Dallas's shoulder, he guided Dallas down the aisles of the store.

My sisters and I picked out our favorite styles and colors, tried them on, setting some items aside for our parents to buy. We finished shopping and met Mom near the beverage area. She took our items and disappeared back into the store while we returned to the car.

On the drive back to our apartment, Lee stopped by White Castle and ordered a couple dozen take-out hamburgers for dinner. When we arrived home, Mom asked us to set out the hamburgers on the kitchen counter and said she would be in shortly. I laid out paper plates, and I placed the hamburgers on a tray for us to serve ourselves. With only four chairs at the kitchen table, we wouldn't be sitting down as a family together.

Mom's bedroom door was left slightly open, so I could see clearly into my parents' bedroom. Mom had removed Dallas's large coat from his back, and she'd laid the coat on the bed. Dallas's torso looked strangely lumpy. Mom unbuttoned his oversized shirt, and she reached her hand inside. One by one, she pulled out stolen clothes: a pair of small blue pants, a sweater, a white shirt, and a flowered blouse. Lee reached inside Dallas's pants pocket and pulled out a gold piece of jewelry. Dallas was puzzled by this situation, but he just stood there while my parents unearthed items from his clothes like magicians at a sideshow.

Mom caught me looking into their bedroom, and she quickly glared at me.

"Stop being nosy, Shirlee!" she screamed from the bedroom.

My eyes looked down at my clothes. I touched my left hand to my skirt, and I scrunched the fabric hard. My right fingers touched the shiny necklace around my neck. I grasped the chain and pulled it down, breaking it so that it fell to the floor and twisted in a pile. Its price tag was worthless to me. I kicked the necklace underneath the dining cabinet. Were my clothes stolen, too? I ran to my room and asked God to forgive me for wearing anything that had been stolen.

It became obvious that my parents had been stealing clothing and jewelry from the store and stuffing them down Dallas's shirt, disguising them under his large coat. Dallas, draped in his oversized winter coat, followed my parents innocently down the aisles. Mom and Lee shopped for the items they desired, and then they shoved Dallas between the clothes racks and stuffed his shirt and pants. Then they'd cover him up, zipping up the large oversize coat, hiding the stolen items. When it came time for checking out, my parents would coordinate, and my mom would usher

Dallas quickly past the checkout counter, and through the front doors. Lee would walk to the cashier and pay for some insignificant item as a distraction while Mom directed Dallas quickly to the front seat of the car. Dallas didn't understand what happened to him, and I didn't accept clothes or jewelry from my parents from that day forward. I would earn what I wore.

At the bank, my boss began to notice the extra unpaid hours I worked. He could see that the long days had caught up with me. I had never complained about working overtime. I was happy to have the job. He told me to take a day off.

The forecast called for clear skies. Outside my window, in the neighbor's tree, birds chirped in unison. My body lay limp, begging for a few more minutes of sleep. My eyelids closed again, and I dozed off for a few more moments of rest.

I had decided that I wanted to spend my day off with Dallas. I wanted to get him out of the house and away from Mom. I planned to take him to Rainbow Beach. My sisters could join us. We would picnic and build sand castles. I'd stop by the deli and pick up a few sandwiches.

Just as I was drifting off, I was awoken by noises in the kitchen. I heard the kitchen cabinet doors slamming. I crawled out of bed and tiptoed to my bedroom door. I turned the handle quietly, and I cracked the door slightly. I peered through the crack in the door. Dallas was standing next to the kitchen cabinet, his hand was holding his right shoulder, his head was bowed, and tears swelled in his eyes. Mom stood over him, her arm raised, and with all her fury, she swept her arm forward, slapping Dallas hard on the shoulder. Dallas held his strength and remained standing, like a broken tulip held together by a single fiber. His vacant eyes tried to process the pain.

Mom stepped back from Dallas. He fell limply to the floor, clutching his shoulder. She bent over him again, and with both hands, she grasped his neck and lifted him from the floor. Dallas whimpered as she released her hands from his throat. He put his hand up for protection, and she slapped him again with all her strength. Dallas's limbs became rigid with fear.

"You better not hit me or cry, boy!" She snapped harshly, her gaze fixed determinedly on him.

Dallas's hands covered his face. His eyes looked toward her in desperation. He tried to stop the tears streaming from his eyes. She slapped him again. Saliva started running from his mouth, and he started to bleed from his tongue. He looked aggrieved, and his eyes became

115

swollen. Then Mom's rage was gone, and there was emptiness in her heart. She showed no emotion.

"Get in the bedroom, now!" Her voice rose in a crescendo.

I ran into the kitchen, trying to keep my tone steady, but my horror at what I had witnessed would not allow me to.

"Mom what did Dallas do to deserve that?" I yelled.

"He wets the bed," she said. "He stinks of urine."

I returned to my bedroom, staring up at the ceiling in disbelief. If only my heart would stop pounding in my ears. I quietly repeated to myself, "Wets the bed?" He had a bedwetting problem, and she was punishing him for it. I had to get Dallas out of here, away from her. I quickly slipped my skirt over my head, sliding it to my waist, and threw my sleeveless blouse over my shoulders and buttoned it. I hurried back to the kitchen.

"Mom, I'd like to take Dallas to the beach with us."

"No! Absolutely not. He's staying in that bedroom."

Mom's moods were unpredictable; she was volatile toward anyone in her path. Dallas was bound to the house, under her control.

"Get to your bedroom, boy!" she screamed again at Dallas.

Through my bedroom wall, I heard Dallas's moans, the sounds of his agony fighting his breath to scream out, as if his wounded body was trying to keep his soul from leaving. Sobbing with passionate abandon, he knew he was helpless against her, knew we were helpless to help him.

Mom found a part-time job as a waitress in a neighborhood coffee shop. She enjoyed this line of work because the hours were flexible, and she made extra money for the household. Her schedule varied between nights or weekends depending on when Lee could be home to take care of Dallas and Jeanine. The coffee shop was located a block from our apartment on Seventy-Ninth Street and Jeffrey Boulevard. Mom served free coffee to the local law enforcement officers, who would stop at the restaurant on a regular basis. The restaurant managers encouraged this. Taking care of police officers was good business. The neighborhood stores felt safe because police cars were always parked outside.

The coffee shop was one of the few places Mom expressed any happiness and some sense of control over her madness. She was talkative and bubbly. To the outsider, she seemed lucid and normal. Mom received a lot of attention from her customers, especially policemen, who came to know her on a first-name basis. Her flirtatious nature ensured bigger tips, and her vanity was fed by her customers' affectionate remarks.

Knowing police officers ensured her place in the neighborhood. On occasion, the black-and-white police cars stopped by our apartment so the officers could chat with Mom. She felt protected just by knowing them. She openly flaunted their presence to the neighbors, particularly the neighbors she didn't get along with, which was most of them. Mom bragged to Lee about her relationship with the law enforcement. She enjoyed making him jealous, and she thought it gave her power in their relationship. But Lee ignored her taunts. My stepfather also ignored my mother's abuse of Dallas, excusing her moods as hormonal and temporary; but as it progressed, Lee began to accept the abuse and distanced himself from Dallas. This was especially heartbreaking since he and Dallas had once been so close.

As a teenager, it was difficult for me to report Dallas's abuse. With Mom's tight relationship with the police, who had no knowledge of the abuse, it would be my word against hers. My sisters and I didn't know what to do or where to go. No clear-thinking person could imagine what was happening to my brother. Who would believe a mother would inflict such evil on a mentally disabled child? Who would believe that the devil could reside within a mother? This painful and helpless part of our lives remained within the four walls of our home.

Mom's work was Dallas's only relief from abuse. No one wanted to be around Mom when she mistreated Dallas. It was too painful, and we weren't able to demonstrate to the world what really was going on in our home. Dallas was abused in isolation, and Mom would only hit him where bruises were less visible. I felt powerless to stop Dallas's abuse, knowing that she would get away with it and that we would be made homeless if I tried.

The alarm clock went off. I set the snooze for another fifteen minutes while the music played. I fell back asleep. I must have slept hard in those minutes because the alarm seemed to go off again instantly. It was Saturday, and I was looking forward to my date that evening. He had surprised me with reservations for a concert. I was looking forward to the happy sounds of the band.

Noises in the kitchen jolted my thoughts. My bathroom door slammed hard against the bathroom wall. Mom was screaming loudly at my stepfather. He was yelling back. It was difficult to understand through the walls what ensued between them.

117

"Get in there, boy!" Lee yelled. "Get in the shower!"

I heard the door open, and I heard Mom rush out of my bathroom and into her bedroom, slamming her door. I opened my door slowly and peeked into my bathroom. My stepfather was pushing Dallas into the shower fully clothed, forcing Dallas to sit on the shower bench. Lee undressed Dallas, throwing his clothes on the bathroom floor. Lee's large hand wrapped around Dallas neck, and he pulled him up. Lee stood back. Then he turned the shower on full blast, and adjusted the knob one full turn to the left, and then back again. He turned it to hot, and held it there, and then he turned it back to cold again. Dallas's blood-curdling screams could be heard throughout the house. Dallas was being tortured in the shower, his face swollen and red from the temperature changes. His cries pushed up from his chest into his throat. In that moment, I almost doubted what I was seeing. My stepfather had been pushed by my mother to abuse Dallas. Mom returned from her bedroom, looking satisfied that Lee was complicit in punishing him.

"That will teach him not to wet the bed!" Mom said, jabbing her finger in the air.

I quickly ran back to my bedroom, my hands cupped to my mouth in disbelief. I slammed the door shut and sat on the edge of my bed. "Oh no! This can't be happening!" I thought. Horrified, I hoped that my eyes had deceived me, but my ears could still hear what was happening. My emotions kicked into overdrive. I covered my ears, helpless to rescue him. Dallas's screams didn't stop until my mother was satisfied that she had inflicted enough punishment for bedwetting.

"Please God," I cried, "help Dallas."

I needed to talk to someone. I dialed Sharyn's phone number, and we agreed to meet in front of the coffee shop. Our friendship had grown, and I knew I could trust her. I confided in her about Mom's abuse of Dallas. We walked the several blocks to Rainbow Beach, talking the entire way about our families, contrasting her life with mine.

My family had no experience being a family together, and we didn't know how to come together. Somewhere in the fog of the chaos, my brother Roger moved into the house, leaving his foster family in Indiana. Traffic in Mom's home was like a highway, our family members passing each other without stop signs, or stoplights. There was no real connection among us. We moved in the world in our own frenetic ways, trying to find our places, our balance in the universe. We were just surviving until life found its balance. We had no family traditions—no family gatherings or dinners—so nothing bonded us as a family. I can't remember one single family dinner in that home where we sat down together at the dining table. The dining room and living room were forbidden zones, never to be used. Heaven forbid we should eat on Mom's dining room table and dirty the plastic tablecloth, or sit together as a family on the sofa and chairs that were protected by clear plastic coverings.

Occasionally, mom prepared a pot of chili or a baked ham and left it on the stove. "Help yourself!" Mom called out to whoever was around. She meant *Take from the stove; I can't be bothered with nurturing you.* We would eat in the kitchen, standing up. There was never food in the refrigerator except the standard fare of ham slices and a piece of steak, which my stepfather would always claim because of his World War II days, starving during battle. He had vowed to never go hungry again, yet our bellies grumbled.

Without cohesiveness to the family, we stayed out late. We came home at late hours after the arguments had quieted down. Our lives were confused. At a time when we should have been focused on preparing for our future, we couldn't concentrate on anything because of the constant chaos. We were unprepared for life because we lacked role models or support. My siblings and I were merely surviving until a time when we could take any path that might connect to a future, any path that kept us away from home. We spent time with our friends and their families and got glimpses of what life and families should be like. We felt unequipped to make it on our own, so we suffered through the family dysfunction. My mother liked it that way. Only she knew what was going on. Only she had power. Only she was in control.

Turmoil tormented our lives. Arguments between my mom and my stepfather echoed through the night with familiar regularity. Mom's moods changed often without warning. She was prone to emotional disturbances. Words flew out of her mouth uncontrollably. Often, Mom's madness energy snaked out of her like heat waves, hot and relentless; her inner anguish bubbled over, chaos always simmering within her. Mom couldn't conceal her inner demons. Her erratic behavior left everyone on edge.

One Saturday I finished my work early at the bank. I came directly home and opened the front door. There was yelling, and it was getting louder. I saw Dallas hunched over in a helpless state. Tears poured from his filled lower lids, and he wore a pained expression on his face. Mom was screaming at him, and her arm muscles bulged as she sharply slapped him. Her beating had caused him to bite his tongue severely, and blood dripped from the corner of his mouth. I ran toward him.

"Stop hurting him!" I covered his head with my hands.

119

"Get the hell out of here, Bitch! It's none of your business!" Mom screamed.

Dallas ran from my arms to his room, and I saw him crawl under his bed; he was insulated from the world outside, living in pain, unable to speak or tell of his private pain. The sounds of Dallas's tortured life reminded me of my distant past. Dallas couldn't control anything—he couldn't even speak to the violence in his life. Somewhere within me, under the numbness and helplessness, there emerged enormous pain for Dallas, hot pain, like the pain from scalding water.

"Dallas, come here! Here's a popsicle!" Mom screamed loudly at Dallas. A few minutes later, Dallas crawled carefully from under his bed. He stood up, his shoulders bent down, his eyes darting in different directions. Suddenly, his smile stretched with tension, and he walked carefully toward the kitchen table.

Mom handed him a popsicle. Dallas enthusiastically held out his hand and grasped the frozen dessert. His eyes dropped, avoiding the sight of her. He had courage to forgive such evil.

"Don't get yourself dirty." Mom scowled at him.

Dallas waited as Mom turned to wash the dishes. He left the kitchen and sat on the living room floor, biting his popsicle. As he sat there, the light and shadows coming through the window created striped patterns on Dallas's hunched back, like a prisoner's uniform. His mouth was drawn in a line of endurance, and his body was postured in resignation. I stood still, observing his forgiveness.

As the beatings became more frequent, Dallas's bedwetting problems were heightened by his anxiety about the punishments, setting off a vicious circle. It was not his fault. Mom and Lee stressed over washing Dallas's soiled sheets daily, and they forced him into morning showers to rid him of the stench of urine. The repeated bed changes and laundry would trigger their rage. Their beatings only exacerbated Dallas's condition. He just peed more.

Over time, the nature of the abuse changed. Together, it seemed as if my parents took sadistic pleasure in hurting Dallas. Their savagery honed in on Dallas's vulnerability, and it swelled their bond. They were the predators; he was their prey. They attacked him to relieve their own pain. They caused him pain to satisfy their own disappointment with their marriage. But the abuse went even deeper than that. Sometimes I wondered if Mom was taking revenge on Dallas as a way to get back at my Dad who had betrayed her.

One afternoon, I came home early from work to change into fresh clothes. The house seemed unusually quiet. When I went to open the refrigerator door for a snack, I noticed my brothers' door was slightly ajar. I walked toward the door and gently pushed it open, wanting to see if any of my brothers were in their bedroom.

My mother was standing next to Dallas's bed, her eyes transfixed on Dallas, and the whole of her hand gripped firmly on the back of Dallas's neck. She held him bent over the bed, his face over the bed sheet, and she was rubbing his nose in his urine. Mom released her hands, and Dallas took a deep breath of air. She tightened her clutch again on his neck, and forced his head again into the urine. She released her grip, slid her hand to the top of his head, and tightly grabbed his hair, pulling him upright. Mom stood back, proud that she had taught him a lesson about bedwetting. Through the narrow crack of the door, she glanced wildly at me, then turned on her bare feet, opened the door wide, and set off, high–shouldered, past me.

I ran to the bathroom, wetted a washcloth, and wiped Dallas's face.

"I'm sorry, Dallas, so sorry this is happening to you." I hugged him tightly, and I wiped the tears from his eyes. I left the room before Mom came back.

In my bedroom, I turned to put the palms of my hands against the closed door, as if to keep the devil away. Waves of anxiety deepened in my belly; what could I do to stop the abuse? I laid face down on my pillow, crying for Dallas. Through my wall, I heard Dallas sobbing with abandon. Mom's mistreatment of Dallas sickened me to the core. She brought her past wounds inflicted by my dad into Dallas's life.

An hour later, my mom called Dallas into the kitchen. "Dallas, get out here," she sing-songed. "I have ice cream for you!" I hoped she felt a tinge of guilt. Before exiting his room, Dallas slowly opened the door, peeked his head out, and looked both ways. He walked slowly to the kitchen table, his head bent. Mom laid the bowl of ice cream in front of him, and he smiled, scooping it to his mouth. His dark eyes sparkled with hope, but were also dimmed with sadness at the same time. He looked up at Mom. Like any child, he would forgive his mother again. He had no choice.

It was a Sunday morning. The house was unusually quiet. From my window, the clouds were taking on an ominous grey color, and they were enveloping the sky. I stared at the ceiling, my arms behind my head, pondering the day ahead.

An indistinct loud sound echoed through my bedroom door. Voices rose and fell like a storm hitting the window. The yelling came closer to the kitchen. There was a thumping sound against the wall. It stopped and then started again. Reluctantly, I tiptoed to my door and quietly turned the knob, cracking it just a bit so as not to be noticed. I held still, so still.

My stepfather and mother were standing in the kitchen, arguing over Dallas. Lee's face was flushed with anger. The sinews on Mom's neck stood taut and she gritted her teeth, white and sharp like a shark's, and she yelled between them. She hovered behind my stepfather, taunting him, moving her body to and fro, the anger and violence raging between them. I watched with fear as their fury collided.

Dallas looked up at them, staring at their pure evil with a look of stupefied wonder and helplessness. Lee bent down within inches of his face. Dallas flinched, his face bracing for the next onslaught, panic rising in his chest, his arms folding tightly against his body. Then Dallas quickly moved away from Lee. Dallas was frightened, his eyes were white-rimmed, and he looked at me, and stretched out his arms. Suddenly, Lee grabbed Dallas, slung him over his right shoulder, and folded his body in half. Dallas was crying uncontrollably; it was the kind of cry that didn't belong in this world, the agony of a body intensely trying to hold onto its soul.

"Stop hurting him!" I cried, running into the kitchen.

Mom answered with a stony face and a solid stare in my direction. Lee scrambled down the back stairs with Dallas's head bouncing against his shoulder, his arms flailing loosely, and his tears hurdling in different directions. I heard the pounding beat of his feet as he descended the stairwell. Lee reached the bottom of the stairs and opened the back door with one hand. He kicked the door hard with his foot, and headed toward the garage. Mom followed behind Lee, her head tilted up like a hunter toward the scent; she ran past me, almost knocking me over.

I followed them out the back door, closing my eyes in disbelief. Dallas remained on Lee's shoulder as Lee ran to the aluminum garbage can. With his left hand, he grabbed the handle of the metal lid and threw it on the ground. With tremendous force, he pulled Dallas down off his shoulder, and with both hands around Dallas's waist, he threw his tiny body into the aluminum garbage container and loudly slammed the lid down on top of him. Then Lee turned swiftly toward my mother.

"There! Are you satisfied?" Lee's eyes threw daggers at my mother.

I ran toward the garbage can. Mom noticed me behind her. "Stay away from him!" she shouted loudly with her finger firmly pointed at me. "I mean it, Shirlee, don't you dare move."

I stood frozen to the spot. "Stop!" I begged. "What are you doing?"

I studied their faces for the devil, and tears streamed down my face. "Don't you dare touch him!" Mom screamed again.

They left Dallas in the garbage can. The two of them went back into the house, quarreling over Dallas. Dallas had soiled his bed again. The stench of urine had once again thrown my mother into a rage.

Suddenly, there was a deadening silence in the house, followed by an eruption of sound. A loud thunder roared in the distance, and dark clouds descended overhead. Tiny drops of rain hit my cheeks. I wiped my face of tears, and I ran back into the house. My feet thrummed on the stairs. I caught my breath and ran to my bedroom, and I leaped over the bed. I grabbed the window curtain and swung it to the side, and I quickly slammed the window open. I peered down at the motionless garbage can. A flash of lightning blinded me, and seconds later, more lightning flashed in every direction, as if the artillery from heaven was targeting all that was bad.

I felt paralyzed. I stared in desperation at the aluminum trashcan, waiting for some kind of movement. Dallas was unable to escape his hellhole, he was trapped in a soundless vault of darkness. For a brief moment, he was safe, locked up in a circle of metal where neither light nor evil could enter. Then I closed my eyes, trying not to etch the violent scene on the backs of my lids. I stayed watch by the window.

More dark clouds gathered overhead, and hard drops of rain began to fall. A loud roar of thunder rolled overhead. Water dropped on top of the garbage lid with pinging noises. Still no movement came from the garbage can. It sat still. So still. Dallas's world rocked from the abyss, his life was balanced between two hells. The longer Dallas suffered, the harder it rained.

Thirty minutes later, the rain subsided, and the arguing had calmed down in the house. I heard Lee's footsteps heading back down the steps to the back yard. Lee walked through the wet grass to the garbage can, removed the lid, grabbed Dallas's hair, and pulled his tiny body straight up. He grabbed his shoulders, and he released him to the ground like a limp dishrag. Dallas lay in a heap on the wet grass. His eyes were filled with fright, and he looked up, taking in all the chaos in a single glance, and then he lowered his head in submission, his mind unable to comprehend such evil. Lee angrily pointed Dallas toward the house. Lee followed behind him.

Dallas was hurting, but he was learning to bear it. People deal with all kinds of suffering. This was all he knew. What human being would throw a child in the trash? This incident was freakish and inexplicable. It's difficult for any right-minded person to fathom such abuse, let alone such abuse by a mother and father upon their own mentally disabled child. Why wasn't the abuse replaced with love and protection for Dallas in my mother's more lucid moments?

The aftermath of the violence rattled my body. I was horrified, and I wondered about the limits Dallas could bear. His strength proved that he was courageous. Surely, no one decides to become an evil parent on purpose, or intends to make an offspring's life difficult. My parents were guilty of gross abuse, but it could never be proved to the authorities. He was abused in isolation, never in public, a secret unforgivable and shameful. But something had to be done.

From my childhood, an instinct had lived in me; I was vigilant, watching, observing, and sometimes judging. I learned as a child to judge good and evil because I'd seen such abuse and violence. I struggled against feelings of hatred toward my parents. I abhorred their abuse, loathed their behavior, and despised their being.

There was a sense of urgency in the air, a necessity to help Dallas. I was going to risk my family unity. I would endure the shamefulness. I would feel the fear that Dallas felt. I closed the door to my bedroom, and I called the operator.

"Please, can you tell me where I can report the abuse of a child?" I spoke in a whisper.

The operator hesitated for a moment, trying to grasp what she had just heard. I could hear her thumbing quickly through the pages. "Here is the number for the Chicago Social Services."

I called the general number the operator gave me and was transferred to a social worker. She said we were not in her territory and that she would transfer me to someone who could help me. Finally, I was transferred to another social worker whose caseload was in our area. I described the abuse that was happening to Dallas, and I gave her my work number. I ended the call with, "Please do something about this." She said she would look into it.

I walked back to the window looking intently at the garbage cans. The rain had stopped, and my fears subsided as the thundering noise quieted in the distance and fell away. The clouds cleared, opening to a blue sky.

It would take me days, sometimes weeks, to rise out of my funk over Dallas's abuse. I was restless, and I showed signs of anxiety, as if I had a hundred tarantulas crawling over my skin. I felt exiled from my parents even at such a close distance; I was unable to connect with their brutality and the chaos, resisting all the way. I was unable to focus, and my life became a blur.

I didn't know if I would ever recover from the hopelessness of our family. Would we ever be like other families who lived with love, protection, and support? I just wanted to soar past the sadness. A month went by, and then another two months, but Social Services never contacted me. There was no action taken to help Dallas.

My parents planned a trip to the East Side of Chicago to visit with Lee's parents, and we drove thirty minutes to the East Side of Chicago. We crossed over the bridge, and the red glow of the steel mills breathed in the distance as a column of smoke bellowed toward the grey sky.

We arrived in a typical Chicago neighborhood; it was an ethnic borough. It seemed that people in Chicago liked it that way. The neighborhood was populated with blue-collar Polish and German residents. Lee was of German descent and grew up in this neighborhood.

Lee turned the car off the main boulevard and passed his parents home. My parents looked over at one another, laughing as if there were something up their sleeve. I knew the look. A couple blocks away, my stepfather parked in front of a new home. In the front yard, a builder's "For Sale" sign was staked to the ground. I figured they must have decided to look for model homes today.

"Shirlee, this is your new home!" Mom pointed toward the house, her face flushed.

I was shocked. A year into living in our new apartment, my parents were always complaining about the high rent and lack of space for our family, but they hadn't warned me that they were buying a new home. My parents liked the element of surprise. There was hardly enough money for food, how could they buy a new house? That's when I learned that Lee's parents, who lived a couple blocks away, had helped with the down payment on the house.

"We'll leave our apartment and move in next weekend." Mom informed me.

"But Mom!" I said. "What about my job? How will I get to work from here?"

"You'll find another job. Now let's go in the house," Mom exclaimed, brushing off my concerns about the job I had held for the past three years.

Our tri-level home was situated in the neighborhood next to the steel mill, close to my stepfather's work. It was one of the only new developments in an established neighborhood of older apartments and homes.

The exterior of our new home was designed with two large picture windows facing the street. The facade was accented with faux stone, and a patch of fresh green sod had recently been installed on the front lawn. In the back of the house, next to the alleyway, was a fenced-in grassy backyard with a separate garage to hold my stepfather's car.

My parents had managed to save enough money to decorate the house. During the week, my mother spent hours shopping for furnishings. She had a talent for decorating. She enjoyed selecting colors for the carpeting, window coverings, and walls. The furniture showed up a couple days later.

On moving day, the air felt heavy and the heat and humidity were high. We sat in the back yard on folding chairs, digging our feet into the cool grass. Inside, my mother orchestrated the movers, directing the placement of each piece of furniture. Mom was in her element. She was never happier.

When the movers left, Mom invited us inside. As we passed through each room of the house, there was plastic everywhere. Custom-fitted plastic covers stretched over the new living room sofa and chairs. Protective runners lay over the traffic area of the living room carpet and down the steps to the family room. I took in a long breath and could feel the heat moving through my throat to the edges of my lungs. Mom made it clear, with all that plastic protection, you weren't allowed to sit in the living room unless you were a special guest; we could only sit in the family room downstairs.

Our boxes were delivered to each room, and we busied ourselves organizing clothes into drawers and closets. I pulled out my binoculars. From my window, I looked at the distant landscape. Long coils of steam pummeled the sky from the nearby steel mill. Smoke rose from tall stacks among rusty steel structures and aluminum colored buildings, reminiscent of an industrial age. Large open doorways displayed massive fire spewing from furnaces. I observed a blackened face and hands in the glow of an oversized oven pushing liquid metal into a vat. The red flame of poured steel penetrated the surrounding atmosphere; orange and gold glowed gently across the workers faces. Men clad in heavy-duty uniforms and masks sat in tall cranes, lifting horizontal steel beams and tending to the movement in all directions. The city landscape and industry was fast paced, continually in motion; as always, it was a stark contrast to Albion.
To my Mom, the house was a place to be admired from a distance, like a museum. This was Mom's first new home, and in her mind, it would be her last. She wanted to preserve the house forever with plastic coverings.

She was proud of her new home. The newness of the house seemed to create excitement in the rest of the family as well. None of us had lived in a new house before.

Lee turned up the volume to his big band music. The music elevated everyone's spirits. Lee ordered a large pizza delivered, and it was the first time we shared food together, standing in the new kitchen. Mom would not let Dallas join us.

"Mom, where will Dallas sleep?" I asked.

"He'll sleep downstairs on a cot next to the washing machine."

They were going to keep Dallas out of sight and in a private area where private punishment could be inflicted. Since Dallas had not been invited to our celebration, I wrapped a slice of pizza in a paper towel and tucked it in my pocket. While mom was cleaning up the kitchen, I went downstairs to the laundry area and handed Dallas the small piece of pizza.

Dallas was now ten years old, and he wasn't allowed to move around the house. He just sat in the laundry room all day, unless Mom decided that he could play on the linoleum floor in the family room. Dallas was never allowed upstairs or on the family room couch. Sitting on his cot next to the back basement door, he would put his hand out when someone walked by, looking for some attention, any attention. When my parents decided to go shopping or leave the house, they only sometimes invited him to go with them. We never understood why there wasn't a special school for Dallas to attend.

His cot was conveniently placed next to the basement bathroom and was a few feet away from the washer and dryer. They tossed his odorous bedding directly into the machine. During the night, my parents woke him up to prevent bedwetting. They'd wake him and hurry him to the bathroom to avoid contaminating the bed and floor with urine. Some nights, my parents were too late to prevent an accident. I'd hear shouting throughout those nights, and I could hear them spanking Dallas hard and then ordering him back to bed like an animal. I heard his whimpers in the night until he fell asleep.

Sometime during our first months in the new home, my other brothers, Roland and Lynn, moved from Indiana to live with us. All my brothers and sisters were finally reunited.

CHAPTER FOUR

Out of the Darkness

After three years at the bank, I gave notice that I was quitting. It was a tough decision. Before we moved, I had received a promotion to work in the bank vault, serving customers with safety boxes. My exposure to coworkers and customers had changed my outlook on life, and I found myself seeking, striving toward, and tasting a better way of life.

But after we moved to the new house, my commute was long and involved three bus transfers. It was unsafe to wait at bus stops at night. In extreme weather it was difficult to stand at bus stops and wait for a bus. Late at night after work, there were fewer buses and they came less frequently. I didn't feel safe.

I would miss the bookkeepers, their bursts of laughter, their homemade dishes of lasagna German chocolate cake, and the celebration at the end of the day when the books balanced to the penny. I'd miss hearing, "I popped!" from behind the large check machine from an exhausted bookkeeper when the books were balanced perfectly. I felt a sense of belonging at the bank. Leaving it would be a loss of security and predictability. I got along with everyone, and no matter what personal event happened in my life, I buried the issues deep inside and maintained a positive attitude; I never shared my chaotic home life with anyone.

Time between jobs, however, gave me time to spend with Dallas, although Mom would never let him engage with the family. He had his place. He was never allowed to leave the cot, never allowed to put his "stinkin' butt" on the furniture. He stayed downstairs on his canvas cot with its foldable wooden legs in the laundry room next to the back door. There was no mattress on the cot, just a blanket and a pillow. He was always on that cot, his eyes swiftly glancing at and moving past objects, unable to hold onto the moment. He held his head in his arms, not seeing, not hearing anything, not understanding, not feeling, and just going through his pain.

Often, Dallas sat on his cot with no shirt on. He wore a large bath towel diaper attached with large safety pins at his waist. It soaked up his urine, and it was less expensive than absorbent underwear from the medical supply shop. The diaper was meant to embarrass him out of bedwetting. It was meant to diminish him. It didn't work. The stressful way they handled him just made the problem worse.

Dallas had developed a love of pens, and he favored gold shiny ones, just like the one kept in my stepfather's shirt. He knew which ones were expensive and which ones were less expensive. And of course, he preferred the shiny, more expensive pens. My parents bought him a large bag to hold his pen collection. When Mom wanted to punish him, she'd take away the bag. The more Mom took his pens away, the more important they became to him. He would take pens off the doctor's desk, in front of the doctor. He started to steal pens from the store, hiding them in his pockets. Dallas wanted some power over something; it was his only sense of identity, his only sense of control.

Over time, his pen collection numbered in the hundreds. If you asked him what gift he wanted, it was always gold shiny pens. But they were too costly to buy. So he settled for pens in interesting colors and shapes. He'd spend hours studying the pens. He liked the bags that he could store his pens in, and he carried the heavy bags everywhere. If he liked a guest visiting our home, he would pick out his least favorite pen and hand to the guest as a gift. This was his generosity.

I spent time with him in secret when Mom wasn't around. I sat down on the cot next to him, making sure the cot would hold my ninety-five pounds. Leaning down toward his face, I kissed him on the cheek and drew him close. I noticed bruises on his thighs and upper arms. My body tightened at my own helplessness to rescue him.

I handed him a red pen and a magazine with pictures. He couldn't read, but the pictures would distract him from his boredom. Moments later, Mom came home from her shopping spree. She entered through the back door, carrying bags from the garage.

"Get away from him! Just leave him alone!" she yelled.

As Mom passed Dallas, she fastened her black beady eyes on him, bumping his leg with her grocery bag. His legs recoiled back away from her, tolerating her savagery. I stood up to leave. I grabbed my purse on the nearby table, and I passed back towards Dallas's cot on the way out. He reached out his hand for mine. I reached back and squeezed his hand as I walked by. I could leave her insanity, but Dallas couldn't.

It wasn't long before my mother was on my case about not having a job. She wanted me to bring in money to help with the household. Her yelling was repetitive and maniacal. After I had exhausted my job prospects in the neighborhood, she continued badgering me. To get her off my case, I would tell her I had an interview and then would hide under my bed. I was scared; I was scared of not knowing how to navigate this large city.

I desperately wanted to work. Getting a job was a way out of the house. I tried interviewing at local banks in the area, but no one was hiring. Each time the telephone rang, my heart raced, and my body filled with anticipation that some job had opened up. I was running out of options. Until one day, I caught my break.

It was early morning, and the phone rang, and I raced toward it, almost tripping over the cord. I picked up the black cradle after four rings. It was a call from an employment agency downtown. My sister had used this agency to get her job, and she referred me there. They were interested in interviewing me the next day. It looked promising!

Rushing to my bed stand, I grabbed the fashion magazine my mother had purchased recently, and I quickly thumbed through the pages. I ran back to the closet, rifling through my clothes for a suitable outfit, looking for anything that matched the fashion model's image. Pulling every hanger from the closet, I ran to the dresser mirror, flinging each outfit against my waist and pressing it against my body. I pulled out a tailored black skirt with a matching jacket. I raced to my drawer and pulled out a cream colored cashmere-like sweater. I threw it over my head, and I slipped into the skirt and wrapped the jacket around my shoulders. Perfect!

I passed the day preparing for my interview, forgetting to eat. My stomach hurt from hunger, and I was tense with anticipation. I ran downstairs to the kitchen. There wasn't any food in the refrigerator, so I drank two glasses of water to fill the void in my stomach. That's when I heard noises coming from the back door. It was my mother. She was creating quite a stir in the garage. She was yelling at Dallas. I ran downstairs, and I stood back where my mother couldn't see me.

"No, Mommy!" screamed Dallas

She raised her hand and hit him again. "Stop looking at me!" She glowered down on his small body.

Dallas choked back tears, the aura of his pain rippling throughout the house. I studied his tiny body, doubled over in its helpless state. He carried constant courage and strength to fend off such evil.

I didn't want to know about Dallas's abuse, didn't want to watch, to hear. I quickly ran up to my room, slipped into my nightgown, and set my alarm clock I pulled the bed blankets back and fell into bed, again using sleep as a convenient escape. I crawled between the sheets with the palms of my hands clasped together and the tips of my fingers resting on the bottom of my chin. I looked to the heavens. *God, I pray that Dallas's fate rise to the summit of human life, his abuse end, and that his abusers have satisfied their need to harm him.* Turning my face to the pillow, a tear dampened the fabric. *Dallas, these tears are for you.* I escaped into sleep.

Leaving for my interview the next morning, the red haze of the East Side permeated the air, revealing its pollution. The nearby steel mills spewed their venomous fumes in the air, and rusty railroad tracks and bridges gave the city a dark and ominous feel. I tried not to breathe too deeply.

The city bus dropped me off at the East Side train station where I could catch my connection. I boarded the Illinois Central train, and it rattled its way toward downtown Chicago. My body tensed with the uncertainty of a new job, but I was excited to have an interview. The city was still unfamiliar and intimidating to me. I observed buildings old and decrepit from years of use, smoke layered within dim glass windows, dogs lying in exhausted heaps on porches with their paws over their head.

A local transient entered the train and sat down next to me. I sat closer to the window, my right hand placed solidly on my purse. His odor permeated the air next to me. As his elbow pressed up against me, I leaned slowly toward the window so as not to offend him. Suddenly, my thoughts raced to my birthfather. I thought back to Dad's drunken revelation that I was not his daughter. It hurt me. How could he know for sure? I turned my head slightly to look at the transient's profile. Could this beggar be my father?

The day heated up, and the sky became dense, as the train neared downtown Chicago. Low-rise buildings swelled into high-rise buildings as we approached the train station. The conductor yelled out my stop. I quickly exited the train to the street level. I brushed off my skirt and shoulder with my hand, and I opened my purse to mist a light fragrance over my body.

On State Street, people rushed in different directions, elbowing their way off buses, crossing in front of cars, and disobeying safety lights. The noise of the traffic swelled to a fever pitch. The city held less terror for its native Chicagoans, but for a transplant like me, the pace was fast and furious, even dizzying.

I found my way to the employment agency off State Street. The Human Resource lady felt confident that my experience would qualify me for the job. With my bank operations experience, I would easily fit into a teller position. She seemed like a trusted and reliable source for anyone looking for a job. She wrote the address of the bank on a note card and said that the bank manager was expecting me.

I entered the First National Bank, passing through its glass turn-style doors. Its architecture was classical; inside were rows of solid white columns, high ceilings, and a marble floor that was like a reflective lake. There were heavy stone sculptures that echoed history. Resting between the columns were panels of bank teller windows. Tellers lined up behind the counters and tended to customers' needs. The busy bank cashiers were handsomely dressed in blue tailored uniforms with the embroidered insignia of the bank on their jacket pockets, and they greeted customers with a smile and fingered transactions on computer machines.

I walked through the lobby to the large walnut desk with a sign that read Savings Manager. I introduced myself. After a little questioning and a short interview, the manager stood up and shook my hand. I was hired! He led me to the head teller in a side room and instructed her to orient me with their policies and procedures. My first assignment was to get fitted for my new uniform. After returning to the main lobby, I gazed back across the vast space of white marble and strong columns. The soft light diffused and softened the space. I felt safe there.

My workday ended as the dark of fall came on quickly, and the city stores' signs turned on, brightening the streets. I walked along State Street toward the train station. The tall buildings towered over me as they emptied out their workers for the day. Vehicles roared softly in the background. Couples passed by arm in arm on their way to the theater. Restaurant windows were filled with couples leaning into intense conversation over plates of fine food. Laughter echoed in the night air, and my belly tightened with an intense feeling of loneliness, a desperate longing to be accepted and loved.

At 20 years old, a new phase in my life had begun. My probationary period ended at the bank, and I looked forward to being a permanent employee. The sense of security calmed me. Each day, donning my blue uniform made me feel a part of something special, part of a family. I

133

enjoyed serving my customers. My co-workers were fun, and we enjoyed time together outside of work. I was making lots of friends, and the guys were lining up to my teller window asking for dates.

After work, I walked many blocks, visiting museums and the Chicago library and shopping at the higher-end stores, seeking advice in clothing trends. I never forgot my childhood in the foster home, and the scent of new clothes once a year during Easter shopping.

The city's heartbeat was enticing. I was maturing in the ways of urban life, becoming aware of its etiquette. I watched the measured steps of people, admiring and studying the habits of the more privileged. I fit my small shoe into their footprints, trying things on, trying things out, eliminating some things and replacing those with better things; I would become a woman worthy in the world. I would leave a footprint of my own some day. I looked for a guidance system to take me to a new place, an entirely new life. I wished time would move forward, hoped for a change in my life to help me lose my memories of the past. But I savored my job stability and seized every positive moment.

I walked Michigan Avenue to the Gold Coast of Chicago where the elite lived. The windows in the tall buildings captured views of the lake. Dazzled by the upscale shopping on Michigan Avenue, I continued walking past landmarks and high-rise apartments designed by notable architects like Ludwig Mies Van der Rohe and Louis Sullivan. I needed to know how the rest of the world lived.

On Friday nights, my co-workers would blow off steam by going out dancing on Rush Street, which was famous for its late-night bars and dance clubs. At first, I was reluctant to join them for fear that someone would get drunk and create a scene. The specter of my father's drunken nights still haunted me. But as I got to know my co-workers and to trust them, I joined their Friday night outings. I even felt comfortable enough to taste liquor for the first time. I learned how to dance and found nothing sinful about moving with a rhythm to music. It was good exercise, and it made me feel good. We would dance to bands until the early morning hour, and, temporarily at least, I was escaping my life at home.

In many ways, this new life was beginning to feel like my own. I enjoyed live theater, museums, comedy, and fine dining. The more time I spent with my friends, the more my old life felt foreign to me, and I became more distant; I found my parents' life repugnant and distasteful in their treatment of humanity, their treatment of Dallas.

It was a sunny day in downtown Chicago. The sky was clear and the air heated up. The city was alive with the hustle and bustle of weekend shoppers. My co-worker, Donna, had invited me to stay downtown at her apartment for the weekend. She lived near the Rush Street area. Saturday was my day off, and Donna invited me to try my hand at tennis. I'd never played tennis, but I was willing to try.

Her apartment was located just a few blocks from the National Armory and a block from Northwestern Medical School, just off Michigan Avenue. Another friend joined us for the day. We walked to the nearby tennis court. There were no tennis courts available, so we would have to wait our turn.

We seated ourselves on a bench on the side of the tennis court, careful not to disturb a game in progress. Two men in their mid-twenties were playing. Both men were skillful tennis players. One player caught my eye. As he moved on the court, he had the grace of a ballet dancer; with each swing, his racket transitioned smoothly, but swiftly, to slam the ball back. The suntan on his arms contrasted with his white sleeves, and his khaki shorts were wrinkled and discolored with stains. The other player complimented him on his win and called him Chuck.

After the game, Chuck and his opponent stepped over to the bench where we were seated. After we'd exchanged pleasantries, my friends and I preceded to the court with our rackets. After some conversation with his opponent, Chuck stepped courtside. He was slow to put his tennis gear away. Then he sat down on the bench and closely observed our play. I constantly hit the ball into the net or outside the lines of the court. It was clear that my friends and I were novice players. Then I swung my racket and accidentally slammed the tennis ball close to Chuck's head.

"I can see you need multiple courts to play," he joked.

He continued to comment on our attempts at tennis. His wit was charming, and I spent more time laughing at his jokes than hitting the ball. When my friends and I finished playing, we went to the bench where Chuck was seated. He introduced himself.

"Would all of you be interested in having a glass of wine at my apartment this evening?"

"That sounds interesting," Donna said.

"We will need to discuss this." I pulled on Donna's arm, and we stepped aside, out of Chuck's earshot. I chimed in with concern about being in a strange man's apartment.

"He seems harmless; I think we should go," Donna persuaded.

"We really don't know him," I pointed out, "he's a perfect stranger."

Donna insisted that it would be safe if the three of us went together. Finally, I consented because we outnumbered him.

Chuck lived in an apartment a couple blocks away from the National Armory and a half block off Michigan Avenue. His apartment was a few doors down from the Northwestern University Medical School and Hospital. He greeted us at the door without his glasses on. He was tall and handsome with regal features and dark eyes that glistened when he smiled. He had a genial smile with teeth set to perfection, and we learned that his father was an oral surgeon who lived on the Gold Coast a few blocks away.

He seated the three of us in the large living room, and he offered us a beverage. He settled into a chair across from me. He spoke with his chin tilted in an air of aristocratic style. Each of his words was measured. He spoke with casual ease in his voice. He exuded a sense of self-discipline, and it seemed like he was someone who never tried anything without succeeding spectacularly. His genteel manner displayed the grace of a man who was trained in etiquette. As he moved his hands, the movement was deliberate, unlike other men who threw their hands aimlessly around while talking. He spoke of the theater—Shakespeare was his favorite— and his love of tennis. He continued his witty comments, which revealed intelligence beyond the norm.

Chuck was in his junior year of medical school at Northwestern, and he shared his apartment with five other medical school students. While most of his roommates were off at exotic islands and countries on vacation, he stayed to teach 150 nurses during his semester off. He preferred to stay and work. He loved teaching.

More conversation revealed that Chuck was raised in Kenilworth, a wealthy neighborhood north of Chicago along Lake Michigan. His parents had recently sold their home there and had moved to the Gold Coast just a few blocks away. It was obvious that Chuck lived a busy but contented lifestyle.

He asked questions about our work at the bank and about what interested us. He looked directly at me with his eyes gleaming and asked, "Do you like Shakespeare?

"No," I replied, a knee-jerk reaction to doing so poorly in my English class at South Shore. It had been difficult to focus on Shakespeare's tragedies when my own home life was such sheer drama. Shakespeare seemed too exotic for my understanding, although I got a kick out of the fact that Shakespeare was married to Anne Hathaway because my last name was Hathaway.

Two hours later, our visit ended. Chuck walked us to the door and asked our names again. He first asked my friends their names, and then he asked me my full name. He paused, and he asked me my name again.

"Shirlee Hathaway," he repeated, "thank you for a fun evening." And he quickly ushered us out the door.

On Monday, I was setting up in my teller unit at the bank and organizing my cash drawer for the day when the telephone rang in our teller unit. One of the tellers said the call was for me. After saying hello into the receiver, I heard a male voice.

"This is Chuck. We met on the tennis court Saturday afternoon. I'm glad I was able to reach you! I had some difficulty with the operator getting to you. I wanted to apologize for pushing you out the door so quickly. I have a difficult time remembering names, and I ran to write down your name."

"Please, no need to apologize," I said, smiling.

"I was wondering if you would be free this Wednesday evening to have dinner and see a movie?"

"Sure, I would enjoy that!" My smile broadened.

"I'd be glad to pick you up from the bank and drive you home."

Wednesday couldn't come soon enough. I shopped during my lunch hour on Tuesday and found a sunny yellow dress. I felt happy in yellow. On Wednesday, I would wear it instead of my uniform. I was ecstatic.

Chuck reserved a table for us at a fine steak restaurant. Since I mostly ate salads, I took a couple slices of meat and gave him the rest of my steak. We discussed my work at the bank and what my hopes were for the future. Recently, I had started attending Patricia Stevens modeling school, and I told him that I had had a shoe modeling assignment at the Palmer House. Then I shifted the conversation from me back to him because I was more interested in who he was.

As he continued talking, I found that Chuck had good judgment. His schoolwork was easy for him, and he was well prepared in his education. We discussed his studies at medical school and his work treating the poor in a free clinic that he had helped to establish. His future dreams included working in a hospital in a far away land. He was someone of great privilege who was willing to give up his privileged life to help others. He made it all seem so exciting. Our lives couldn't have been more different.

Chuck and I dated over the next few months. He represented everything that was good and honorable. His disposition was gentle and stable; his integrity beyond reproach, and his wit was sharp and colorfully animated. He made me laugh. He gave me a peace of mind that I had never known in my life.

On a brilliant sunny afternoon, we arranged to meet for tennis. It was on the same court next to the armory where we had first met. On that day it was empty. After Chuck gave me a few instructions and some advice about holding the racket, we played a game. I was no match for him. I watched Chuck's swift figure move across the court in brilliant competence. He moved gracefully and deliberately, balanced and triumphant.

Soon I was hitting the ball aimlessly in all directions. Chuck was laughing heartily while he kept my wild shots in play with agonizing effort. He could have smashed the ball back to my side and ended the game, but he was not playing to win; he was playing to make a connection. After an exhausting hour, Chuck approached the net. My heart beat rapidly as he leaned over kissed my lips. The game was finished, and we collapsed on the grass next to the court, feeling no desire to move beyond that moment.

Chuck and I played tennis regularly on the court where we met. We enjoyed the entertainment Chicago had to offer: plays at the Blackstone Theater, Second City comedy, matinees, and art museums. Chuck and I could talk about everything.

My world was no longer dark; it was light. I began to see the world through a kaleidoscope with a full spectrum of colors, tones, hues, and textures. The light brightened my life with a colorful palette. I was just feeling. I was just experiencing. I was in my element. I wanted to walk away from my history.

It wasn't long before Chuck asked me if I would be interested in moving to the Gold Coast. He wanted to spend more time with me, and he wanted me to live closer to him. He knew of three female medical students who had an extra room below his apartment.

I thought hard about his offer to move close to him. I felt safer with him than I had with anyone in my life. But I wanted to be with him for the right reasons, and not just take this opportunity to move out of my chaotic home. That would be dishonest and unfair to him, and it would be an easy decision in my self-interest. I wanted this relationship because we were compatible, with common interests, and because we cared for one another, and we saw the possibility for a future together. Although I worried about leaving my siblings behind, at 21 years old I was not prepared to care for them financially. If I was to have an impact in their lives one day, I needed to find a better path for myself. Ultimately, it was who Chuck was that made the decision easy. I said, "Yes!"

One Saturday evening, Chuck and I hailed a cab on Michigan Avenue and drove a few blocks to a forty-story high-rise residential building on Lake Shore Drive. We were meeting his parents for dinner. The doorman greeted us, and we took the elevator to the thirty-eighth floor. We got off at a private foyer with a shiny marble floor and an ornate entrance door. A large black ebony table with fresh flowers and a tall mirror sat against one wall. Chuck rang the bell to the apartment. The maid, Josey, dressed in a black uniform with a white apron, answered the door. She had been with the family for many years. She welcomed us in.

I was immediately drawn to the large windows and expansive views overlooking the Chicago skyline and Lake Michigan. Chuck took my hand, and he walked me closer to the windows to see the view. Overhead the clouds formed in the sky like castles in the air with fantastic shapes and profiles. Down below I saw other low-rise and high-rise buildings clustered in neighborhoods, and handsomely carved painted entrances on stone apartment buildings embellished with shiny metal hardware. Lake Michigan was to the south and was blue, clear, and bright with calmness. I walked to the other side of the living room, and I saw a landscape of buildings and landmarks, a history that I wasn't a part of. On the street, pedestrians bustled to and fro on the sidewalks and crosswalks. Traffic was stopped, anxious to move to another destination. From this height above Chicago, I saw my life from another perspective. I saw that I was denied the safety and security of just being a child living without violence, without hunger or chaos.

I turned to enjoy the spacious living room, which held furnishings of exquisite taste. The setting revealed the splendor of their class. There were several areas to sit, sofas I could actually sit on. There were no plastic coverings. Near the corner window was a black grand piano where Chuck played for his mother.

His mother and father entered the room. Chuck gently grasped my hand and introduced me to his parents. Chuck resembled his mother, herself a picture of grace and poise, regal in her rank in society. She spoke softly, and she tilted her head up when she spoke. She was devoted to his father, and she looked admiringly at him during our conversation.

His father was distinguished, and he was daringly dressed in a colorful suit with black and white shoes. He enjoyed intellectual conversations about philosophy and world events. A wordsmith, he would occasionally present unfamiliar words for discussion—words outside my vocabulary. Since I was an ace speller, I challenged him to spell the words.

Josey rang the handheld dinner bell. Dinner was served. We walked to the dining area situated on one end of the large open room near the kitchen. The long walnut dining table was surrounded by twelve upholstered chairs. Chuck seated me next to him. Rays of amber light streamed through the large window onto the dining table, rendering a peach glow to the room.

At the table, I stared down at the costly china plates and the fancy hors d'oeuvres before me. I enjoyed the stiff freshness of the white tablecloth and the sunlight sparkling on the silver. Polished wine glasses glimmered reflections from objects around the room. Each place setting was set with fine china and silverware. Folded white linen napkins were placed carefully next to each place setting. Josey returned to the dining room, serving us each tiny portions of food on our plates. I wondered if she would be joining us, but she returned to the kitchen.

Conversation around the table was slow and deliberate, and everyone had terribly proper manners, which made my life seem inadequate because our conversation was always interrupted by my mother. The formality of listening and discussing events in each of their lives was such a contrast to my home life, where we never sat down at the table to eat together.

Chuck's father owned a successful oral surgery office in downtown Chicago. His patients were politicians and celebrities, and he wanted Chuck to be an oral surgeon like himself, I learned at dinner that Chuck had once wanted to become a playwright, and he had enrolled at Amherst College in Massachusetts to study playwriting. Chuck joked at the table that he was asked to write the school play his second year, and that he had put in a lot of effort to create his best work. He then presented it to the president of the college for approval. But while reviewing the play, the president fell asleep. Chuck immediately changed his focus to medicine. There was ripple of laughter from his parents.

I had imagined for myself, and had expected someday to find, a relationship filled with peace, love, and hope for the future. Being with Chuck was a dramatic shift in my life; it was surreal at times, as if my world flipped from a black-and-white one to a colorful, three-dimensional world filled with love, hope, and security. I tried hard to live in the present, but it was as if Chuck had turned the programming to a new channel and a different future.

Ten months later, Chuck invited me to a party hosted by a friend of his. He handed me a camera and asked me to change out the film. When I opened the camera, I was surprised by an engagement ring made of a jade stone setting surrounded by diamonds inside. With his small salary from teaching nurses on his semester off from medical school, he had met with a jade dealer, selected the stone and chosen the custom setting. At first, I thought the ring was a gift. I didn't know he was proposing to me. I accepted his proposal

Without warning, my mother went out and bought my wedding dress without me. Luckily, it fit perfectly, and it was beautiful. She intruded into other areas of my wedding, adding stress to my life. She wanted my sister to be the Maid of Honor, but I wanted my best friend, Carole, to stand next to me on this occasion. I wanted my sisters to be the bridesmaids, so neither would feel slighted about not being the Maid of Honor. Dallas would be my ring bearer.

Our wedding took place at the Northwestern Hospital Chapel. We minimized expenses by having the ceremony at the medical school chapel. Chuck's hours in medical school kept him with a heavy load, so we timed it conveniently with his routine medical rounds. It was a simple wedding, and both our families attended. My stepfather walked me down the aisle, and I detected some awkwardness from my Dad that he had not been chosen to give me away. But I couldn't count on him to not show up drunk. Grandma didn't come to my wedding because she was fearful of driving in the car with Dad, who often would stop at bars along the way.

The wedding and reception left little time for conversation between my parents and Chuck's parents, which reduced the chasm between our families social and economic differences: the blue collar parents meeting the university-educated parents. More importantly, though, the separation between our parents was a way to preserve my wedding day without drama from my mother. The wedding and reception seemed to go by so quickly; it was a complete blur.

After the wedding, it was difficult for me to reflect on how things had changed now that I was married. The disarray in my life had never allowed me to plan for the future, but instead forced me to live in the moment. I had married a man whom I trusted more than anyone to love and care for me, to provide the stability and safety I so desperately needed, and I wanted to spend the rest of my life with him. I married a man who became my husband, and who, in four months time, would become a doctor.

Chuck accepted a medical internship in San Francisco. He would spend a year at the San Francisco County Hospital rotating his internship in various medical specialties. We would be moving soon. Since we didn't need a car in Chicago because of the public transportation, Chuck found a caravan car that needed to be transferred to California by the owner, which meant we would only have to pay for gas. It was a four-door Cadillac with just enough room to pack our wedding gifts in the back seat. We had few possessions between us, though Chuck had his family-heirloom Art Deco Grundig cabinet radio, which he carefully stored in the trunk. Chuck attached a homemade *Grapes of Wrath* sign to the back of our car.

We were off to California to find an apartment. I wanted to be the best wife possible, but I had no good role models in my life, except maybe Donna Reed. I would try to be everything good, and I would reject all that was bad. My new life would be my best revenge. I could change my future because I understood my past. I would show the world my personal best. I said good-bye to my family, not without feeling some guilt at leaving my brothers and sisters behind, especially Dallas; I would miss them. And I thought to myself, *Dallas, I'll be back for you some day.*

The sky was overcast with grey clouds on the day of our departure. We would leave Chicago and drive south through the Midwest to New Mexico, Arizona, and California.

The farther we drove from Chicago, the wider and deeper the sky seemed. As we approached the southwest, there was a heat spell. In the dry desert, the high temperatures scorched the landscape; vegetation withered in the hot sun, curled up, and blew away. Horses hung thin in the arid heat, their skin stretched over their hips like slings. The car air conditioning felt cool to my skin. We drove on. The colors of the land ran rich with seams of honey and gold. At the day's end, the long rich sunset was rimmed with amber and purple, and then it was abruptly dark.

During the days, we took turns driving. After many miles of driving along the highway, we were stopped for a speeding ticket. We had to pay the ticket in a small town up the road. On our way to pay the fine, we stopped for a large soda. Chuck placed his cola on the dashboard, and I slowly drove off.

Driving into the small town, I kept my eyes peeled for any building that could be part of the judicial system. We had to pay at the local judge's office, which was situated in a small white house along the main street. Chuck spotted a dilapidated white clapboard house and a sign that indicated the judge's office.

"I believe we just past it. The small white house on the right!" Chuck exclaimed.

Forgetting the large soda sitting on the dashboard, I immediately swung the car into a quick U-turn.

"Oh no!" Chuck yelled, recoiling as the super-sized soda swept across the dashboard and landed in his lap. He was covered in cold, sticky cola. Wet ice cubes scattered across his new slacks. His eyes were widened in disbelief as he looked down at his soaked lap.

"Whoops!" I said, and I bit my lip. Suddenly we both began to laugh wildly. After that, I believed our marriage would make it.

We had been driving for three days, and sightseeing along the way. Somewhere in the desert, we stopped for dinner. As we walked from the car, the heat from the sun was stupefying. We settled in for the night in a local motel. I pushed back the drapes and looked outside and up to the heavens. I gazed up at the clear stars shining like endless silver tubes of light, years and light years long. And then I fell asleep.

We left the hotel and drove steadily for hours in the heat, and the earth passed under the car at warp speed. Objects blurred outside, and our senses numbed. We steered the wheel mindlessly, following the white line on the pavement. From the flat of the desert, we saw in the distance the waves of bluish and purple mountains coloring the horizon. The ridges of the green hills kept moving closer as the car sped down the highway toward our destination. Finally we arrived at the shocking granite mountains dotted with tall pine trees. *Welcome to California,* read the sign.

We drove over the California border and through uninterrupted fields, newly paved highways, and stretches of mountains, high and low. Houses tenderly sat on the hills. I realized the beauty of California was not easy to come by; it was a state of such detail and loveliness. The undiscovered awaited us.

We headed north through California, up highway 101 to San Francisco. We drove through the East Bay and Oakland and made a loop through Marin County so that our grand entrance to San Francisco would be the Golden Gate Bridge. To my naive surprise, the famous bridge was not actually golden. But I found a new meaning in the bridge's orange rust color and its studied engineering and magnificent views of San Francisco. The Pacific Ocean with its transparent waves and rocky cliffs lay on one side of the Golden Gate Bridge, and the San Francisco Bay lay on the other. I observed the coiling cloudlets of mist above the water, which concealed the colorful cityscape beyond.

San Francisco is a city made of hills and landscapes that are sensual and exotic. It is a city of extremes; it's bizarre and beautiful in its sophistication and devotion to immediate gratification. I observed the colorful Victorian homes accented with gingerbread designs that lined the sides of streets and boulevards. As we approached Union Square, the heart of the city, the sounds of iron clanged from trolley cars. We found parking underneath Union Square, and we walked up to the square. I stood in awe of the world-class restaurants and shops. The city was alive with cultural experience. A parade had just ended in Chinatown, and the last of flowing multi-colored dragons streamed down the streets.

Outside, the cool fog misted the air. We retrieved our car from the parking garage and drove to Lombard Street, famous for being the most crooked street in the world, and we saw its sinuous curves flow from top to bottom. It was time to return our caravan car, so we drove the car to the Nob Hill garage and dropped it off.

The sun descended behind San Francisco, and the magnificence of orange and amber filled the sky. Chuck held my hand as we walked through the Nob Hill Square, once the home of silver kings and railroad barons. This neighborhood's noble residents enjoyed magnificent views of the San Francisco landscape. Grace Cathedral dominated the Square. We stepped through the carved doors of the chapel: The church is designed in French gothic architecture and is a famous replica of Notre Dame; its spires are heaven bound, pointing towards the sky. At the entry of the church was a labyrinth, and we deliberately walked and turned and twisted through the maze until we reached the end. The maze reminded me that marriage could be a bit like a maze, with unexpected twists and turns.

We sat down at one of the pews, studying the intricate interior of the church. The tall ceiling kept our eyes fixed upward to the heavens. I closed my eyes, intent on replacing my childhood memories with joy, happiness, and love. I was filled with the warmth of love and security— what I desperately longed for. I was married to a wonderful man. I had an opportunity to begin a new life. I needed to feel different, and San Francisco fit the bill.

The next day, we found an apartment in the Sunset district of San Francisco, next to Golden Gate Park. Our furnished apartment was in a modern-style building, with an open-air lobby landscaped with a Japanese garden. It was pleasing, and the neighborhood felt safe. The Pacific Ocean was several blocks away.

Chuck would return to Chicago for the next three months to finish medical school while I stayed in San Francisco and set up the household. When Chuck returned to San Francisco, he would have to immediately start his internship program, and I wanted to have our home ready for him. Also, I wanted to have some time to find a job that would help with the monthly bills. Chuck sent money for the rent and groceries, but he was also saddled with medical school expenses.

With the banking experience on my resume, I landed a job interview at the University Medical School in the accounting department right away. It was a low-paying job, but my salary would help with some personal expenses.

Life was good.

A couple months into my job, my energy level began to feel low, I began to tire more easily in the late afternoon, and my stomach felt nauseated. I couldn't explain my cravings for garlic dressing on salads. Something about my body felt different.

Chuck called after his rounds at medical school, and I explained how I was feeling. He recommended I visit a gynecologist, and he said he would find me one in San Francisco. He would book a flight to San Francisco in about two weeks, but then would have to return to Chicago to finish out his medical degree.

The following week, I walked slowly home from the office, observing the myriad of shops along Judah Avenue. The ocean breeze from the Pacific masked the other midday scents, and the salty air filled my nostrils. I entered the lobby of my apartment building, and I stopped by the interior Japanese garden and noticed the new spring plantings. I took the elevator to the second floor, and I placed the key in the apartment door. The door opened quickly.

"I wanted to surprise you!" Chuck said, opening his arms to me. I fell into them, ecstatic.

He had been planning to surprise me all along. He couldn't wait to see me, and I was deliriously happy to see him. I embraced his warmth, and the smell of him filled me up. We caught a cab that evening and went to dinner. We discussed his medical school experiences and my job, but we mostly talked about our future life together.

A few days later, we received the test results from my visit to the gynecologist. They were positive. We were having a baby! Chuck made reservations for a comedy club. That evening, we took a cab to the Broadway comedy club. Once we started laughing at the jokes, we couldn't stop. We didn't know if the comedian was that good or if it was the news about the baby that made us giddy.

Chuck finished out his medical degree, and two months later, he returned to San Francisco and immediately started his internship program at the San Francisco County Hospital. His desired profession was in the field of emergency medicine, and this hospital had its share of emergency cases.

As a medical intern, he was required to work many long and painful hours. Sometimes Chuck was on call working away from home for a couple days at a time, only to come home and sleep a few hours before returning back to the hospital upon waking. It was part of the rite of passage to becoming a doctor. Doctors before him had put in the same sacrifice, and he was expected to do the same.

And so our new life began together. Living in this foggy city, my life was brighter, clearer, and sharper. We were starting a family. Despite having so many siblings, I had never discussed having babies with my mother or foster mother, so the process was alien to me. I had no friends or family in California to discuss my pregnancy with. I never anticipated what was happening to my body. I was healthy except for a growing belly. When I reached the latter part of my ninth month, I could feel strong movements in my stomach.

That month, coincidentally, Chuck's medical rotation was in the obstetrics ward, and he was busy delivering other babies. I stayed in the doctor's bedroom at the hospital. Between his rounds of delivering other babies, he checked on me frequently. He was putting in long hours, and he looked exceptionally tired. It was Friday night, and my contractions were feeling stronger.

"I believe it's time to go to the hospital," he said, a wide grin breaking through his exhaustion. He sped me to the obstetrics ward at St. Luke's Hospital. After fourteen hours of labor, our eight-pound baby boy was born. The nurse laid Baby Scott close to me. He was rosy cheeked with black thick hair. His shiny black eyes were alert. His head was normally shaped and not misshapen. My hand gently caressed his head, being careful not to touch the tender spot on top. I knew he couldn't see perfectly, but our eyes slowly studied each other closely. I touched his hand, and his tiny fingers wrapped around my finger, sealing the bond between us. Everything about him seemed perfect.

The nurse removed Scott from my arms and handed him to Chuck. The tiredness in Chuck's face from his grueling schedule and staying up with me during labor just melted away into a deep smile. His eyes twinkled and his face lit up.

Chuck embraced his son and tears of happiness sprang from my eyes. As always, though, the past intruded. For a brief moment, my joy was interrupted as I remembered that Dallas's entrance into the world had been so different from my son's. A father's violence stole Dallas's chances for a bright and healthy life on earth. Dad changed God's plan for Dallas.

I called the family to share the news of Scott's birth.

My sister Diane answered. "I'm so happy I have a nephew! When will we be able to see him?" Her voice was filled with anticipation.

"I will be there in a couple of months," I answered. "How's Dallas? Have Mom and Lee been abusing him?

"They're cruel to him; they won't stop hurting him." Diane whispered.

"I'll be there as soon as I can," I promised.

That fall, a month after delivering Scott, Chuck encouraged me to enroll in college. Since childhood, the idea of college had seemed remote and impossible. My foster mother said I would only clean houses, but I still dreamed that some day and somehow, I would graduate from college. In what field, I didn't know. The idea of getting an opportunity to fulfill that dream was intoxicating.

Nevertheless, when Chuck suggested that I register right away, my stomach tensed, and my body started shaking. I felt echoes of my foster mother's words and they shook me to the core of my being. "I was not worthy! I was not worthy!" I felt anxiety spread throughout my body; my nerves were pulsing rapidly, and I started to have a panic attack. But how could I share these feelings with my new husband? Registering for college was a part of his way of life: college was simply a step in life's sequence of events.

For a moment, I found myself fabricating excuses. My baby needed me at home with him, and how would I have time to both study and take care of Scott? I didn't even know what I wanted to be. The night before registration, Chuck could see that I was nervous. "Honey, I'm taking the day off tomorrow, and I will go with you to register."

The next day, as promised, Chuck took the day off from his busy work schedule. We secured Scott in the back seat of a used car we had recently purchased, and we drove across the Golden Gate Bridge to Marin County College. Together, the three of us stood in the registration line for hours. It didn't seem possible that I was getting the opportunity to enroll in college. Chuck held my shoulders, calming my nerves, and making me feel safe. Scott became fussy, and Chuck stepped aside, changed his diaper, and fed him his bottle. When he brought Scott back to the line, I held Scott in my arms, his head tucked tenderly on my shoulder. At last, I filled out all the necessary paperwork. I was now a college student.

My classes began right away. I wasn't over my fear of attending college, but one teacher who taught an interior design class took a special interest in me. She made a difference in my life. She pointed out my strengths and guided me to improve my weaknesses. In a light-bulb moment, I realized that I wanted to design hospitals in order to affect how patients felt in a hospital. I would change the hospital's institutional look to reflect a hospitality look, like a hotel, so that it would be a place to visit and not feared.

I was especially concerned with providing people with special needs a place in the hospital designed for them. I wanted them to be able to sit with dignity in a waiting room, to lower the reception desk to a height that fit the needs of someone, say, in a wheel chair. I knew from Dallas's

147

experience that, at the time, there had been little thought given to the special needs of the disabled. I wanted to help change that.

Our airplane descended from 35,000 feet and lowered over the northwest side of Chicago. I had taken the week off from school so that I could share my two-month-old baby with my family. It had been around a year since Chuck and I had left Chicago, and it still looked the same. The Chicago sky was overcast, with ominous clouds rising above. The sun glinted in a corner of the city, and then it faded as rolling dark clouds closed the gap. The city looked the color of rust amid the smoke spewing from the factories. In the distance, high-rises rose from the earth.

I arrived to a crowded Chicago airport. Carrying Scott in my arms, I followed the signs to the baggage claim area. I passed strangers and imagined them as travelers escaping their ordinary lives and traveling to exotic destinations.

After gathering my baggage, I checked out the airport rental car and headed south to my parents' house. While driving, I studied the familiar landscape for any changes. The pulse of the city held the same energy. Passing near downtown, I remembered the city with fondness. Michigan Avenue and Rush Street were the beginning of my changed life. That was where I met my husband.

By now, the heat of the day had broken, and the light dimmed on the southeast side of Chicago. I exited the freeway. My muscles were tense, and my stomach tightened; I was anxious to see my parents, but I was also excited to share my new baby. I pulled the rental car in front of my parent's house.

Mom's large picture window was open to the street. My family saw the car pull up and came rushing out to greet me. They stood patiently by the car while I wrapped Scott's blue blanket tightly around him and then I got out. Diane stepped forward, and I placed Scott in her arms. Scott cooed at her affectionate words, and Diane's face lit up. She studied his every move.

Even though a year had passed since I had been home, the place still had its newness, as if my parents had moved in yesterday. Mom's colorful plastic flowers centered on the coffee table brightened the room. Lee's music was blasting, and for a moment, the sound made me happy. I was honored to sit on the plastic sofa in the living room, which was reserved only for special guests. Of course, like all guests, I would only be special for about three days.

"Lee, turn the music down!" Mom shouted. It was just like old times.

I was happy to see my brothers and sisters. Sissy had moved out and was living in another state. Roger and Roland were now in their late teens, were living at home, and were trying to find their way. Lynn was in Indiana, moving back and forth between my dad and mom's house, not knowing where he belonged. He wanted to be part of the family and spend time with his siblings, but Mom had totally rejected him at no fault of his own. She gave no reason.

I looked around for Dallas.

"Mom, let Dallas join us in the living room," I begged.

"Nah," she replied, grimacing. "Leave him in the laundry room, leave him alone." There was no way she could be convinced. She ruled her nest, and that was the way it was.

On the third day of my visit, I was sitting in the rocking chair putting Scott to sleep when I heard noises coming from downstairs. I heard voices yelling, objects being thrown, and cries from Dallas. I jumped up with the baby in my arms, and I ran downstairs. My stepfather had a large leather strap and was beating Dallas over his head and body.

I rushed toward them. "Stop hurting him!" I cried, clutching Scott closer to my chest. "Please, stop hurting him!" Lee towered over Dallas who, at twelve years old, was half the size and weight of someone his own age.

"Get out of here," Mom yelled back.

They kept it up in defiance of my pleas. The blows left welts on Dallas's flesh as he underwent the flogging passively. Shaking with anger, I ran up the stairs to the bedroom. I closed the door and pressed Scott closer to my chest. His sweet smell sent tears streaming down my cheeks, landing on top of his head. I never wanted his ears to hear such violence. I never wanted him to see such violence. I never wanted him to experience such violence. Dallas must have been abused more than I knew about. I felt helpless to stop it. I had called social services before, and they had done nothing. Who would believe me?

I laid Scott down on my sister's bed, and I threw our clothes swiftly in my bag. I picked Scott up and I grabbed the rental car keys and left the house, my parents unaware that I had left. I drove a few blocks on the main boulevard.

I pulled up to a phone booth tucked in the corner of a gas station, and I called Chuck. I told him I would be visiting his parents sooner than planned. I sat the phone on the cradle. After seeing what I had seen, I had to try again. I rifled through my bag for change to make a second phone call. I called information, and they connected me to Chicago's Social Services.

"Please, I need your help! No, no, my brother needs your help." The words were running together in my state of agitation. "My parents are abusing my brother, and I need you to protect him. Please."

"Slow down, Ma'am! I'll put you through to a social worker," the receptionist said. After a moment, another voice came on the line.

"Can I help you?" The voice at the other end said with a rushed tone.

"My brother needs your help. Can you do something?" I pleaded.

"I'll transfer you to the right department. Hold on please!"

"Hello?" Another strange voice with a slow accent answered.

"My brother needs your help. Can you do something?" I repeated, desperate. "He is being abused by my parents. Can you protect him?

"What's his name? Where does he live?" She asked matter-of-factly. I gave her Dallas's information.

"I'll look into it, Ma'am," she said. Then she hung up.

I returned home, packed my suitcase, and spent the rest of my visit with Chuck's parents before heading back to San Francisco. Weeks passed, and then months passed, without a return call from Social Services. I phoned my sister to see if anything had changed. Nothing had changed.

"Are they still hurting him?" I asked.

"Yes, worse than ever!" She told me. "Oh Shirlee, what can we do?" I wanted a relationship with my parents, and I hoped that one day I could influence their behavior. The authorities had not responded as far as I knew, and if they had spoken to my parents, there still wasn't any change for Dallas.

Though difficult to admit, soon, the tragedy of Dallas's life deepened my desire to remove myself from his life. I know it was a failure on my part. The unuttered words about his plight followed me, and I kept my feelings buried within me.

A year after Scott was born, Chuck and I settled into our new home in the East Bay of San Francisco. College had been put on hold for the time being, and I could now focus on trying to get my brothers Lynn and

Dallas out to California. We planned a vacation to see my family in Chicago.

After the disaster of my last visit, I had reconciled with my mother and Lee in the interest of seeing my siblings. Dallas was never discussed. That was the way it was with my parents. I had to ignore the obvious abuse of Dallas, or I was entirely out of the picture. So much was at stake with so many of my siblings. I was going to capitalize on Chuck's good will in order to help my brothers. With Chuck's likeability and credentials, maybe he could convince Mom to let them move to California.

A few days after we arrived in Chicago, we had convinced my parents that Dallas and Lynn would be better off living with us in California. After all, Chuck was a doctor who could help Dallas with learning. Dallas was almost thirteen years old and still not in school. And Lynn, now 14, had ping-ponged back to Mom's so he could be with his brothers, but he wasn't happy living there. We could help Lynn, too, because his grades were failing; this was an opportunity to tutor him and bring his grades up. Besides, Mom could use a break from the boys.

With much reluctance, Mom finally agreed that the boys could move to California. I was flooded with relief. Since we were driving back to California, we decided to buy a weekend trailer. With the four of us, and Baby Scott, we would be more comfortable on the trip back. With the little money left in our pockets and some negotiating skills, we bought a used trailer. We would turn the trip into a vacation, visiting landmarks and tourist sites at national parks along the way, and the boys would be able to see another part of the country outside of Indiana and Chicago.

We said good-bye to the family and headed west, stopping at campgrounds along our northern route, talking around campfires, and taking short hikes. Lynn and Dallas were safe, and we were off to a hopeful beginning.

Dallas was still very small for his age. He looked to be about seven years old. Signs of distress from the abuse were becoming evident in his behavior. He would act out. He would take pens and hide them in his pockets. He had not been taught to enunciate words—the only sounds he made were grunts. My mother talked at him, not with him. We had our work cut out for us.

It was the middle of summer when we arrived in the San Francisco Bay area, and Dallas and Lynn settled into our neighborhood. Even with Lynn's shy nature, he was able to make a couple of friends. While caring for Scott, I would spend time helping Dallas with his speech, teach him new things, and watch that he didn't take things without asking. After being taught to steal while shopping, it was a challenge to teach him differently.

151

We enrolled Lynn and Dallas in school—we put Dallas in an exceptionally good school for children with disabilities. We tried to observe his behavior and learning abilities, but some days were more successful than others. His retardation and the struggles from Mom's abuse were a barrier to his learning. Because of his inability to speak, no one knew his thoughts. No one knew his pain. We had many days with setbacks.

But at times, Dallas was a willing student. It was apparent some things were difficult for him to grasp. Understandably, he had a lot of emotional and psychological issues to overcome. But he was safe in our arms, away from my mother.

Several months into the school year, Lynn's grades had improved from F's to high B's. He was making remarkable progress. He was also coming out of his shell and laughing more. Chuck had spent a lot of time teaching him how to study to improve his grades, and as a result Lynn's self esteem grew.

Now, we were a happy family. Chuck had embraced my brothers and was supportive in helping them better their lives. They had the best medical care and a family that loved them. But all of this was about to change.

One night, the phone rang. We were seated at the dinner table, and I didn't want to interrupt our meal. Chuck wasn't on emergency call that evening, so he was relaxed and entertaining my brothers with his wit and humor. Then, the phone rang again. And then immediately, it stopped. When the phone rang a third time, I reluctantly picked it up.

My mother's voice screeched over the line. "I want those boys on a plane tomorrow!" I physically stepped back, as if trying to get away from her command.

"What?" I exhaled the word.

"I want those boys on a plane tomorrow, period."

"But Mom!" I said. "Dallas and Lynn are doing so well! Lynn's grades have improved dramatically. His report card went from D's and F's in Chicago to B's here in California. Dallas is progressing with his speech and is doing well in his special needs school. Please let them stay!" I fell to my knees.

There was no discussion. No explanation. No forewarning. In fact, just the week before, I had called to update her on their progress, and she had even seemed faintly pleased at the news. So the call didn't make any sense at all. Mom was unpredictable and erratic, but I had hoped she wouldn't interfere in my brothers' progress, or in their lives, again.

Why would she yank my brothers out of school on a whim? We had put so much effort into helping them, and now she wanted them back in Chicago?

"Tomorrow!" she yelled, and the phone clicked.

Later, we surmised that social services had called Mom to inform her that someone was coming by the house, and if Dallas wasn't there, Mom would not receive the monthly check she took in each month for his care. That evening, after the shock of having to send them back, we booked their tickets to Chicago at great expense, and the following day, we drove them to the airport. At the gate, Dallas was confused, not understanding what was happening. Lynn, who understood all too well, clung to me, and then to Chuck. Sending them back to my mother broke my heart.

Over the next few years, a distance started to develop in my marriage. Chuck's schedule in the emergency room was intense and required long hours. We planned to move closer to the hospital to reduce his driving to the hospital, and, because as a family, we wanted to spend more time together; we needed to spend that time together. Scott was ten years old, and at an age where he needed to spend more time with his father. Also, Chuck and I had less time to play tennis, which was a common interest between us.

We decided that we would build our dream house. Chuck and I drove over the Oakland hills to the town of Alamo to scout out properties. We heard Alamo was a great place to live. Scott would be entering the third grade, and the grammar school was excellent, the weather was sunny, the days were warm, and the night temperatures were comfortably cool.

Spring had come late this year, and the hills surrounding Alamo were a lush green color from the winter rains, so different from the dry golden brown of summer. Pink cherry blossoms were in full bloom; their fragrance sweetened the air and lifted my spirits as we drove through the neighborhood looking for vacant lots to build a home. Afterward, we parked and walked through the small downtown. The evening was quiet and blissful. We stopped at a café to order a cool beverage. I called the babysitter to check in on Scott, then we continued walking until the night darkened. We looked up at the black sky punctuated by bright stars. This was just what we needed to quiet our busy life. After much consideration, we decided to purchase a lot and build a house in Alamo.

I had recently started college again after a long absence, but I decided I would again put my education on hold in order to further our plans to build a home; it was more important to me that Chuck be closer to the hospital so that he could spend more time at home. We worked with a building planner to design our dream home. Several months later, we finalized our building and landscaping plans, and we deliberated over several contractors' bids for the house. Building permits were issued. The completion date was set.

Though we'd committed with a contractor, his promises of meeting the deadline were soon ignored. It took twice as long to finish the house than we expected. There were weather-related delays, deliveries of certain materials that didn't arrive on time, and the distraction of the contractor's other projects. To accommodate changes in the schedule, we had to move into two separate rentals in six months. Our life felt constantly in limbo. If only we were finished with the house, we could settle in, and our life would feel normal.

The stress of feeling unsettled in our life was taking its toll on both Chuck and me. As if building a home wasn't enough, the moves to two different rentals and having our possessions scattered between storage units while our home was being completed, added to our stress. At thirty-two years old, I felt stuck in so many ways: the house, my schooling, my marriage. Finally, a very long year later, the house was completed.

We had only been in our new house a short while when the phone rang. "Shirlee, we're driving to California to see you!" The voice on the phone was unrecognizable.

"Is that you, Mom?" I asked, holding the cradle closer to my ear.

"We moved to Florida a couple months ago, and we'd like to visit you and stay for a month," Mom continued. "Your sister, Jeanine, will come with us. We're packed and ready to leave in the morning."

Mom never offered a polite salutation, nor collaboration. She just informed us of her plans.

This was a particularly bad time for a prolonged visit from my mother. Chuck and I had not yet recovered from the lengthy building process, and we needed to settle quietly into our home together as a family, without outside distractions. Nevertheless, I felt too guilty to refuse them and, as always, was nervous about the repercussions of denying my mother. She would take it personally and become irate, shutting off any contact with Jeanine and Dallas. Besides, another part of me wanted to share my changed life with my parents, as if to say, "See, you could change your life, too. This is what our family could be like."

154

"Of course, we would love to see you," I said. "Will Dallas becoming too?"

"Nah! He can't come," Mom replied dismissively. "He'll stay in a facility here. They'll watch him when we are gone." I knew there was little possibility of pushing Dallas's visit further. If she had brought Dallas, there might have been a possibility that I could keep him here for a while.

Dallas had become another family Ping-Pong ball. Since his return to Chicago, my mother had begun calling the assisted state-run facility to care for him when she tired of him. The facility was designed to give caretakers the occasional break from the difficult care of the intellectual and physical needs of individuals. But sometimes Mom left Dallas there for days or weeks. Then she'd drop in spontaneously and tell them she wanted him home again. To the chagrin of the staff, everyone marched to her orders. Dallas's routine would be upset again without consideration for his needs. She had custody of him, and that was the way it was. The facility was the only respite that Dallas had from her abuse.

Over the years, I had been able to keep a civil relationship with my mother because I desperately wanted a relationship with her. A healthy relationship. I enjoyed talking to Mom until the conversation turned into gossip. I tried not to get involved with the family chaos, but there was always a family member calling about what transpired with Mom and Dallas. Mom and Diane were constantly arguing with one another. My sister's concerns were mainly about how Dallas was being treated. My mother's concerns were about maintaining power over every family member, dividing and conquering. I wanted my mother to talk about her grandchildren, and I wanted her to stop gossiping about my siblings' lives. I wanted her to stop abusing Dallas.

Ten days later after my mother's phone call, I heard my parents' car pull into the driveway. Lee honked the car horn, announcing their arrival. He pulled to a stop and Jeanine burst out of the car and ran excitedly toward me. At fourteen, she looked almost grown up. A part of me was excited about their visit. They were my family, and they would be the first guests in my new home. I knew my mother would be proud of my life. Inside all of us is the need for approval from a parent, even a bad parent who had moments of redemption. My family settled into the guesthouse, which I had prepared for them. They would be comfortable there. There was a large living space with a sofa and a fireplace, a small kitchenette for preparing food, a ping-pong table, and a billiard table for their entertainment. The guesthouse offered a view of the surrounding hills and the tennis court and the pool, where Lee could smoke his cigarettes and take a break from my mother's constant hounding. Mom didn't have conversations with people, her words only demanded or criticized, and the tone was always crass or angry. Lee tolerated it most times.

I was putting away the dishes after dinner when I heard arguments coming from outside. We lived in a quiet neighborhood, so it was an anomaly to hear such arguments. In the evening air, the sounds grew louder, and the voices escalated; I heard fists pounding against a table and loud voices speaking over other voices. I listened carefully for where the voices were coming from. I slid open the kitchen patio door, and I carefully leaned in the direction of the guesthouse. My parents were standing face to face, pointing fingers at each other, yelling at the top of their lungs.

"Oh no!" I said, cupping my hands to the side of my face, looking at the scene before me.

My parents had brought their issues into my home. I knew from the past that if I tried to interfere and calm them down, the fight would escalate, and they would turn on me. A half hour later, they were obviously tired or running out of things to argue about, and there was a sudden calm.

After a restless night, I prepared breakfast for my parents, and I took a tray to the guesthouse. Mom was in a good mood. After we had eaten, Mom was excited to show me something.

"Come here. I have a surprise for you!" she said.

I followed her into the bedroom, and she pointed to the bed. I was shocked to see my comforter had been changed out with a new blue floral bedding. She stepped back, the palm of her hand and her arm stretched out with pride, waiting for my approval. I looked to the window where my simple shade had hung. It had been replaced with a white rod and drapery made of matching fabric. What was I to say; the color scheme didn't match my color scheme for the home.

"Mom, you shouldn't have spent so much money doing that." I hid my disappointment that she'd changed my bedroom without consulting me. After all, I was studying to be an Interior Architect, with only one year to go before completing my college degree, and I enjoyed the room the way I had planned it.

"Ahh," she said, smiling with satisfaction. "It didn't cost anything. We took it from a motel on the way here."

"Great, they stole it! Now what do I do? "Which motel did you take this from?" I hoped that I could contact them after my parents left and make up for what had happened.

156

"Nah. They won't miss it. Besides I can't remember which one."

It was a very long month. Finally, my parents were packed in their car and were ready to head back to Florida. I hugged Jeanine goodbye, and I waved to my parents with a momentous feeling of relief.

Not long after my family left, I stood outside on the patio watching the movement of the sky. The sky was shifting with grey clouds, and the warmth of the morning had disappeared. *Is this what life is about? Constant change?* I thought of my chaotic childhood and teenaged years: I was like a cog in a piece of constantly moving machinery. My whole life had been filled with anxiety and uncertainty that kept me in motion physically and mentally from sunrise to sunset. Now I had the perfect life, a wonderful husband and son, and a beautiful home. But I was feeling restless and lonely. It was unexplainable.

At times in my marriage, I felt exhausted by trying to emulate the Donna Reed version of perfection through my over-eager efforts to make everything perfect in order to correct my past. I felt determined to right my dysfunctional childhood, and create a different life in my own marriage. It wasn't my husband's fault; this was my own deficiency. My need for approval and attention and for physical demonstrations of love was more than my husband could provide in his busy schedule. My childhood left me needier than the average woman.

My purpose was to love and care for my son, Scott, but now he was in school most of the day. Chuck's schedule at the hospital, along with his long hours on emergency calls, left me feeling alone. His medical writing and speaking engagements were filling up the other parts of our life. By his own admission, his work had become his mistress. I was ill-equipped emotionally to handle this, and I felt alienated from my husband's affections. He was busy saving the world in the emergency room. I was needy for attention from him. I was like a bougainvillea stretching its branches, as if to say "Please notice me! Notice my beautiful colors, my form, my being: acknowledge my contribution to humanity."

Now, my life was too perfect. My body was used to sheer chaos, and now I had it all, and I didn't know how to be in this life. Unfortunately, my husband and I had lost our connection to one another, and he could do little to guide me.

Standing on that porch, I detailed the myriad ways I had failed my marriage. Shame came over me, and it overwhelmed me. The whole world felt as if it was spinning on its axis without me, and I couldn't stop it. I felt it leave me like something warm and comfortable covering me on

157

a cold day. My skin had gone icy with shock. Fear cut into me just like it did in my childhood, where I felt no one was there to protect me.

After twelve years together, Chuck and I finalized the divorce papers. I was on my own once again. My happy life was no more. It was the only security and true love I had ever known, my only happiness, and I let it slip away.

The telephone ring shook me; the clock indicated two in the morning. It was my dad; he wasn't sleeping, and he wanted to talk. For years, he had been ill with emphysema, and his illness was worsening. He was unable to sleep lying down, so he slept on his knees in a prayer position next to the bed. His veteran's benefits had refused him the oxygen tanks that he needed for breathing. He didn't have the strength to fight the system. Chuck had become involved, and he had set up oxygen in his home along with a portable tank to carry on his back. But now, the oxygen equipment was no longer enough to relieve his suffering.

His breathing was labored, and his voice was raspy, and he sporadically coughed hard for what seemed like minutes. I knew he was in pain, but he rarely complained. We talked until four in the morning. With my brothers and sisters all moving away years ago, marrying and living in different parts of the country, he felt alone. He was afraid. He was afraid of dying.

After the phone call, I turned the lamp off, and I leaned back on my pillow and stared at the ceiling. I thought about the way my father had lived his life. The good times were few. I thought hard, remembering with fondness the drives we took to remote lakes with our fishing gear, the lakes surrounded by the black silhouettes of trees and bushes in the distance against a dark sky. Dad would place his fishing gear in the rowboat and navigate quietly with oars around the lake until he could feel the right spot for catching fish. He was always right—he couldn't afford not to be, as he had several mouths to feed when he returned home. I never questioned the many boats he borrowed from the shoreline. I thought they were his boats. I only found out later that they belonged to strangers who docked their boats on shore. In the late hours of the night, he justified it because they weren't using them, and he was just borrowing them to feed his family.

But mostly, I remember that Dad defied Grandma, and maybe God. His misdeeds affected my mother and the entire family, changing all of our destinies forever. Dallas's injury at birth changed God's plan for Dallas. I wanted to believe Dad could have been different. I wanted to love and respect him in the way most daughters love their fathers. But he had made it difficult.

Three weeks later, Dad passed away. After Dad's passing, the family gathered for the funeral, which was held back in Albion. Grandma was in her mid-eighties, and had outlived Dad, who had died when he was only in his mid-fifties. My siblings were all in attendance, yet we each mourned the passing of our father in our own way.

In the following years, my siblings and I grew even further apart. All of us migrated to different parts of the country. When we were young, phone calls between us were frequent, but as each sibling created his or her own family and life, the phone calls happened less often. And distance and travel expense made it difficult to spend one-on-one time together.

Given how rarely we saw each other, I was excited when the family sent out invitations for a reunion to celebrate Grandma's ninety-fifth birthday in Marion, Indiana. During Grandma's reunions, we had always found a way of setting aside differences, if only for the moment. I missed seeing Grandma. I missed Grandma's laughter. I missed her stories about my visits with her during my childhood. They reminded me how Grandma's goodness and love carried me through the dark times.

Chicago's O'Hare airport was busy, as usual. I picked up my rental car and drove to Indiana. Driving through the rolling countryside and small towns reminded me of my childhood. Each town had a courthouse square to anchor the town, but the heat of summer left the sidewalks barren except for a few pedestrians. It was a contrast to the urban living I had grown accustomed to.

I arrived at the hotel where the family reunion was well underway. My family was gathered around the courtyard swimming pool, and my nieces and nephews splashed and screamed in the pool, and their aunts and uncles were seated in chairs along the poolside in conversation. My brothers and sisters gathered around me for embraces. It was wonderful to see them. I missed our crazy senses of humor, through which we always demeaned one another, but with affection.

From across the room, Grandma was seated in a chair overlooking the pool. She looked like she was in good health and good spirits. She wore the same style of black oxford shoes and handmade floral print dress that she'd always worn. Suddenly, she glanced up at me, her glasses slipping on her nose from the humidity of the pool. Her face beamed, and her smile stretched from cheek to cheek. I ran toward her and kneeled down next to her. I tilted her glasses back onto her nose, and I reached for her hand.

"It's wonderful to see you, Grandma!"

"I'm so happy to see you, too!" she said as she reached her arms out for me.

I stood up and pulled a chair next to her, and it seemed like we talked for hours.

The cake was brought out. Afterward, as I was leaving for the airport, there were the usual promises from family members to visit California—generally ending with a rub about "those people in California!"

One week before Thanksgiving, my best friend, Yvonne called me. She had a surprise gift for me. She had scheduled a session with a psychic. Although I had never been to a psychic, I had been curious about other people's experiences with them. I appreciated her gift, but I decided I would not build up any expectations from her predictions.

The next week, Yvonne picked me up from the architectural firm where I was working. We drove north up the coast to a small town called Bolinas, just north of San Francisco. The quiet scenery and cool breeze along the California coast was a refreshing change from our busy lives. Like long-time girlfriends, we talked the whole drive about our single lives.

We were getting close to Bolinas, but we were having difficulty finding the entrance to the small ocean town. This town was a hippie enclave left over from the sixties, and they treasured their privacy. A sign identifying the town could sometimes be found at the road entrance, but someone would always take it down so tourists wouldn't wander into town.

After some exploration, we turned into the road leading to the small coastal town. Yvonne pulled up to a Victorian apartment house. We were greeted at the front door by a woman in her late thirties wearing a long dress. Her hair was pulled back in a tight knot. She wasn't wearing a turban on her head, sitting with a crystal ball. She looked normal. It was the psychic.

We stepped into the apartment, which was vacant of furniture. She borrowed the apartment especially for these occasions. The psychic invited us to sit down on the carpeted floor next to an unlit fireplace. The room felt cool. She mentioned that if we wanted to tape record our conversation that she was quite comfortable with that. Yvonne had seen her a couple times before and was prepared with a tape recorder. I didn't know what to expect of this meeting.

The psychic began: "You have thirty minutes each. Who would like to go first?"

"Shirlee, why don't you go first?" Yvonne said, nudging my shoulder with hers.

"You can ask me anything that comes to mind," the psychic said.

For a moment, I gathered my thoughts and wondered what I should ask of this stranger. I started out by asking about my career. Then about my son, who was now seventeen; I wondered what his future held. I was also curious about family members, and certainly about my future in love. At thirty-nine years old, I had been divorced for five years, and although I dated frequently, I was determined not to marry again until I had met the right man.

The psychic's answers concerning my family seemed to be right on, particularly when she was describing specific characteristics about them. It was like I was having a regular conversation with a friend—not at all like I imagined it would be.

The psychic mentioned how religious my Grandmother was, and she said that my son would work for my company one day. Soon, my time was almost up. She told me I had five more minutes to my session, and she asked if there was anything else I wanted to ask. I thought for a moment.

"Why don't you ask about your birthfather?" Yvonne chimed in.

"Oh, that's a good question!" I said excitedly. It hadn't occurred to me to ask about him.

"What do you know about your birthfather?" The psychic asked.

"I know a few things my mother told me," I hesitated.

"Go on, please," she encouraged.

"My mother had a brief affair with him when she lived in Hawaii, but she decided to marry the father I grew up with. My mother said his name is Walter Maynard Leonard. He was from Cleveland, Ohio. I also know he had a gunner named Red Draught whom my mother particularly favored."

The psychic considered what I had told her. "Your father is closer than that," she said. "He is in Arizona. In fact, he was in the center of Arizona, but he recently moved southeast of there." She didn't explain a reason for his moving.

"Is he healthy?" I asked.

"Yes."

"Do I look like him?"

"You would be surprised!" the psychic responded—a very non-committal answer.

She instructed me to take out a newspaper ad in the central part of Arizona. She wasn't specific, and she didn't say where. She said that a friend would contact him and that he would call me. My reading came to a close, and Yvonne proceeded with her reading. After Yvonne's session, we drove back home. I thanked my friend for her gift, and we talked all the way back about our lives without referencing the psychic's information.

Later that night, I returned home. I asked Scott if he would like to hear the tape recording of my session with the psychic. We both sat down together and listened to it. But when I heard her words for a second time, I found the psychic less credible.

On Saturday morning, I slept in later than normal. But after breakfast, I thought, *I'm going to pull out a map of Arizona.* I laid the map on the table, and I swept my hands across the sheet to the corners. The psychic said my birthfather had lived in the center of Arizona, but that he'd recently moved south. I looked for the largest city located near the center; it was Phoenix.

Without hesitation, I picked up the telephone and dialed the Phoenix operator.

"Operator, could you please check for a Walter Leonard in the Phoenix area?" I asked.

"I have two numbers, ma'am," she said. "Would you like both?"

"Yes, please."

I dialed the first number, and an elderly lady answered the phone. She hadn't heard of the name my mother gave me. I studied the second number, and thought I was being silly and foolish. But I dialed it anyway. It took me to a voicemail. *Well, I can't leave a voicemail saying that I'm looking for my long-lost birthfather.* I called the operator in Phoenix again and suggested she try outside the Phoenix area. She gave me a third telephone number, and I dialed it immediately. The telephone continued to ring without an answer. I hung up, and I gave up calling for the day.

The following Monday morning, I sat at my desk and began my day's work. Under the paperweight on my desk was the piece of paper with the third phone number. I picked up the receiver, paused, and laid it down.

But something compelled my hand to pick it up again. My fingers began dialing the third number without hesitation.

"Hello," a man answered with a pleasant voice.

Without hesitation, I said, "I am looking for my birthfather." I blurted the words out before he could hang up on me. There was silence.

"Could you tell me more about him?" he asked.

"Well, yes," I said. "My mother told me his name was Walter Maynard Leonard."

"Well, you've reached a Walter MaGruder Leonard. Tell me more."

"He met my mother in Hawaii during the war."

"Well, I was in Hawaii during the war. What else do you know about him?"

"My mom said he was from Cleveland, Ohio." I continued.

"Well, I'm from Cleveland, Ohio."

My pulse was racing. "Walter, did you have a gunner who was killed on your plane whose name was Red Draught?"

"Yes, I did!" he exclaimed.

"Then I believe you're my birthfather," I gasped.

I had just experienced the wondrous work of divine intervention—a previous prayer uttered in silence to find my birthfather. My will was determined with certain clarity, and my best friend was an instrument to this miraculous event. After talking on the phone some more, we decided that I would come to Arizona for a short visit so that we could meet in person.

The skies were clear over Tucson. The airplane flew over the desert, and mountains hailed in the distance. Tall cacti, feathery trees, and manzanita bushes dotted the sandy landscape.

The airplane landing was smooth. While exiting the airplane, my brain felt in an ethereal state. Could I actually be meeting my birthfather? I was staying for the weekend only. After all, we didn't know each other. We'd never met before; never had been a part of one another's life. Would there be other family members to meet?

At the terminal, the crowd was large. Some families stood anxiously waiting while others joyously reunited. My birthfather and I had exchanged photographs, but his picture gave me only a hint of his appearance. I carefully panned the crowd, wondering if I would recognize my father. What if my birthfather didn't even show up to meet me?

My eyes made another pass through the crowds of people. I saw a hand in the air waving intensely, looking for a connection with someone. A white-haired man in a bolo tie broke through and was waving his hand like an unfurled flag in a strong wind. He moved closer to me with exuberance. He raced toward me with open arms.

"Shirlee! Shirlee!" he called out.

"Hello! So nice to meet you!" I said as our arms stretched toward one another.

"Where is your wife, Phyllis?" I asked

"She's waiting in the truck out front."

Before my arrival, my birthfather had asked me if I would be interested in having our picture taken for a national magazine. I was reluctant, since this was our first meeting. As I was unfamiliar with my birthfather, I declined the interview. It was difficult to know how this reunion would end up, and turning it into a national issue made me nervous. My birthfather's best friend from high school decided to come anyway. He flew out from New York for this special occasion. He was associated with the entertainment magazine that was interested. He stood quietly beside my birthfather, and then he suddenly disappeared.

Outside the baggage claim, an old camping truck parked at the curb moved forward and stopped in front of us. My birthfather's wife of forty years was seated firmly in the driver's seat. He asked that I sit in the middle seat between Phyllis and him. For a moment, I caught myself repeating under my breath, "perfect strangers, and I just got into a truck with someone I don't even know and I'm headed to an unknown destination?"

During the drive, Phyllis occasionally spoke with a soft voice and a twinkle in her eye, but since my birthfather was the talkative one, she mostly just listened intently. Even though my birthfather and I had talked over the telephone about how I found him through my friend's gift, he wanted to hear it again in person. Driving back, I could see his hands were small, very much like my own. Although growing up people commented about how much I looked like my mother, I could also see a slight resemblance between his face and mine.

"May I ask where we are going?" I asked, trying to be casual.

"We are headed to the small town of Tombstone, about an hour south of Tucson," he replied.

My birthfather and his wife had lived in Phoenix for thirty years, and they had recently moved southeast to Tombstone, just as the psychic had indicated. On the drive to their home, I learned a little about their life. Phyllis was an author of several published novels. Her books contained stories of the history and romantic lives of the people in the southwestern United States and Mexico. For thirty years, my birthfather and Phyllis were partners in an insurance business. They were both fluent in Spanish from their many travels to Mexico and South America.

An hour later, we arrived in Tombstone, a western-style town that I had only heard about in television and movies. The town was smaller than I had imagined. We spent the weekend catching up on our lives. My birthfather still had pictures of my mother when she was eighteen years old. The photos were stuffed into a large tin can that he stored in the garage. My father filled in the gaps left by my mother. He was twenty-four when they met and was a handsome navy pilot in the war, and he had dated my mother for four months.

My birthfather pulled out pictures of his parents and grandparents and some photos of his sister and her children. Ironically, his sister lived within twenty minutes of my hometown in California. Now I had a whole family that I had never known existed.

My birthfather told me about his days in World War II. He was stationed in the Saipan Islands. While flying, his plane was rear ended in the air by a squadron member. The static electricity between the planes caused his plane's gas tank to explode on impact, killing my birthfather's gunner and friend, Red Draught. My birthfather ejected to safety and fell in the ocean, badly burned. He was rescued a few hours later, and he was picked from the ocean and taken to a burn unit.

Not knowing if he would heal from his wounds, my birthfather wrote my mother a letter stating that he was badly burned. She rejected him after that. His efforts to connect with her were never successful. Over time, he fully recovered from the burns without any scarring. The doctors thought that being in the salt water may have kept him from being scarred for life. Finding my birthfather helped bring closure to that part of my life. Other parts of my life, however, remained unsettled. A couple months after the reunion with my birthfather, my mother phoned. She wanted to be a part of the reunion. The hairs on my neck stood up. She wanted to plan a trip to Arizona to see him, and she wanted me to meet her there. She wanted to bring my sister's baby, too, and to relive her experience with my birthfather when she was eighteen and pregnant. I told her that I wanted to know him better first, and that I wanted her to meet him later. Furthermore, I told her it was not a good time for me to get away. My work schedule was too busy. But again, she cajoled me to meet her there, ignoring all of my protests.

"I will set up the airline tickets, and I'll pay for your ticket," Mom insisted. I knew this reunion wouldn't have a good outcome because my mother's vanity was at play. "Mom," I said, "I'm sorry, but this is not a good time for me to go."

"You bitch!" Her voice grew louder, her words meaner. "You selfish bitch!" she responded with an impatient tone that showed her lack of control in any situation. She slammed the phone down.

When I had made contact with my birthfather, I didn't tell my mother his telephone number or his address. I knew that she would do whatever she could to eventually destroy our relationship if she wasn't the center of attention. To Mom, this wasn't about the celebration of this divine experience; it was about her reliving her teenage years.

I was trying to put my life back together, piece by piece. For a couple of years after Chuck and I divorced, life was a struggle. Chuck was spending time overseas and support payments were uncertain and inconsistent. Faced once more with my childhood fears of being homeless, I made the decision to finish out my college degree while simultaneously working full-time and being a single parent to Scott. Our future could be imperiled if I didn't get my college credentials and have job stability. I had no family to fall back on, and I continued to live in the East Bay of San Francisco, so Scott could be near his friends; it was the one constant I could give him.

While trying to navigate this chaotic life post-divorce, I met a man. He was attractive and fun, and he appeared to be an escape from my busy life of uncertainty. But as the relationship developed, he stopped being the person he had been to me in the beginning. Parts of his character revealed themselves, dark as a cavern; he was a carouser and an alcoholic, and he was verbally abusive to me. His lies, manipulations, and apologies were endless. My full-time curriculum in college and my thirty- to forty-hour workweek left little time to end the relationship. And the efforts I made to rid myself of him never worked. He always promised he would change his ways. The situation echoed my childhood; it reminded me of my Dad's issues with alcohol. It seemed that life's events had brought me full circle.

Now, at last, I was strong enough to make a change. I had discovered my birthfather, resolving that painful part of my history. With my college degree in interior architecture finished, I had been hired to design health care facilities and corporate offices for a major health maintenance organization --- my dream job. Scott, who had always been determined and focused in his life, was preparing to go to college himself. And I had recently bought my first home. My son and I were going to be safe.

I needed to move on with my life. The anguish from this relationship was more than I could bear. More important, I saw my son was being impacted by this man's presence in our lives. After many failed attempts to end the relationship, I was determined to end it, tonight.

I drove into a parking lot across the street from Wanda's bar, and I pulled the car alongside a telephone booth. As I sat for a few moments in the yellow light of the streetlamp, I stared across the boulevard at the neighborhood bar. The exterior was plain, and with the entry door closed from the world outside. The bar sat in between a hardware store and a furniture store. I suspected that he was dating another girl—not that I cared. I didn't blame the woman. He was a master of deception. She probably heard the same lies I did. But I just needed to catch him in a lie to end it. He had been trying desperately to bring us back together, so he had been claiming that he was faithful. I realized I would need to show up in person and find them together.

I slammed the car door and walked toward the unlit phone booth. The air felt crisp, and vapor shimmered in the light. My body was chilled from the cold, and my legs shook with anxiety. But my mind was filled with the determination to move on with my life. I opened the phone booth door and picked up the receiver. My palm was damp from my shaky nerves, and the phone slipped out of my hands. Retrieving the cradle, I dropped coins in the phone slot, and my other hand closed the folding door behind me. With all the courage I could muster, I called the bar to see if he was there. He was.

I crossed the boulevard and pushed through the heavy doors. I was in a place I would never be found: a dive bar. I walked into the dark and cavernous world where the walls were a dingy color and were layered randomly with history and brawl. A pool table dominated the room, and a jukebox sat at the back wall. Behind the bartender hung a large mirror and shelf, haphazardly holding up bottles of Jack Daniels. People were seated on barstools, listening to the jukebox, hovering over their distilled drinks in a sweeter and headier place.

I paused after I entered, and I saw him seated at the end of the bar with his back to me. His black hair shined in the cool light, and he held his arms around a beautiful girl. At first, he didn't see me enter the bar, but the other men in the bar turned around and stared at me. Then, suddenly, he

167

turned toward the entrance where I was standing. His arm dropped swiftly from her shoulders like a lead balloon. His face looked shocked to see me. I had caught him, and we both knew it. His unfaithfulness was revealed to both of us. This was the end of the lies, and the end of the relationship, and we both knew it.

Standing at the opposite end of the bar under bright fluorescent lights, I glanced at my reflection. The lighting made my skin look grey and unhealthy. In the distant shadow, my eye caught sight of my boyfriend leaving the back door with his arm around the shoulder of the girl. I gave a sigh of relief.

The atmosphere inside the bar echoed my childhood. It left me with the smell of alcohol reeking heavily in my memory. I remembered standing outside a local bar begging my father to come home; I remembered how the residue of abuse and carousing meant chaos would ensue when Dad came home. My body tensed. I felt unclean all over again. In a way, I wanted to understand my dad's attraction to bars—it was like I was facing head on such a dark period of my life. I sat down at the bar and ordered a club soda with lime.

Strangely, for whatever reason, I took this moment as an opportunity to understand my dad. The dank smell of liquor and tobacco permeated the air. People congealed together as a single family, listening to one another's woes. I engaged with the people sitting next to me at the bar. They made me feel welcome under the circumstances. Surprisingly, I found them warm and congenial, not at all like the belligerent drunks I had imagined. But maybe it was still too early in the evening. I could see the allure that brought alcoholics back. Little did I know that the journey inside this place would change my life.

An hour later, the bar started to fill up. I had been in conversation with a woman next to me, and I didn't notice someone standing a couple barstools away from me. His back was gorgeous. He was a tall, elegant figure of a man with distinctive good looks who held the air of celebrity. He exuded inherited wealth, and was a fine representative of the human species. His brown hair was swept back on the sides, but a hint of hair fell on his forehead as well. This dreamy man had the distant charm of a man who doesn't know he is attractive to women. He commanded attention in almost any crowd. But what was he doing in a dive bar?

One of the patrons at the bar walked away, and he sat down on the barstool next to me with his back to me. He subtly turned his head slightly in my direction and then back the other way. Despite his incredible good looks, he appeared humble and shy. He possessed the amiable reticence admired by men and lusted after by women. He looked like my first television love. I leaned over in his direction and said, "You look like Ricky Nelson!"

He didn't answer back, and I didn't think much of his lack of response. I continued my conversation with the woman next to me.

The pool table was the center of attention, and I was interested in playing. In the background, a bright light shone down on the green felt. Two men were playing pool, and the last ball was on the table. The game was over. I saw him sign his name, Blake, on the chalkboard to play a round of pool. So I placed my name under his name. *What a nice name, Blake.*

Blake would be my opponent. Moving toward the pool table, he stopped short. He asked if I would break the triangle of balls. Grasping the wooden pool cue, I picked up the chalk and rounded it over my cue. Leaning my thighs against the table, I bent forward, feeling my flat stomach and the slenderness of my body. I placed my pool cue against the cue ball and struck it with force, breaking the balls in various directions.

It was Blake's turn. He examined the table and location of the balls, and he leaned into the pool table. He lifted his cue with his right hand and chalked the tip gently with his left. He leaned toward the table and bent down to find his line of sight from the ball to the pocket. His left hand steadied the top of the pool cue.

Suddenly, he lifted his head, and his eyes looked directly at me. Our eyes locked on one another, and our gaze seemed to last an eternity. A steady stream of warmth entered my body, and our spirits transfixed, blocking out any noise or movement in the room. My heart pounded fiercely. For a moment, time stopped, our eyes frozen and fixed, and a surge of energy went from the top of my head to the floor like a bolt of lightning surging down a tall erect pole and exploding in both directions. While we held our gaze for a moment, everything around me except him was out of focus. Something transmitted between us; we had the ability of somehow bridging time and space.

The rest of the evening, we seemed to gravitate toward one another, alternating between games of pool and glasses of wine. Throughout the evening, I'd glanced back over my shoulder to find Blake looking at me from a distance. He smiled the kind of smile one considers deeply. The room would remain still for that moment; the jukebox would stop playing. Conversations would come to a halt.

As the hours passed, Blake awed me and charmed me at the same time, soothing my inner anxieties. We sat on a bench together. He told me his dreams of being a movie scriptwriter and said he had written a dozen scripts and hoped that he could submit them one day to the Hollywood studios.

"Why don't you live in Hollywood?" I asked.

"I don't want to live in the Los Angeles area. My family lives there, and I visit them often, but LA is a different place.

"Someone dropped coins in the jukebox, and the music began to play.

"Would you like to dance?" Blake reached his hand out.

"Of course!" I hopped off the bench.

We centered our bodies on the dance floor. The melody was familiar, and the rhythm was slow enough to dance close to him. The song playing was "Teacher" by George Michael. My emotions sent electrical notes to my soul. The tone of the artist's voice hit a chord that profoundly penetrated my heart. As I leaned my head on his shoulder, I didn't know what it was that I felt in Blake's presence, nor what his purpose or reason would be in my life. The moment felt beyond anything I had ever felt before.

"What are you doing in this bar?" I asked him. "You don't look like you belong here."

"Neither do you!" he interrupted, and then we laughed together.

My friend, George, and I were walking by, and we saw the pool table inside, and he said, "Hey, let's jump in for a quick game of pool."

Blake was here on a whim. Just like me. It was a fluke that we happened to be here, at the same time. I was glad to hear that.

We dated for the next two months, and I got to learn more about him. He was born to a line of people that used their leisure for thinking, spinning brightly colored dreams of the future. He looked at life as it was, and he accepted the universe and his place in it. He lacked arrogance and conceit, which made him even more appealing to everyone.

He had gentleness and grace, which made me feel good just being around him. He displayed an ironic wittiness and sense of humor, which captured the attention of any audience within a few feet of him. We savored every delicious moment together. I felt an immoveable certainty within me. He made me laugh. He made me feel. He made me happy. Something felt so right. Of course he won my heart.

A year and half later, Blake and I were married. The wedding took place in Oklahoma, where he spent summers with his grandmother. He traveled to Oklahoma before me, and he and his grandmother planned our wedding.

CHAPTER FIVE

The Shadow of the Past

I was bent over the car seat removing the shopping bags from my car, when the mailman's tires rolled up behind me. He handed me a letter addressed from Chicago. It was a letter by Dallas's court-appointed attorney requesting my response to Dallas's abuse. A guardianship hearing date had been set by my sister Diane. She was taking legal action to remove Dallas, who was now in his twenties, from my mother's home. The family battle had begun.

Diane would put herself in peril by siding against my mother with certain family members and by alienating my brother Roger. "Just leave it alone!" Roger had told her.

But Diane felt prepared to gain guardianship of my brother. She called me and asked that I send a letter of support. With only half of the family sending letters of support, I knew that writing a letter to the Judge would break the family apart. Was it a necessary part of the legal process to pit each family member against each other, some for and some opposed to my mother keeping guardianship of Dallas?

Living 2000 miles away made it impossible for me to deal with Dallas's situation. Diane lived close to my mother, and she had more current information on how Dallas was being treated by my parents. I asked myself, *Is my sister strong enough to go up against my mother and the*

172

dissenting family members? Is she strong enough to take on the challenges of managing Dallas's special needs? Can she manage his life?

I knew the responsibilities to care for a mentally disabled person could be enormous and overwhelming. Love alone is not enough to provide the intense care and management needed throughout each day. Often, in our society, the heroes and heroines who provide unselfish love, patient support, and proper care for the physically and mentally disabled go unnoticed.

My parents were not equipped to care for Dallas at so many levels. There should have been support services to train them how to deal with his special issues. They needed relief so that they could take a break, or take a trip from Dallas's needs. How would things have been different if my parents had received the support they needed to help Dallas?

In recent years, Diane had been showing signs of emotional weariness. The close proximity to my mother had put her in harm's way of my mother's constant verbal attacks. Her heroic attempts to rescue Dallas failed, but the harder she tried to save him, the more my mother used Dallas as a way to control and manipulate Diane, refusing to let her or other family members see him. Diane was worn down, her health diminishing. I was certain that the burden of caring for Dallas would be difficult. But the question remained: Was my sister capable of shouldering such a burden? No other family member would step forward to rescue Dallas in a proper way. After much consideration, I didn't feel my sister would be able to manage Dallas's life. Was there a better way to do this?

From the moment I moved to California, I had been focused on my own family life. It was too painful to think of Dallas from a distance, and I didn't have to witness the frequent abuse—only the retelling of it that was passed along to me. At times, my sisters were getting along with Mom and the reports of abuse seemed to stop. Then, Mom and Lee moved to Florida to retire, moving Dallas and Jeanine with them. I needed a strategy to help Dallas, and to bring the family together. Over the years, I had remained on good terms with the whole family. I had also stayed on good terms with my mother, as long as Dallas was not part of the conversation. Through different siblings, I kept informed on what was going on inside the family—what was going on with Dallas.

I lived on the West Coast, so the distance kept me outside the minutiae of family chaos. I didn't want to create any more problems for my siblings. My siblings had struggled to wade through their lives into adulthood. They had suffered enough during our childhood, living separately in different foster homes.

Immediately, I sat down at my desk and jotted notes on a clean white paper tablet, documenting the past abuse of Dallas by my parents that I

173

had witnessed. I wretched over, grieved over, each abusive event. Sitting back in my chair, I let out a sigh.

I formed a strategy to help Dallas and my parents. My parents would get counseling to cope with their issues around Dallas. Mom could get help with her extreme moods. And if Mom and Lee could learn how to discipline Dallas in a healthy way without abusing him, that would help keep the family together. Lastly, a specialist could help with Dallas's incontinence issues, which only worsened as he grew older, with Dallas suffering at Mom and Lee's hands as the laundry piled up in proportion to his age. I wrote a letter to the Judge.

My letter would recommend to the Judge certain programs and counseling to help my parents learn how to cope with their issues and how to cope with Dallas.

I was convinced my plan would work for everyone. I was sure mom would be pleased about my plan. I valued honesty, and if I was going to hurt my mother with a letter sent to the court, I wanted her to know in advance what I was doing. Regardless of whether I told her or not, she would receive a copy of the letter through her attorney when the court documents were filed with the court. With my strategy complete, and my letter to the judge finished, I was confident I was doing the right thing for my family.

I picked up the telephone to call my mother, but the receiver leaped back onto the cradle. My hand trembled, unable to hold onto it. I took a long deep breath, picked up the receiver again, and dialed my mother. Each ring was shrill, long, and accelerated. Mom answered the phone.

"Hello, Mom. It's Shirlee," I said. "I hear you're having some beautiful weather in Florida since you moved there. No hurricanes."

"It's better than Chicago weather, than shoveling snow in winters," she groused.

"Um, Mom," I paused, thinking of the best way to open this conversation. "I wanted to share something with you." My voice sounded uncharacteristically nervous. "I understand Diane is going to court to gain legal guardianship of Dallas.

"That bitch! "

"Mom, don't you think Dallas would be better elsewhere? Isn't it hard for you—"

"NO! Dallas belongs here with me," she yelled into the receiver.

"Mom, I don't know what the answer is, but I've written a letter to the judge, and I want you to hear me out. I want you to know where I'm coming from. I don't want to do anything behind your back."

The other end of the line was quiet. I proceeded to read the letter.

"Dear Judge, I live in California, I have been witness to the abuse of my brother Dallas by my parents—"

Before I could go any further, my mother cut in. "Stop, stop! You f-----g bitch!"

"Please Mom, just listen! Mom, please! I feel that at the end of this letter it will help you, Dallas, and the family. Just hear me—"

"You f-----g bitch!" she screamed into the phone with sheer intensity, and she slammed the phone down.

I was speechless. I was calling to inform her of my strategy without going behind her back. She knew the truth about abusing Dallas. God knew the truth. Dallas knew the truth.

I laid the letter on the desk in front of me, wiping the tears from my cheek. It felt like my last desperate attempt to unify and keep the family together. I leaned forward in my chair, and folded my arms on the desk; my head fell down on my arms, and the letter slid to the floor. I was too exhausted to retrieve it. I wanted to finish the letter. I wanted to fix Mom. I wanted to fix the family. I believed I was building a bridge for the family by recommending the support of professionals. Instead, I had built a tall fence between my sisters, my parents, and myself.

The court hearing to consider Diane's petition for guardianship of Dallas was set in Chicago. I was unable to attend due to my heavy work schedule. Although her bid for guardianship had divided the family, I did not feel any resentment toward Diane's efforts to do what she felt was right for Dallas. It took courage on her part to try to rescue Dallas. There was no clean way to do it.

My letter to the judge never arrived. In the end, I could not bring myself to mail it. Although I personally was not convinced at the time that Diane was the best-suited guardian for Dallas, I felt that she had enough support from other family members to win the case without my support. Diane's attorney presented her case in the court, but failed to convince the judge that she would be the best guardian. The court appointed an attorney ad litem to manage Dallas's case. Dallas would remain with my parents.

After the court hearing, family relationships were further strained between siblings. Because I didn't send my letter to support her in court, Diane would not forgive me. She met my phone calls to heal our relationship with deep resentment. She blamed me for losing the case. What she failed to recognize was that she didn't lose the case because of my not supporting her; she lost the case because she didn't convince the judge she would make the best guardian for Dallas's life. Still, my decision not to support my sister haunted me. Could my letter have made a difference? Did I make the wrong decision?

I was losing hope that, as adults, we would be able to remake our present lives together free from the shadow of our past. By creating our own families, independent of the dysfunction, we could express our own values, traditions, and lives separate from my mother's influence. My hope was that we could share with one another a fully functional way of being in the world by helping each other bridge the differences. I was wrong. We were disconnected from one another. And Mom was always in the middle of our lives, controlling the dysfunction.

What now was to be done? How would Dallas be rescued?

Grandma passed away. She had lived to a healthy one hundred and half years old. She outlived all of her friends. And she had finally entered the gates of that heavenly place she had so often spoken of.

Blake scheduled our flight to Indianapolis. I was grateful for the long flight to reflect on my memories of Grandma. Throughout her life, she had been the anchor for our family; she served as example in difficult times by remaining calm, prayerful, and in control of her spirit. God must have wanted her to live a long life to help us through our childhood and into adulthood.

It had been over a year since my last visit with her. But I remembered her as if she was sitting beside me. I cherished our many walks to church, listening to the rhythm of her black heels tapping along the sidewalk, and I was grateful for her patience with my orneriness as a child, her unfailing faith, and her kindness.

She spent most of her life in Albion, but she had later moved to Marion to be near Dad, and my aunt and uncle. Over the last few years, our family reunions had been about celebrating Grandma's life. If there were tensions or disagreements among family members, they were erased momentarily so as not to taint our reunions. At one point, my husband had compiled and edited a tearjerker video about Grandma's life, and we shared it at the family reunion. Grandma was loved by everyone she touched. She was loved by me.

176

Before Grandma's passing, there had been disagreements among my sisters and my aunt and uncle regarding her hospital care. Some members of the family wanted more done to save her life, and other family members wanted her to go to heaven without extraordinary measures, as God and Grandma would have done it.

When we arrived at the church, my family was standing in front, except for my sisters, who didn't attend the funeral out of protest over Grandma's hospital care during the last days of her life. The organ music began to play, and we entered the sanctuary. Grandma was laid to rest at the front altar. I walked up next to her and placed my hand on her arm. *I will miss you, Grandma.*

Soon after the viewing, the service began. The pastor spoke of Grandma's life, but he could only speak about the part of her life that she had lived in Marion. He didn't know what an indelible mark Grandma had left on our lives; her steadfastness, humor, and love, which would carry us forward. He couldn't speak about the purity of her life, the likes of which I had never known. He couldn't speak for the parts of Grandma's life when she worried about my sisters and brothers, especially Dallas.

It was early spring, and the snow had melted in the Sierra Nevada. The snow had been plentiful during the winter, and the water released from the mountains gushed along the American river. It was time to plan our annual rafting trip with friends.

Family and friends were invited the night before to bring their sleeping bags and stay at our home. On Sunday morning, after breakfast, we caravanned forty minutes to the American River, where we met our guide. The guide walked us through the safety tips. We collected our wet suits and helmets. With everyone wrapped tightly in their orange safety vests and white helmets, we boarded our three different rafts.

Scott paddled forward in our boat. His face lit up with the anticipation of our rafting adventure. I watched his confident paddling, and it filled me with pride. He was comfortable around water, and he shared my love of nature. It gave him respite from his intense work. I was proud of his single-track mind that helped him succeed at his passion and follow through with his vision of becoming a software engineer. He had grown to be quite handsome; his black hair glistened in the sunlight, and his tanned skin spoke of his healthy fitness. He was strong in spirit.

The river was a mix of calm and white water, which added to the thrill of white water rafting. I enjoyed water adventures, but I had been leery of the water since childhood after my dad threw me into the lake without swimming lessons, expecting me to swim. That was his idea of how to teach a child to swim. Struggling to stay afloat, I had thrashed around in the water while his attention drifted elsewhere. My fear of drowning had never left me.

The raft maneuvered down the river through calm waters. Immediately, the paddles splashing began between friends and added to the competition and fun. Blake was animated and witty, engaging with everyone. A little ways downstream, I could see an intense rapid. I carefully watched the guide approach the white caps with our raft parallel to the foam, dipping the raft to and fro, almost tipping it over. We had taken these rapids in previous years, and this was not the way the other guides had approached them. Soon, I became concerned with his experience as a guide.

After a couple more hours of rafting, we stopped along the riverbank. The rafting company set up a picnic. We joined our friends and enjoyed swapping our rafting experiences. When lunch was over, we headed down the river and let the water wash away our cares.

Several miles later, we approached Devils Rock, where the rapids were the strongest. Two large rocks appeared in the distance. The treacherous narrow path between the two rocks made it difficult to cross through to the other side. I turned behind me, observing our guide. He began paddling furiously and yelling for help to avoid the large rock. He didn't have control of the raft. Suddenly, the raft veered swiftly and vertically upwards and washed up onto the twenty-foot-high granite boulder and filled with water, lodging our raft solidly in place. My body fell completely backward. Seconds later, a tremendous force sucked my body out of the raft and under the white caps through the narrow passage and down the river. I was underwater and unable to breathe. I was unable to surface or see where I was. I was drowning.

Though I was submerged under water, the waves periodically elevated me to the surface, giving me seconds to breathe. Up ahead, I glimpsed at a large granite rock directly in my path. I remembered to put my legs and feet downstream to avoid hitting my head. But the water was so strong that it pulled me underneath the rapids again. I looked up at the crystal-clear water bubbling above my head. I couldn't breathe. The moment felt serene in an odd sort of way. I was as close to death as I had ever come. The water level seemed to rise, and my head was forced down again. *I think I'm going to die.*

Then, once again, I resurfaced. I caught a half breath. My eyes looked toward the impending large rock. I moved my arms quickly, and with all my strength, I swam as hard as I could to the left side of the river. In the distance, I saw a raft move swiftly toward me. Dripping water blurred my eyes. I couldn't see who it was. My hands swept the water from my face, and I looked up. Someone was standing above me, calmly reaching his paddle out over the raft. I grabbed the oar, and he pulled me onto the raft. It was Scott, handing me my lifeline.

I could see that Blake was not in the raft.

"Where's Blake? Where's Blake?" I screamed. Blake had been sucked out of the raft along with me.

"Don't worry, mom, another raft has rescued him," Scott reassured me.

I was reminded how precious life was, how precious my son and husband were to me. How, in just an instant, one event could change everything in your life.

After a fourteen-year absence from my parents in my life, I received a call from my mother telling me that my stepfather's health was failing. I thought this would be an opportunity to reconcile with both of them. My stepfather had been suffering from lung cancer and emphysema from years of smoking, just like my father had.

By the time I was able to fly to Florida, my stepfather had passed away. My career responsibilities made it difficult to attend his funeral. A part of me felt sad that I had not seen my stepfather in so many years. I enjoyed being with him in our early years together. He was interesting to talk to, and, in the beginning, we had lots of fun going places like Riverview Park in Chicago, miniature golf courses, restaurants, and dances with Mom. I would miss the part of him that tried to make the family work.

I had regrets; death always makes you think about the person who died. I wished I had spent some time understanding him. I wished I had spent more time visiting him. He could have been a wonderful stepfather, if my mother would have let him. His decency was corrupted by her. I wanted to ask him why he allowed my mother to rule with such evil that divided the family. I wanted to ask him why he put up with her, and why he engaged in Dallas's abuse. Why didn't he leave her, rather than be drawn into her world of mistreating Dallas. Why? Why did he take that journey with her?

I saw what my mother's vanity and evil did to him, but his scars were less visible than Dallas's. Over the years, Lee's relationship with Jeanine was tenuous at best. Mom interfered in their closeness, and she did her best to keep the center of attention on herself. Jeanine had often absented herself from their life to escape the arguments at home, and upon Lee's death, he still had not reconciled with his only daughter. I know that must have saddened him. Mom never permitted any closeness between Lee and Jeanine unless she controlled it, even at the end of his life. Only my mother attended his funeral; no other friends were in attendance, and even Jeanine did not go. She would mourn him in her own way.

In Florida, the weather forecast predicted extreme heat, with tropical storms settling in the gulf coast. Hurricane weather could destroy buildings and lives. Yet I booked my flight to Florida amid the stormy forecast.

So many years had passed without my mother in my life, yet I continued to wish I had a functional mother. I admired my friends' relationships with their mothers. They shopped and cooked together, shared events, and celebrated Mother's day. They built positive memories and created lifetime bonds. I had made up my mind not to expect anything from my visit. After so many years, my intention was to see if I could bond with my mother and sister. I wanted to see how Dallas was doing, and how Mom was treating Dallas

When I arrived, I realized that I hadn't brought the directions to my mother's home. It was late in the afternoon. Mom was expecting me. I called my sister from a telephone booth, and I asked her for Mom's telephone number.

"Please come by and visit me on the way to Mom's!" Jeanine begged.

"I've been up since four o'clock this morning to catch a flight from San Francisco, but I'll visit you tomorrow," I promised. "Please understand, it has been a long day of travel."

If I hadn't felt so tired from wrapping up my work before leaving California, I would have taken the time to see her that evening. Jeanine sounded hurt. Her voice sounded desperate.

While driving to my mother's house, I thought about the life Jeanine had lived with my parents. She had it rough growing up in my parents' home. The constant bickering and arguments between them were relentless. Her tiny ears were exposed to such hateful conversations, and the abuse of Dallas.

Now that Jeanine was an adult in her early thirties, she was unable to forge a mother-daughter bond because Mom had turned her own father against her. Jeanine was saddened that the division between her and her father had been Mom's doing. Mom had to be the center of the universe with Lee—there wasn't room for any other planets.

I arrived at the entrance to my mother's private community. The security guard studied me carefully and reviewed my identification. By the security guard's reaction to me, I assumed my mother had previously expressed her paranoia at the security gate.

"I am here to see my mother." My voice was simultaneously laden with trepidation and excitement. The security guard waved his hand. I drove past the security booth and navigated the winding paved road through the large community of manufactured retirement homes. The front lawns were decorated with plastic pink flamingos and sun-faded plastic flowers where natural flowerbeds would usually rest. I rolled down my window and listened to the crickets playing fitful songs in unison. The address led me to a neatly-groomed yard and a white aluminum house.

Mom's house was situated on a flat, shade-less property surrounded by green lawns. I pulled into Mom's driveway and parked alongside her car. She was standing in front of the house, her body moving nervously with anticipation. Her face seemed to clash against the bright outfit she wore. She stared at me through the windshield. I saw an icy demeanor, incongruous of a welcoming mother.

Opening the car door, I breathed in deeply. Familiar with the California dry air, the sweltering summer heat sizzled, and the humid air burned my lungs. My blouse stuck to my moist skin as the fabric moved with each breath. Feelings of happiness and sadness alternated through me like ocean waves. Mom's face was older. There were deep lines by the side of her face, which was framed by powdery white hair. Her beady black eyes stared hard at me, darting fast with a suspicious look.

I closed the car door and walked slowly toward her with my arms outstretched. We hugged with a distant coolness. Mom was guarded in her affection. She invited me into her home. She led me to her bedroom and indicated that I would sleep in her room. She would sleep on the living room sofa during my stay. I knew better than to voice my objection at taking her bed. This was the kind and generous side of her. It was her way of making me feel welcome and special. For me, it only magnified how much I wanted her to be this way all the time, to my siblings, and especially to Dallas. I wanted to love her unconditionally.

We sat in the living room on the sofa. The seating no longer had custom plastic over the fabric. She brought me a beverage and sat it down on the coffee table. We discussed general information about family members. I asked how she was doing with my stepfather's passing. She pretended to be powerful and in control, doing her best to distract me from her grief, her mistakes. She blamed the world for her unhappiness.

I surprised her with Lee's Purple Heart framed in a large shadow box containing his war pictures and other medals. She had given it to me earlier, and I felt it should be returned to her now that he was gone. I wanted to honor his days in Normandy during World War II. She seemed surprised that I would return it to her, and she was more impressed with the box than the sacrifice and memory.

181

It wasn't long before general information about the family turned into gossip. She didn't see the pain she had caused the family. She saw the universe through her own window, as clouded and distorted as it was. She didn't feel the pain she had caused Dallas. Her own perceived power stemmed from ignorance and stupidity, yet she wanted me to believe that she was different than she had been in the past.

"Where is Dallas?" I asked, hoping he would be able to join us in the living room.

"He's in his room." Her tone, cold and crass, meant for me to leave him alone.

Mom stepped outside to wrap up the garden hose. I walked to Dallas's bedroom and peeked inside. He sat at his desk with his shoulders low, his head half-lowered. His hand tightened his shirt collar close to his neck—an embrace missing from his life. His eyes looked out over the dining room. In the center was the highly polished dining table and its early-American seating, a place where his urine-shamed butt was never allowed to sit. He was watching football, a game he liked and seemed to understand. His room was neatly organized, military style, clean, everything neatly in its place. Mom made sure of that.

"Hello, Dallas do you remember me? I am your sister Shirlee!" I said.

"Yeah!" He looked at me and smiled.

Dallas's eyes were sad and veiled, and his glance moved swiftly away, gliding off and past objects, unable to hold onto the moment. He still couldn't mouth more than one or two words at a time. He was punished for trying to talk. Mom didn't want him to talk. Then he'd be able to tell. He'd be able to tell about the abuse that happened to him. Horrific abuse that any clear-thinking person would never believe one human being would do to another, let alone a mother to her own special needs son.

Moving closer, I went to touch his arm affectionately, but he immediately pulled back. The only touching he knew was hitting, so he withdrew his arm to defend himself. Dallas had been abused so much that he couldn't stand human touch anymore. I bent closer to him.

"I won't hurt—"

Suddenly, Mom was behind me.

"Leave him alone!" She yelled. I immediately left the room, knowing I could inflame the situation further. She would only take it out on him.

The most important thing in Mom's reality was her sense of control and power. She was mission control, controlling every move in space, pushing the security button to stay away, closing down communications between Dallas and me. Dallas was imprisoned by his mental capacity, and he was physically constrained to an aquarium rather than allowed to swim in an ocean.

In that moment, I felt a desperate wish to help Dallas, to make up for my failed attempts to rescue him, and my guilt at having no time to rescue him because of my busy career. In this vast world, people have the opportunity to build their life in their own way and image, but Dallas was imprisoned in his own world, left without the choice to choose life, fulfillment, and happiness.

Our lives couldn't have been more different. My freedom to do what I wanted was unconstrained. With my home three thousand miles away, I could see no way to help Dallas. If I completely severed relations with my mother, I would never be able to help him. During my stay, she wouldn't allow Dallas to spend time with me. I hadn't earned her trust and loyalty enough to be allowed to bond with my brother. My only hope was time.

While reconnecting with my mother, I learned that she also didn't want me to see Jeanine. Soon after I arrived, our conversations became about problems between her and my sisters. Family gossip was rampant. In my mother's singular world, she didn't want to bring the family together. She would settle with fighting and then making up, and whoever was in her camp at the moment was part of her life. Part of Dallas's life.

Now, Jeanine and Mom weren't speaking to each other. Mom gossiped about my sister and about what she had done to her, convincing me that this was not the right time to call her. This was code that I shouldn't see Jeanine while I was visiting. I knew their tempestuous relationship. I knew Mom.

In coming to Florida after so many years, I had been hoping for a family reunion, yet, once again, I only found division. I weighed my desire to see my sister against my desire to preserve my relationship with my mother. It was a loss either way. The issues between Mom and my sisters made me feel guilty. Regretfully, I found it best not to see my sister during that visit.

Each day of my visit, Mom was like a different person. Her moods shifted from wanting to do things for me to making my life miserable by attacking me or someone else. She didn't have friends, but she always needed an enemy. She never asked for help for her dysfunction. Her dysfunction felt familiar and normal to her — she thought everyone else was wrong. There could be no family intervention because the family was so divided. My mother saw to that. She lived her life ruining other lives, lashing out at everything and everyone around her. She created chaos for days, and then she slept for days. I didn't know what to do, but the chaos my mother encouraged among my brothers and sisters kept everyone distant from one another and unable and unwilling to focus on helping her.

I was hopeful that with my life's experience and education I could begin to try to help my mother get the intervention she needed. I knew I had to approach her gingerly. If I could get her better, Dallas would have a better life, and my brothers and sisters could come out and be supportive and loving to each other. Mom could come out from behind her veil of secret abuse and change her ways. She would be able to see the harm she had inflicted for years on Dallas and on my other siblings.

I believed my mother was intelligent, but she was frustrated by the limits in her life. She lacked education and a way to express herself in a normal society. She was emotionally unequipped to articulate her needs. She had left the protection of her parents in Hawaii and moved to Albion, where she suffered under my father's abuse. The aftermath would express itself for years to come.

During the week I spent in Florida, I tried to get mom to see a doctor about her moods. Getting help from a specialist would help with her anxiety and depression. But she would have none of it. I tried to convince her that taking medication for anxiety would help her relationship with her other family members. Again she refused to hear it. She couldn't be convinced to get the help she needed.

"Mom it will help you cope better. You will have a better relationship with the family." I pleaded.

"I don't take drugs of any kind." she barked.

But she would take diet pills on a regular basis to lose weight because that was part of her vanity. She valued beauty and money. I flattered her for her good health and her ageless beauty. I complimented her on her decorating of her home and her choice of beautiful colors, and, briefly, something would light up in my mother's face, but then she would wonder what you wanted from her. She was a desperate woman in need of constant attention.

Although Mom had physically changed in her aging years, her vanity remained. She seemed indefatigable. She was always motivated and on a mission to stay ahead of her perceived enemies.

One day, Mom wanted me to help her organize her affairs. I considered her business private. I didn't want to know about her finances. But Mom was in one of those moods. She wanted to change her will. Delving into her financial affairs was uncomfortable for me. She had preconceived notions about who would receive her inheritance. It was as changeable as the weather in Florida. This was the game she played, to disinherit those who she thought had betrayed her recently. From my perspective, anything left of her inheritance should go to better Dallas's life in the future and to make up for the wrongs done to him. It should all go to enhance Dallas's life and care.

We sat at the table in her screened porch area overlooking the expansive back lawn. She laid out her papers and scattered them on the table, stopping for a second, digging her fingers into her lowered brow in confusion. There was my stepfather's birth certificate, papers about my stepfather's pension. She wanted me to see if there was more money that could be had. My stepfather had retired many years before, and she had hope that I could find more money from his steel worker's pension. She wanted to increase her monthly retirement. Having Dallas helped with her income.

I caught her eyes darting around, and then through me, as if she knew my thoughts. She had a curiosity that was sharp at moments; she was always seeking loyalty, piecing together the past, and framing the present. The strange manner in which it seemed that her naked thoughts held me for a moment in utter contempt gave me chills. Her eyes were intent, and her mind moved quickly through some realm only she comprehended. She was testing me to hear what I would say. Did I believe in her truth?

I studied her closely for some sign of regret about dividing the family and for her abuse of Dallas. Suddenly, her volatile spirit shot up from the deepest depression to excited happiness, and she was grateful that I was going to help her organize her life and that she could know something about the life I made for myself and that it might rub off on her. In that moment, I realized that we hadn't been living with my mother. Dallas hadn't been living with my mother. We had been living with an undiagnosed illness. No, I wasn't a doctor, but the signs had been evident for years. But how do you help someone who refuses help? How do you help someone who is comfortable in that dark place, controlling and hurting others, and who refuses the care?

At Mom's insistence, I contacted the steel mill, and I learned that it had closed many years ago. The company now handling the pensions was curt in responding to my questions regarding additional monies owed. Perhaps Lee had other retirement monies? The possibilities were bleak, and Mom's mind stirred as if a tornado had gone through it. Her thoughts were swirling with perceptions, innuendos, and gossip about family members, looking for the cog in the wheel that fit this moment.

Mom's impulses were constant, and changing her will was her latest form of outrage. She decided to set up an appointment with her attorney to change her will for that same day. She demanded I be in attendance. Mom yelled for Dallas to get in the car, and he slipped into the backseat behind her, where he was out of arm's reach. She dropped him off at his day program, which provided some activities, outings, and work responsibility, and we continued to the attorney's office.

At the attorney's office, I explained to him that I didn't feel comfortable being there, nor did I feel comfortable being involved in my mother's affairs. He understood; he had dealt with my mother's maniacal behaviors before. I shifted in my chair as my mother rearranged her assets. She always trusted my judgment, but my advice that she include everyone in her legacy fell on deaf ears. My feeling was that Dallas should benefit from her life savings to make up for the wrongs and to improve his quality of his life; she owed it to him.

On the way back, we stopped by Dallas's day program to pick him up. My mom introduced me to Linda, the director of the facility's program. Linda had an angelic face, and spoke softly. She studied my mother carefully, as my mother spoke rapidly with her hands animated in the air. I detected some discomfort from my mother, as if Linda knew more about my mother than she wanted to expose.

In the car on the way home, Mom hastily began reciting her past decade of woes about my siblings and their spouses. The depth of emotion in her voice made the gossip harsh to my tender ears. These siblings were my flesh and blood, and she was speaking so hatefully about them. Did she know I loved my brothers and sisters? Did she know I cared about their spouses? What part of this was true? She was always convincing. This was how she controlled the family; it was how she kept one sibling from talking to the other, kept one against the other. I changed the subject.

"Let's get something to eat." I suggested. It was the only way to spend time with Dallas. He was never allowed to join the family, and he was always forced to stay in his room until it was time to go shopping. She wouldn't leave him home.

"Can Dallas come with us?" I asked, glancing at him huddled in the backseat.

"Yeah, we'll take him." she said, as if he was an afterthought.

Mom drove to her favorite buffet restaurant, screaming at cars along the way, slowing down, glaring at whoever passed her and inconvenienced her life. I tightened my seat belt. After a tumultuous ride, we pulled into the driveway of the restaurant. After a sudden stop, she swung her head toward the back seat where Dallas was sitting.

"Get out! And behave yourself!" she bellowed at Dallas in a harsh tone.

We followed the buffet line and filled our plates. I found a more private table where we could sit. I kept the conversation more general, so gossip about family members was limited.

"Stop eating like a pig!" Mom yelled at Dallas.

Patrons of the restaurant turned around quickly to see where the rude statement came from. Dallas's eyes dropped, abandoning his sight of her. He lowered his head, as if embarrassed at being excoriated in front of me. I smiled reassuringly at Dallas and started gathering our dishes. My mother's display had caused me to lose my appetite.

It was hard to feel the way I did about my mother. I wanted to love her unconditionally. I worried about her coping without Lee. Earlier in my life, I had made arrangements to take care of her in her elder years. After all, I was her daughter. At times, she had done kind things for me. She had put me in modeling school when I was nineteen, and she'd paid for my braces.

I'd assume that as she aged she would soften her moods and be less controlling and become too weak to abuse Dallas. But even in her mid-seventies, she was still hell bent on dividing the family. I couldn't risk her toxic nature in my life. No money on earth would be enough to tolerate her destroying my marriage. I would let the other family members salivating for the leftover inheritance take care of her. They would soon deserve it.

Dallas was another matter. He was the most vulnerable. She had complete and utter control over his life, and she let everyone know that, from the family to the government institutions that were trying to help him. She took great pride in that control.

The distance between my siblings had remained a painful reminder of the dysfunction of our early childhood, as did the painful and constant thorn of Dallas's abuse. My mother continued to use Dallas as a pawn in her relationship with all of us. I wanted to walk away from my family's history and pretend it didn't exist. But Dallas was where he was, and the family was still divided.

The Florida sun shone through the window on my face, creating a warmth and calmness inside me. Surprisingly, I slept well on the last night of my visit, even after a tense day with my mother. I would be flying out the next morning for California. I missed everything about my husband, especially his humor and gentleness that held me through difficult times. I also missed my son, who had stayed steady and strong through the chaos of my divorce. From the aftermath of my divorce, I tried to create an independent life for Scott and me by finishing my college degree and securing a stable job. It took too long. He suffered along with me through the financially tough times. He held the values and the goodness his father and I had taught him.

In the kitchen, Mom opened the refrigerator, rummaging through the shelves to make breakfast. With her back to me, I took a moment to check on Dallas to see if he was awake. I quickly tiptoed toward his room. His door was slightly ajar, and he was sound asleep on his bed with his blanket secured over his face.

I needed to cleanse my body of the Florida humidity and heat. Wrapping my bathrobe around my body, I returned to the bathroom where I removed my robe, placing it over the glass shower door. I stepped into the shower. After a minute, the hot sprayer scorched my shoulders. I quickly adjusted the handle. Suddenly, a loud noise shuttered the shower walls. At the sound, I felt a swoop of intense emotion that was difficult to contain, as if a volcano had burst within me. I couldn't see, but I heard violent noises in the house.

I heard my mother yelling, her voice getting louder, and then I heard her crashing through Dallas's bedroom door. Horrified at the sounds coming from the other room, I quickly stepped out of the shower, careful not to slip on the linoleum floor. I wrapped the towel securely around my body and tucked it under my arms. I stepped on the bedroom carpet and picked up my pace, running toward the bedroom door, and flinging it wide open. Mom stood over Dallas, her arm raised high. The force of her blow to his head swept his face blank.

"Get your stinkin' body out of bed!" my mother screamed.

Dallas sat up on the bed, his hands pulling the blanket tightly around his body. He pulled back against the wall, a stunned reaction to this abrupt violence. Then Mom saw his eyes move quickly from her face to his helpless body. She struck another blow to his body. There was silence.

Mom hurriedly walked out of Dallas's room towards the kitchen, her face pinched in anger and her fist tightened as she rounded the corner. Dallas lay still on the bed with both hands covering his head, knowing that any minute she could fly back into his room with even more fury.

I tiptoed towards him. Dallas's eyes met mine. He had a resigned look about his lot in life. But Dallas and I knew that if I comforted him, it would get worse.

"Dallas, did mommy hurt you?" I whispered to him.

He reluctantly shook his head sideways. He couldn't say yes. He couldn't say yes to the authorities.

"Stay away from him, Shirlee!" Mom yelled from the kitchen.

"Mom, did you hurt Dallas?" I asked, seeking an admission of her guilt to take to the authorities.

"No, I never touched him!" She screamed at me.

I hadn't seen all the violence, and Dallas never cried out. Dallas learned from the past to never cry out loud because Mom would abuse him even more. If I called the police, they would want sound evidence of the abuse. Mom was cunning with the police; they didn't frighten her. After all, she thought they were her best friends, just like they had been in Chicago. How many police had she befriended in this town? She would deny that she had hurt Dallas. And Dallas would deny that Mommy hurt him out of fear that he would remain in the home and be further punished. Where did Dallas get his strength each day to tolerate the abuse? This was all he knew of a mother's love.

Many years ago, my sister had made an effort to take him away from my mother, but she had failed. How could I do any better in this situation? Mom was a master of concealment. She was able to conceal her private demons outside the home. She abused Dallas where she thought the bruises wouldn't show: on his back or on his head where there was hair. I was visiting from out of state. It was her word against mine. Dallas couldn't talk and defend himself. I knew that if I reported her, it would be on me to prove the offenses. Who would believe a mother could be so cruel?

I closed the door to the bedroom and sat down on the hard fruitwood chair, staring outside the bedroom window. A neighbor's colorful bougainvillea embraced the side of the house, growing, maturing, and thriving in the sun. I watched the neighbor tending to her bougainvillea. She trimmed gently, molding and supporting each of the narrow branches in a direction that supported the whole of the bush. Here I was again, unsupported and helpless to rescue Dallas.

It was late Saturday evening, and I sat up on the bed and doubled the pillows behind me, resting my hand solidly against my face. I longed for the profound love and stability of my marriage. It was all that I had dreamed of since I was a teenager. I missed my husband terribly. I jumped out of bed, preparing for my last night with Mom and Dallas. I packed my suitcase with gifts from my mom. She enjoyed giving me clothes and jewelry. I believed that she paid for them now. The risk of stealing would

189

be too high, and I had seen her buy these items. She always wanted me to dress well. She knew it could bring me opportunities — opportunities she never made for herself. She never resented my better life. After all, she was proud of my life, and she lived vicariously through my successes. I was happy to share that part of my life with her. I longed for her to change who she had become. I wanted to do so much for her. In her rare moments of clarity and balance, she could be generous and fun. I longed for the impossible.

After the long day, the temperature outside was still hot and humid. The mosquitoes buzzed in the night. I had the window cracked slightly, and a gust of wind broke the silence in the room. I set my ticket on top of my packed suitcase. I opened the bedroom door and retired early for my flight in the morning. I lay on the pillow and closed my eyes, thinking back over the week's visit. I realized there had been few moments of mother-daughter bonding, and I felt disconnected from my mother, unable to relate to the darkness inside of her. There was a heavy silence. I fell into a deep slumber.

"Get up! Get up, stupid!"

It was the middle of the night, and my mother's voice was reverberating throughout the house. I rose out of bed, my need to know what was happening greater than my terror of finding out. I tiptoed towards Dallas's bedroom. Mom stood over Dallas's bed and slapped his head with her fist.

"Get your stinkin' ass in the bathroom! Now!"

Dallas awakened. He had been sleeping soundly, the blanket drawn tightly to his neck, and his pillow hiding his head. Shrinking in dread at the sight of Mom above him, he recoiled below her body, moving to and fro. Pain was etched solidly on his face, and a flash of fear overtook his helpless body. Dallas raised his arms to protect his head.

"Don't you dare try to hit me!" Mom yelled, and she slapped him again. She backed away from him, pointing toward the bathroom. Dallas jumped out of bed and ran to the bathroom.

This was still part of Dallas's nightly routine. He suffered facing her rage over the bedwetting, night after night after night. As always, her outbursts kept him anxious and on high alert, and he just urinated more. Once my mother went back to her bedroom, he would fall into a deep sleep, escaping her madness. He did not understand. He was lucky on the nights she felt too tired to expend such hateful anger.

After a week with Mom, I left Florida discouraged. After all these years, she had not changed. I had such a bittersweet relationship with her. She made it difficult to get close to her. Mom sought to be no different. Chaos, control, and Dallas's abuse were all she knew. She didn't know how to be any other way in the world.

In late October, the leaves on the branches turned yellow and orange, beckoning me to prepare my backyard for the winter chill. I raked the fallen leaves and trimmed the remaining flowers of the season. I caught a glimpse of myself in the window. Sections of my hair fell loosely to my shoulders. I looked closer at my reflection, and my face was etched with lines from too little sleep, and my eyes looked dull. *Am I seeing a reflection of the person I want to be? Am I serving the purposes I was sent to serve?*

Inside, the telephone rang loudly. I laid aside my garden tools and ran into the kitchen. The phone rang again. I removed my gloves and picked up the receiver.

"Mom padlocked Dallas in his room," a heavy smoker's voice said matter-of-factly.

"Who is this?" I adjusted the cradle on my shoulder. I must not have heard correctly.

"It's your sister, Jeanine! Mom padlocked Dallas in his room. She won't let him out. He can't even use the bathroom."

Hearing this, my breath failed me.

"Have you called the authorities?" I asked.

"Nope, it won't do any good. When the police get there, Mom makes it sound like nothing is wrong, and Dallas can't talk."

Somehow I believed her.

"Mom turned off his television and lights."

"What does he do if he can't use the bathroom?"

"She left him with a urinal bucket in the closet."

"How does he eat?

"I don't know."

I felt a fierce urgency. The laws against abuse were being enforced these days. Dallas had to be rescued. Once and for all, I needed to make sure he

191

would be free from my mother's hands. After I hung up with Jeanine, I dialed Social Services in Hernando County.

I was shifted to various departments until I finally got in touch with Dallas's caseworker. She was from Puerto Rico, and it was hard to understand her words, but she expressed interest in hearing about Dallas's situation. I said that she would need to send someone out right away. If my mother found out that she had been reported, she would remove the lock before anyone got there and would repaint the door.

The caseworker allowed me to talk for almost an hour about Dallas's abuse over the years. The tone of my voice added to the urgency. I reported that I had witnessed abuse firsthand in my late teens before moving to California. Other information of his abuse that I related to her came from my sisters, whose descriptions of the abuse fit with my own descriptions. And I had no reason to disbelieve my sisters. We couldn't make up stuff like this. This was what horror movies were made of.

"You must get out to the house right away!" I begged her.

She assured me that they would follow up on it. Three weeks later, the caseworker called me. She didn't say when she went out to the house. She'd met with my mother at her home. She'd asked to see Dallas in his room. When she'd approached Dallas's bedroom door, she'd noticed fresh paint on the doorframe. The walls had also been freshly painted. She inquired about it, and my mother said she'd called in painters just recently. The social worker spoke to Dallas briefly, but it was difficult for her to understand him.

This was bureaucracy at its best, but it was better late than never. However, nothing came from the report. Dallas remained with my mother in spite of the concerns. Dallas suffered through this ordeal, imprisoned in his jail, and though he was free from a pad-locked door, he was not free of abuse.

Not long after this incident, my brother Roland called me. It had been many months since I had heard from him. His voice sounded high on the phone, and I could hear a slight buzzing of insects in the background; after a heavy rainfall, Louisiana, where he was living, teemed with insects. Roland asked me to hold on while he slammed a window shut, and the buzzing stopped.

"Hey, Shirlee, did you hear Dallas isn't with Mom?" he asked.

For a moment, I caught my breath.

"No!" I exclaimed. "What happened?"

I was puzzled. Roland was closest to Mom, visiting her and calling her often. He had the least contentious relationship with her. He ignored the obvious problems with Dallas. How could he not know where Dallas was? Did he really believe that I knew? What could have happened? Was Dallas all right? Was he safe?

"I don't know. I thought you would know something about it."

"Is he with Jeanine?" I logically inquired. She occasionally would pick up the pieces when situations weren't going well with Mom and Dallas. He would stay at her house until Mom calmed down.

"No, he's not."

"How long has he been away from Mom?"

"About a month," he said.

"A whole month? I will do what I can to find out where he is. I'll call you back later."

I sat down on the chair behind me to collect my thoughts. Why else would Roland have called me? I hadn't heard from him in many months. My family believed I knew where Dallas was, and that I had somehow created this situation. Mom always had to believe that there was a family member conspiring against her, so this time, the conspiracy had traveled three thousand miles west to my doorstep.

Without further delay, I dialed the operator for the telephone number of Social Services in Hernando County. I was routed to various people before reaching the director of the Association of Retarded Citizens (ARC), a community-based organization advocating for and serving the intellectually and developmentally disabled and their families. The director seemed to have intimate knowledge about Dallas's case.

"Linda, I am Dallas's sister from California," I introduced myself. "I just received a call from one of my brothers who said that Dallas was no longer living with my mother. Can you help me locate him?"

"Yes," Linda replied, "Dallas is temporarily staying at this facility in Spring Hill until we find a more permanent placement." She knew Dallas, and she knew my mother and sister. "He is doing fine, but he refuses to go back to your mother. He has indicated that she hurt him."

Relief spread throughout my body. "Linda, I believe that many years ago I visited Dallas at Spring Hill. I am Dallas's oldest sister from California."
"Yes, I remember you well!" Linda said.

193

"Well, thank you," I said, taken aback. "You have a stellar memory. Are you sure you don't have me confused with one of my other sisters?"

"No, I know your sister, Jeanine, who lives in town. But you left me with a very favorable impression," Linda said emphatically.

I was amazed that someone would retain a memory of me from the past. Linda discussed Dallas's history and life over the years. She spoke about the chaos he often lived with under my mother's care. Dallas was a part of the many programs provided by the facility. My mother often moved him in and out of the programs that were benefiting him. My mother had the reputation of being highly crass and unpredictably moody. The staff often wondered which one of them --- she or Dallas --- should really be residing in the facility. Mom needed well-deserved breaks from caring for Dallas, and so she brought him to the care facility. Dallas definitely needed the breaks from my mother, too. But this last time, he refused to go back to her.

"Mommy crazy!" he exploded to the facility coordinator. He didn't have the words to describe all the abuse that had happened to him. But he could describe Mom's behavior as being abnormal.

The staff had been suspicious of the abuse for quite some time. On occasion, they found bruises on Dallas's body that indicated that he may have been abused, but it was difficult to prove. When questioned, Mom always had an answer, and Dallas had a difficult time explaining what had happened to him. After all, he would be further harmed for telling because he knew he would be back in my mom's care again soon. Mom was careful to never hit him in public or outside the house where neighbors would see it.

In the past, Dallas had refused to go back to my Mother, but he had been encouraged by staff members to go home, or he would go because Mom would hold his prized pens and Nintendo hostage, refusing to give them back to him unless he came home with her. But this time, it was different; he had had enough. And, this time, an astute staff member had actually listened to Dallas's desperation, and decided that if Dallas did not want to go back, they would not send him back. The world around him hadn't protected him. Dallas rescued himself.

As we discussed Dallas's case, Linda stated evidence of problems in Dallas's life. She seemed concerned for his future welfare. She envisioned a productive life for him if his life was managed with love and a careful eye. She thought he could thrive in a different environment; she had Dallas's best interests in mind.

"Shirlee, have you considered guardianship of Dallas?" she inquired.

"No, I haven't given it any thought," I confessed. "I live in California, and I think my chances would be slim in obtaining guardianship."

She encouraged me to file for guardianship right away, and said she would support me. So many questions surfaced quickly in my head. What would the responsibilities entail? Now that Dallas had rescued himself, how would the family respond to my move for guardianship? Like Diane, would I put myself in peril because my mother and my siblings would judge me and blame me. I knew I would be risking what fragments were left of my relationship with my family. I took a deep breath, leaning back in my chair. I laid the phone in my lap and pushed the speakerphone on.

"Linda, let me talk about this with my husband. But if I choose to go in this direction, I will need all the support you can muster."

"You have it!" she pledged.

Linda's encouragement shifted my life from darkness to light. My conversation with her gave me clarity, and I understood my higher purpose. It set me in motion, as if some energy propelled me forward. My goal and purpose was to obtain guardianship of Dallas. The path to rescuing Dallas had been opened.

The next day, I awoke to a brilliant sun shining through the windows. I was happy with my life. My son was independent and doing well. I loved my husband. We enjoyed our life together. We liked the freedom of our work and travel. Outside of our work, we had few responsibilities.

Over dinner that evening, Blake and I enjoyed our view of the Sierra Nevada from our dining room window. The sky was clear, and in the distance, I noticed that the snowline on the peaks had risen.

"Blake," I began, "I have something to ask you. I would like your support in obtaining legal guardianship of Dallas."

"Please go on," he said, his eyes on mine.

"Yesterday, my brother called and asked me if I knew where Dallas was living. His question caught me off guard and puzzled me. It was like he was testing me to see if I knew the answer. After I hung the phone up, I made several calls to Florida and discovered where Dallas was living." I paused. "Blake, life has not gone well for Dallas. The family has not protected him from Mom. She's been abusing him." I took a deep breath. "What would you think about petitioning for guardianship of Dallas?"

Blake thought about all I had said. "How will this impact our life?" he asked.

"I don't know," I said, "I only know that he's my brother, and we have failed to protect him. There may be legal costs, travel, and, of course, I don't know how the family will react."

"Shirlee, you have my full support," Blake placed his hand firmly on mine, securing my role and my purpose.

The morning after Blake and I had our conversation, I escaped to the stillness of nature, which had always brought clarity to my life. The hiking trails in my community were surrounded by undulating hills, Tuscan-style homes, and oak and cypress trees. For a brief moment, the landscape carried me far away to Italy. I parked my car at the foot of the trail, checked my water supply, and tightened the bow on my hiking boots.

I breathed in the clean morning air and enjoyed the scent of early spring. I continued down the shaded trail, walking more slowly than usual. The birds chirped melodious tunes while squirrels scampered around. I was happiest in nature. A gaggle of geese flew over me and landed on the lake, one by one, splashing sprays of water into the air. Two geese started fighting, and the larger goose repeatedly pecked the smaller goose hard with its beak. I picked up a rock and threw it near the dominant goose, scaring it away.

Over the years, our family had been faced with what seemed like impossible conflicts: violence in the home, near starvation, foster homes, abuse, and alienation from one another. There had always been tension in the family defined by sharp words, commands, criticism, yelling, and fighting; seldom was there rest from it all.

But now that we were adults, I could not understand the divisions. I could not understand why we could not come together for Dallas's good. What words could I speak to my sisters and brothers who weren't thinking clearly about a better life for Dallas? He needed to be where abuse and neglect would never happen again. Staying in the town where Mom lived would leave Dallas at risk.

My sister Diane's efforts to rescue Dallas didn't go unnoticed; she had paid the sacrificial price of being shunned, even considered crazy, by certain family members. My brother Roger was AWOL when it came to Dallas. His life was unaffected by the abuse Dallas suffered. Those who wanted to keep the family waters calm appeased Mom while sitting back and calculating their inheritance. My brothers Roland and Roger would never let their children spend time alone with my mother and rationed their own time with her, yet they let Dallas's life continue in her home with full knowledge of his abuse.

I turned to my own shortcomings. I had married years ago and moved to California, away from the family. For many years of my life, I was preoccupied with raising my son on my own, getting a college degree, and building a career. It left little time and money to regularly visit my family. They must have felt I had left them behind, abandoned them. Over the years, a new marriage and other life events made it difficult to bond closely with my siblings. The family dysfunction often got in the way. Our lifestyles didn't intersect, and we had less and less in common. But my supportive married life and my strong values from childhood, along with my religious foundation, could not excuse any more failures to rescue Dallas and to finally go beyond a seemingly impossible reach.

Crossing over the weeds to an uphill trail, I reached soft grass. I realized I had walked nine miles. I had to get back for a meeting, and I found a quick path to return home. My hand reached for a solid tree branch, and I used its strength to pull myself up to the higher trail, crossing over to a new path. I turned around to admire the tree's beauty and its strong support with only shallow roots to hold it up.

CHAPTER SIX

The Battle for Dallas

A couple of weeks later, Dallas left the ARC facility and was placed in a residential home for the disabled. He would reside in the same town with the mother who abused him, and the sister who had failed to protect him. But at least for now, Dallas was safe. I needed to keep it that way.

At the residential home, Dallas was assigned a team of people to care for him, including a man named Ken who, as Dallas's team captain, would oversee his daily activities and monitor his issues. I unclipped the team captain's phone number from my leather-bound schedule, and I called Ken. His voice resonated with genuine concern and interest in Dallas's well being. Ken would be in charge of housing and protecting Dallas. After further conversation, Ken revealed he had studied Dallas's file extensively and that he knew a lot about my family in town. He understood which family members created chaos in Dallas's life. He said that Dallas had left my mother's home and had refused to get back on the bus to see her.

Ken asked Dallas daily if he wanted to see my mother. He had Dallas sign a contract every day that confirmed his refusal to go back to her. We planned that I would phone Dallas at the residential home.

"Dallas, would you like to talk to your sister, Shirlee?" Ken asked him when I called.

"Yeah!" he responded enthusiastically.

"Dallas, would you like me to visit you in Florida?" I asked cautiously when he came on the phone.

"Yeah!"

It had been five years since my last trip to Florida when I witnessed my mother abuse Dallas. My mother and I had been estranged since then, which meant that I had also not had any contact with Dallas in five years. Would he remember me? Would he want to see me? His vocabulary only consisted of a handful of words.

For the first time in years, Dallas was accessible to me by telephone any time of day, unless he was at his day program. Dallas refused to talk to my mother and Jeanine, who also lived in town, perhaps feeling that Jeanine had not protected him. The care home respected his wishes. On a daily basis, they asked Dallas if he wanted to talk to either my mother or sister. They documented his emphatic response as "NO!"

The team captain understood Dallas's situation. I was willing to share the events from Dallas's childhood to help him get to the core of Dallas's issues. I explained about how he would take things, particularly pens. The team captain kept me updated on Dallas's progress, and I continued to fill in the gaps of Dallas's history.

When Dallas came to the residential care home, he wouldn't let anyone touch him or hug him. But he was showing some progress by accepting hugs and praises. Touching now meant something positive to him. He still didn't make eye contact, but he was slowly coming around to briefly looking people in the eye.

The team captain worked with Dallas to gain his trust. He knew just the words to use to get Dallas's attention and to connect with where he was. But Dallas still had a hard time building trust with women because of my mother. Dallas was acting out with some of his behavioral issues, such as leaving the property and stealing pens. He had a fear of the unknown, and he worried that he'd be sent back to my mother, back to the violence and abuse.

Furthermore, Dallas's health was poor. The care home was trying to balance his medications to help him cope with his anxiety and his depression, as well as the current changes in his life. They were trying to get him to eat healthier foods. For the first time, Dallas was able to decide what he wanted to eat and drink. He was able to go to the kitchen and open the refrigerator and find something to eat, which he had never been allowed to do at my mother's. He could sit in the living room with the rest of the residents. He finally had freedom in his life.

But he still wasn't with his family. Surely, that would be the first choice for the state authorities, to have Dallas with a functional family member who would look out for his best interests.

My purpose was to imagine the possibilities for Dallas's life. He endured the suffering in a malevolent home ruled by evil, but he never lost his desire for joy, never let his pain win its permanent victory over him. Others had failed, and it was now my moral responsibility, and my purpose, to do what was right for him.

Two weeks later, I called Jeanine in Florida to tell her that I was going to petition for guardianship of Dallas. In a final gesture of reconciliation, I wanted to explain my position.

"I just feel I would be better qualified to help Dallas. You and the other sisters had ample opportunities to save Dallas from the abuse, but whether through bad luck or good intention, Dallas has always wound up back with Mom. I love you, and please don't take this personally." The unuttered words in my mind spoke loudly: *Please believe in what I can do for Dallas.*

I knew for Jeanine that this meant competition for Dallas. Since she was the last baby of eight, Jeanine was constantly seeking approval from her siblings, and she often determined her self-worth based upon how much approval she received from other family members. She was the only sibling who lived in Spring Hill, but she had failed to protect Dallas, failed to report the abuse.

Now in her thirties, Jeanine had opened a care home for the elderly, and, legally, she had a responsibility to report any abuse. However, according to court records, no abuse of Dallas had ever been filed. Jeanine also benefitted emotionally and financially from Mom during this time; she would not be able to refuse her. Her own life had spun out of control, and she often left her own two babies with Mom to raise while she was absent from their lives. How could she manage Dallas's life when she couldn't even manage her own, or deal with Mom's issues? Unfortunately, she seemed unfit to be Dallas's guardian, but I suspected she would nevertheless take up the mantel.

That night, I was restless and couldn't fall asleep. I sat up on the bed with my arms wrapped tightly around my knees, wondering when my family would get this right. I felt devastated and overwhelmed in my position against the negative forces awaiting me. Heavy waves of emotions washed over me.

My siblings did not know about what I had seen before Dallas entered the world, but the image was forever etched in my memory. I was the oldest child. They were not yet born, or were not there, or they were too young to understand.

We had been so close as children, but I had lost my sisters Diane and Sissy when Diane petitioned for guardianship of Dallas so many years ago. Over the years, we had continued to be divided, and we never knew a normal family life. I couldn't call them to discuss Dallas's future or tell them how well his life would thrive under my management. All I wanted to do was make him safe, give him a stable life, and help him with his health issues. But I was now seen as a threat and an enemy to my family.

Suffering has many forms, and it touches each of us in a different way. For Dallas, his suffering began with the violence inflicted upon my mother before his birth. When he was born, the umbilical cord wrapped around his neck, and the lack of oxygen affected his brain for the rest of his life. For the next thirty years, he suffered abuse from my parents. My mother, who had power over Dallas, used that power in a way that prevented any good from coming to him. And we siblings, for whatever reason, had been unable to come together to protect him.

My eyes looked upward toward heaven. Visions of hope overtook me. I would move forward in my plans to rescue Dallas. I pushed the thought from my mind just for the moment and fell asleep.

Seven weeks later, Blake and I arrived at the Orlando airport to more agreeable and drier weather. Our meeting was set up with the residential care home, and after that we would take Dallas for a couple days to Disney World.

We found our rental car and drove for an hour and half. We arrived at the two-story office building in Spring Hill, parked next to the stairs, and climbed to the second floor. We were meeting Ken, the team captain, at his office for the first time.

We stepped into the sparse office waiting area, and Ken was there to greet us with his strong handshake. I observed his movement and his words. His face showed someone who had experienced life at its deepest; he was wise, and he had compassion that no Ph.D. program could teach.

Suddenly, there was a slight movement in the background, and Dallas came forward with his arms outstretched. The team captain had surprised us by arranging for Dallas to be waiting there when we came in for our meeting. Dallas and I embraced for a few minutes. Ken stood aside, observing our welcome and Dallas's reaction.

"Do you remember me?" I pulled back to look at my brother. "I'm your oldest sister."

"Yeah!" he said.

I studied his face. His eyes sparkled, but his skin was dull, and the lines from the abuse were prominent in his face. I reminded Dallas that a long time ago he had come to live with me in California, along with our brother Lynn.

I stared into his eyes. "I really missed seeing you!" I said.

Dallas's face lit up immediately, and we held each other again. It was difficult for his eyes to hold my gaze. I gently cupped my hands around his head, bringing his attention back to my eyes, our steady stare helping him connect to me. Dallas was excited to go to Disney World.

There was a brief meeting with Linda, the director who had encouraged me to file for guardianship. She informed me of Dallas's plight with my mother along with the issues from his acting out. In his new residential care home, Dallas was struggling to make adjustments. After our meeting, the director excused herself, but only after she revealed that she was enlisting support from another community services coordinator to back me as well. With the team captain's support, and the support of the director, I felt a surge of hope and an eagerness to take action to help Dallas.

Ken brought to my attention that Dallas needed some personal items, such as clothing, a desk, a computer, a desk chair, and a backpack to store his new pen collection. I asked Dallas if he needed anything else.

"Church," he said. He wanted to go to church. Church held a special meaning for him. Though Mom didn't attend church, someone had taken him at some point. We left the director's office and drove down the boulevard.

"Dallas, can you show me how to get to the church?"

As we drove down highway 19, Dallas pointed us in the direction of Cortez Avenue, and we made a right turn into a parking lot. The church was slightly hidden among the trees.

"Dallas, the church may not be open," I warned him, "but I will check in at the office."

We got out of the car, and Dallas followed closely behind me. A kind lady approached me as I came toward the administrative office. She looked at

Dallas, who was eagerly pulling on the handle of the church door. I turned back to the lady.

"My brother would like to enter the sanctuary and pray. I know it's locked, but would you mind?"

For a few seconds she studied Dallas with some familiarity.

"I will be happy to unlock the door," she said. She reached in her pocket for the sanctuary entry keys and glanced back at Dallas, giving him a slight nod.

As she opened the door, Dallas passed swiftly by her.

"We won't be too long," I said. "Thank you." We smiled at one another as Dallas charged down the sanctuary aisle toward the altar.

I walked behind Dallas. He quickly kneeled down at the altar, as if he'd been lost in the desert without water and had found an oasis to save his life. Dallas placed his elbows solidly on the wooden altar rail, clasping his hands together. His eyes looked up at the cross. He began to pray, elevating his voice to make sure God heard him.

"Power, Power! God, Power! Dallas, Power." Dallas begged, holding his eyes to the heavens. His voice rose, and his upper body heaved forward and backward. He closed his eyes tightly.

"Power, God! Dallas, Power!"

Dallas was praying for control over his life. He wanted to be free of all that was bad. He just wanted his life to be better, to be free of abuse. He had forgiven so much that had happened to him. He was a man of few words, but God understood him.

I kneeled down beside him, clasping my hands under my chin. I closed my eyes tightly, so I would never lose the memory of Dallas's birth. I remembered how he came to this earth at once a radiant being, but then how God's plan for him was changed in an evil and destructive moment. The unintended consequences of Dad's actions changed Dallas's life forever. It had changed God's purpose for him . . . or had it? We all learned so much from his sweetness, endurance, and forgiveness. The world had learned.

"Thank you, God!" Dallas opened his eyes, and in the next moment, he jumped to his feet. He stood strong and felt in control. He walked from the sanctuary through the church doors and outside. I followed behind him. His posture was erect and hopeful; he held his head a little higher.

Outside the church, the clouds retreated and the skies cleared. The sunlight seemed brighter. In that sacred moment, I deepened my commitment to helping Dallas. Life is a driven struggle, and I had set my goals on bringing Dallas to a better place. My family would disagree about the plan for his life. It would be an emotional as well as a financial sacrifice for my husband and me, and it would mean alienating certain family members in my life.

We arrived early to the gates of Disney World, figuring that the morning crowds would be lighter and less overwhelming for Dallas. The colorful and artful landscape beckoned us inside. We walked down "Main Street" past the gift shops and toward the rides. Dallas observed each ride, and if he didn't want to go on a certain ride, we just moved on.

"Two tens?" Dallas asked. He wanted money. It was his way of asking for money to buy pens or something meaningful to him. It was his way of having control over something in his life. Having his own money empowered him. He wanted to be able to own without it being taken from him. In the gift shop, he wanted to buy the shiniest gold pens he could find to add to his pen collection.

Later that evening, we left Disney World, and we drove to a local pizza parlor. I wanted to know what had happened at Mom's. By now, I was beginning to understand his words better. I could only communicate with him through simple questions because he only communicated with one or two words, and the rest of his words were often unclear. But I didn't want to lead him in his words.

"Dallas, do you want to see Mommy?"

I moved toward Dallas and listened closely to his voice. His face suddenly went devoid of shape, and he became distant, and he was unable to grasp the moment.

"Crazy! Mommy crazy!" He blurted out, pointing to his arm and head.

"Mommy hurt!" I knew his simple words could never describe the violence he had endured.

In further conversation, Dallas expressed his desire to live on his own. He wanted independence from his abuse, and he wanted control over his life, the ability to make his own choices. Even though he wasn't capable of living alone, he felt that he would be better off in his own world. He had already met with satanic forces in his home. What other dangers awaited him outside that he hadn't already experienced? He wanted a safe home where he would be protected.

I leaned my arm on the back of his chair and gently brushed my hand against his short hair cut, exposing a thin, five-inch white scar on the side of his head, as if something sharp had cut him straight across his head, or as if a straight bat had slammed hard on his skull. A chill went up my spine.

I felt more anguish over Dallas's abuse and toward my family and their inability to rescue him. Although my sisters made heroic efforts to save him, they failed to protect him, as had I. Suddenly, I had a flash of pure fear that as my siblings matured, Dallas would get lost in the state system. It became clearer than ever that I had to work toward Dallas's happiness and provide him a life free of chaos and filled with sound predictability. I would help him achieve some form of happiness within the limits of his ability. I knew what must be done.

That evening, we checked into our hotel. After settling in for the night, Dallas picked up the television remote and channel surfed to a program of his liking. He found the Animal Planet channel. He intently watched a segment on abused animals being rescued by Animal Control. Dallas eyes were glued to the rescue. I thought of how long it took for him to be rescued from his mother's abuse. Yet, he rescued himself.

"Dallas, let's go to bed. When we wake up, we can go back to Disney World, the happiest place on earth!"

Dallas smiled and flipped off the remote. He rushed to the hotel door and locked both the upper and lower door bolts and quickly slammed the metal door guard securely against the door. He checked the sliding glass balcony door. With the palm of his hand, he locked it hard.

"Bad people, out!" He said aloud.

He wanted to keep bad people out. He wanted to keep Mommy out.

When we returned to Spring Hill, the director of the facility referred us to a guardian litigation attorney in the area. I immediately called his office and spoke with the secretary. She said that he had recently undergone surgery and was not presently taking cases.

I called the director again to ask for another referral, and she suggested a second attorney. I called his office, and his secretary put me through to his line immediately. I introduced myself. The attorney readily announced his 50 percent fee without listening to my concerns and before knowing the reason for my call. I explained that I was looking for an attorney to represent me in obtaining guardianship of my mentally disabled brother. I explained there would be competing family interests.

"What is his name?" he asked.

"Dallas Hathaway."

"Hathaway ... Hathaway? That sounds familiar." He paused for a few seconds.

"I'm representing a woman named Jeanine, and her mother, for this case already."

"They're my sister and mother in Spring Hill," I told him.

"Yes, let me review this file." He paused. "Jeanine said she only had one sister in her family."

"Oh, that's interesting," I said. "How about her seven other siblings?"

"Can you fax to me the list of the other family members?" the attorney requested.

"Certainly," I said. "You will receive those in the next half hour."

I knew it. I had a sinking feeling that my mother and sister would try to ambush me. Despite their contentious relationship, they had come together against me, their new common enemy, who wanted Dallas to remain in Spring Hill. They had retained legal representation and set an early hearing. By not notifying the other family members, it guaranteed their win. Dallas might have to move back with my mother, where he would be abused again.

How was I going to find a skilled guardianship attorney to represent me in Florida? I picked up the telephone, and I immediately slammed it back down on the cradle. I hesitated for a moment, and again I picked up the phone, holding it tightly in my fist. I called a female attorney whom the director had also referred to me, hoping she would have compassion for Dallas's plight.

After a brief conversation, I explained I would need representation. She said she would find out about the case. An hour later, she called back. Indeed, my sister and my mother had set a hearing in two weeks to gain guardianship of Dallas. No other family members had been notified about the hearing. If I had not happened to call their attorney, the hearing would have happened swiftly, and no other family members would have even found out about it. My attorney rescheduled the court date for six weeks later.

I informed her of the reasons I was going for guardianship of Dallas. I detailed the information about Dallas's life and the ongoing family difficulties. This would be my opportunity to right Dallas's life, and she said she would represent me in court.

Walking along the sunny Florida beach, Blake and I gazed at a knot of pleasure boats bobbing like ducks on the ocean water. A family reunion gathered nearby under a shade tree, and rumbles of their laughter and full-throated roars shook the sand. A mother and her daughter hugged each other with loving embraces; it was a picture of what was missing in my life. It was a reminder of my family's dysfunction. It was the calm before the storm.

I scheduled a meeting with the attorney to go over the case. She warned us that judges in Florida do not often award guardianship to families living out of state. She said that in the past, judges had awarded out-of-state family members guardianship only for the guardians to abandon them. I would never do that, but I could understand the court's concern. My confidence was now waning over this bit of news. Surely the judge would discern between my goals for Dallas and my family's goals for Dallas.

At my first meeting with the attorney, she informed me that all my sisters had partnered to oppose me. Oppose me for what? I felt shocked and betrayed. I felt that their actions were just repeating my mother's dysfunction. Why couldn't my family get it right? Why couldn't we put aside our egos and control for the sake of Dallas? I didn't necessarily question their motives, but their methods.

Now it had become clear that my sisters had joined together to plot against me. Over the last few months, my sisters' telephone calls to me had seemed more saccharin than sentimental. Their conversations had been a ruse to find out if I was going for guardianship and to get a hint of my strategy. My sisters bonded together whenever they took on an enemy. I had to ask myself why they were so gleefully scheming against me? But I was still open to mending our family relationships, hopeful that we could work together. Dallas would benefit by our willingness to get along.

Despite my hope for an amicable resolution, it was no use. They had formed a plan to discredit me, challenge me, and defeat me. Their collective pursuit of me was repugnant to the core and indecent, and it didn't serve Dallas's best interests. Part of this was their savage resentment toward me, their fear that I might be successful and that I might do what they were unsuccessful or incapable of doing. They knew that with my accomplishments, I could best manage Dallas's life while their lives were often in chaos. They were unable to control their own lives, let alone Dallas's special needs.

Sometimes I rack my memory for anything that I might have done differently. Maybe I used the wrong tactics. But bolder measures or gentler messages seemed to raise their ire either way. It felt like tribal warfare against my own flesh and blood. I could find no way to heal the family. Their rejections and assault blocked any of my efforts to help them understand why they had failed. If they couldn't control Dallas's life, they didn't want me to either.

It was a no-win situation. Egos were involved, and family kingdoms were breached. My sisters still didn't understand why I was getting involved this time. They didn't understand that I had made efforts in the past to rescue Dallas. They didn't understand why it was that, though I lived far away, I now had the time to help Dallas. I felt suspended in space between the desire for a family without conflict or competition, and the fight to win Dallas's battles.

Their ruse wasn't about Dallas; it was about control. Since my sisters were unable to free Dallas from the abuse and chaos, they should have given up, or gotten out of the way, or supported me in my determination to win for him. I wasn't competing against their past noble efforts to rescue Dallas. I was just determined to succeed where they had failed. I came to the conclusion that to win for Dallas, I would have to lose most of my family members. This division was putting a toll on me and my other family members. It saddened me.

But I had to do what was right for Dallas's life even if it meant further disunity in the family. Rescuing Dallas at my peril was unhappy, yet necessary. Because I'd been estranged from my family for so long, I knew how to love them from afar, but I didn't know how to win them over. We were all fighting a familiar issue: our family's inability to come together to rescue Dallas. Within my family there were two worlds, and I was caught between the two. Mom was still in the background controlling the direction of things. The family was plotting to deny me a victory. They would deny Dallas a victory.

It didn't seem like I would have enough time to strategize and review everything I needed to prior to the hearing. I knew the judge wanted to know how Dallas's benefits would be transferred. Our attorney had no information for us about the benefits. I felt alone in the wilderness, not used to these government programs. My attorney didn't smooth out this wrinkle for me.

I researched California state and local agencies for transferring Dallas's benefits, and I was told that Dallas would be covered in benefits when his toe crossed the California line. But I needed the information documented for the trial. I couldn't get the agencies to put anything in writing—it was a Catch-22: the main agency said Dallas has to be living in California for the interview to take place. This wouldn't work because Mom wouldn't even let Dallas visit in California.

Meanwhile, our attorney requested family letters in support of my guardianship of Dallas. Why did we need to have their letters of support when we were on the opposing side? The idea seemed irrational. A couple of months later, my sisters submitted letters to my attorney stating that my husband and I would take Dallas to California and would never bring him back. But my attorney didn't tell me that before I came back to Florida. Had I known, I might have found California representation to help me with the process. But Blake and I were heading back to Florida for the hearing.

Outside, the weather was humid, street lighting lit up the night air, and thunder roared in the distance. We checked into the only hotel room available in Spring Hill, too tired from our day's travel to drive to another town.

I placed the room key in the lock, but the door was stuck because of the humidity. Blake leaned against the door and forced it with his shoulder to push it open. When I entered the room, it was dark and damp. I'd always disliked dark, damp, and moldy places, because they reminded me of the moist basement cellar in Albion with its pungent odor of mildew, and of the time I was shocked by the exposed light switch. At that moment, I longed for the dry and sunny weather in California.

The next morning, I felt a chill from the wall air conditioner. I rolled over next to Blake. The heat from his warm body was comforting. Still exhausted from planning for the guardianship case, I fell asleep again for a few more minutes. Then I was startled awake, my mind restlessly thinking about the fight ahead against three sisters and my mother.

After my shower, I reached for my light blue suit. I thought it would be a calm and trusting color to wear at the hearing. I needed all the help I could get. I rifled through my suitcase for my white pearl necklace. I couldn't find it. The cold fluorescent lighting was inadequate for a hotel room, and it created dark shadows in the suitcase and made it difficult to find certain items. I would feel naked without my necklace. Did I leave it in California? My matching high heels were also missing. Did I forget them in the rush to leave home? I found a pair of casual dark flats. I quickly slipped them on my feet. Standing there, I felt as though I was going into the boxing ring too short for the fight and without my gloves.

Feeling my mother's vanity surface within me, I glanced in the mirror. My hair looked frizzy from the humidity. It looked unkempt. I wanted my hair to be straight and shiny, like it was in California. I felt unclean all over. I took another shower.

My nerves frayed, and my body shook with anxiety at the thought of facing my family issues. I had no clue why certain family members wanted to fight against me. They had hardened their hearts toward me. Their inner voices propelled their thoughts throughout their day, and these were the same voices that justified and explained their lives to themselves.

My family had lost all sensitivity and had given themselves over to sensationalism about what would happen to Dallas if he moved to California. They ignored their understanding of Dallas's abusive and neglectful situation where he was, and they were unable to comprehend the risks to Dallas's future if he stayed in the town where my mother lived. They separated from the truth because of their willful ignorance about Dallas's plight. The difficulty was that we couldn't come together as a family. Mom had implanted poison in my sisters' thoughts and words.

One of the greatest causes of my family's disunity was our vivid imaginations: We imagined someone gossiped about us, imagined the gossip was true, imagined someone's words were meant to harm us when they were meant to help us, imagined issues were greater than they were. We would all be surprised to know that most of the time, our other family members rarely thought about us in our absence.

The last thing I wanted to do was divide my family further apart. My goal was to get Dallas into a stable and permanent situation where his environment was nurturing and would make up for the horrific years he lived. I wanted to bring the family together in a functional and managed way around Dallas life. Wasn't the goal here to protect Dallas from further abuse? I finally had the time to help Dallas. But I never thought I would need to wear boxing gloves in court to punch out the words that were untrue about my husband and me.

The sky took on the look of an impending storm. Suddenly, there was a tremendous downpour. Blake reduced his speed and drove slowly to the courthouse in Brooksville. The tires rhythmically turned over the black wet pavement. Blake turned on the windshield wipers, and the squeaks against the glass heightened my anxiety. My nerves were shattering at the onslaught I was about to endure.

"Please speed the car up so we get there on time," I asked.

Blake tried to console me; he knew me well. He noticed my constant shifting in the seat. He leaned over and placed his warm hand on my knee.

"Honey, we have plenty of time to get there."

I could always count on his voice and demeanor to calm me down. My drumming nerves were about everything in the past: The lies, gossip, manipulation, and neglect were all culminating in one stressful reminder of my childhood. All my memories of my dysfunctional childhood created raw feelings and panicked nerves.

By now the rain had subsided. We arrived to the main street square, where the modern courthouse filled every square inch to the edge of the sidewalk. I looked for the green lawn to soften the edges of the razor-sharp corners of the building. Blake pulled the rental car in close to the front door. I observed cars swirling in and out of the parking lot, and I looked for signs of my sisters and mother. It had been many years since I had seen them. I wasn't sure I would recognize them.

I unzipped my purse and removed my powder puff from the case. I reached over to position the mirror toward my face, and my skin was wet with perspiration from the humidity. The hair I worked so hard to straighten with the dryer was beginning to curl in all directions. It reminded me of the hot nights in Indiana, when my parents would fight in the cruel humid heat. It felt like bugs were crawling over my skin. I quickly threw the air conditioner on high and patted the shine on my face to a dull, dry surface. Blake walked around the car and opened my door. I could always count on him to be the consummate gentlemen in any situation. I could count on him, period.

I approached the front doors of the Brooksville courthouse. They were tall and imposing. I pressed my shoulders against the heavy glass doors, and I pushed them hard and entered the main lobby. My shoes pounded on the stone floor, echoing loudly. My heel occasionally slipped at an unexpected rise in the floor, but I held steady until I reached the security line.

I was met by the security guard and was directed to the security clearance area. In the distance, I observed a coiffed white-haired lady with pale skin sitting unnaturally still. It was my mother. Seated next to her was a likeness of my sister, Jeanine, but her full face was unrecognizable. Both women were waiting for this moment to challenge me, and both hoped for and had prepared for the fight, but at the same time dreaded it.

As I cleared through security, my mother raised her head as if to discern something from a great distance. She was looking at me. Her eyes were transfixed, intent in concentration, and she squinted. Then she noticed me, and she jolted upright.

"Why can't you be thin like Shirlee?" Mom's voice chastised my sister with an edge of sharpness. Their arguments about my sister's weight transmitted across the lobby. Obviously my sister had heard this mantra too many times before. She didn't deserve to be compared to me, and I didn't deserve to be hated for my body type. They sat restlessly in their seat until the bailiff called us all into the courtroom.

For a brief moment, I longed for the family I wished I had. I wanted a mother who was stable and kind, someone to talk to about motherly things in life. I wanted a sister I could hang out with and have some bond of commonality with, someone I could share conversation about our children with. Someone I could laugh about our differences with.

I could not understand my own feelings. At times I questioned my own rationality in rescuing Dallas. This hearing wasn't about hurting my family or creating disunity, but my actions furthered the disunity in our family. It was the price I had to pay. This was not a battle I chose to fight, but I had to fight it. Nevertheless, throughout the process, I would have no ill-feelings toward my family.

My trembling jolted me back to realty. Simultaneously, my body felt the weight and emptiness of my decision. Dallas must be rescued at any cost to me. I would be shunned and excoriated by certain family members. The system had failed Dallas in the past. He had always wound up in Mom's hands. I needed to assure Dallas wouldn't be abused in the future and that he'd be free from the instability and chaos in his life.

The memories of the violence that happened to Dallas remained in my mind, as well as the encouragement and full support of certain authorities here in Spring Hill to go on. It reminded me that this challenge was about saving Dallas from further abuse and uncertainty in the future. Hopefully, from these proceedings the court would recognize the truth about Dallas's situation and rule in my favor. My will and determination would have to prevail. Yes, I could do this, but it would take time.

Inside the courtroom, a walnut table was centered in the small room, and the judge's desk was attached at one end of the table. My attorney entered and sat at her preferred seat to the left of the judge. She thought that side of her profile made a better impression on him. I sat next to her, and Blake took the chair next to me. Dallas's attorney sat next to the judge. A court reporter settled in at her desk in preparation of the start of the hearing.

A few minutes later, voices grew louder outside the courtroom door. Then Jeanine and mom's attorney entered the room. Mom followed and walked toward her seat, glancing at me with an air of belligerent defensiveness, as if declaring her resentment toward me.

The judge entered the chamber, sat down at the head of the conference table, and he motioned for the witnesses to be seated. Mom straightened her back, tilted her chin up, and quickly settled in her chair, arranging and rearranging her purse, pressing away the wrinkles of her pants. Mom had not lost her delicate features, but her face would transform to malicious hatred when she glanced in my direction. I looked back at her for a deliberate moment, and I wished she could have been a different mother. Our family could have been different. Once again, I let the thought of what I'd wanted my family to be like, fall into the abyss. It was too painful to imagine what could have been.

It had been years since my sister and I had seen one another. She was seated across the hard wooden table from me. Our eyes locked, and for one moment, our natural sisterly love rose to the surface. In spite of the issues, we simultaneously reached our arms out over the table, embracing one another. I held tightly on to her. It was strange: we had never spoken an unkind word to each other. Only our ears had been filled with my mother's ugly accusations and gossip about one another. The war had been in our minds.

Close up, I noticed for the first time how utterly Jeanine had changed. She was now grown up, with her life story etched in her face. Her eyes were punctuated with a bit of deviousness from surviving my mother's wrath. Wrinkles of sadness deepened in her eyes from years of battles with Mom and from not reconciling with her father even at his death. Her lifestyle choices had also left her face emotionally scarred. Jeanine had always been even tempered, living amazingly through the anger and violence in the household. As a child, she had no choice.

She was my baby sister, the one I strolled on Chicago streets, showing her glimpses of another world away from the fighting in my parent's house. I remembered those precious moments when I wrapped her tiny body in the soft cuddly blanket and held her close to my breast. My mind then flashed back to when she was in her mid-teens and she came to stay with me in California. Mom had begged me to help turn her life around. She had been hanging out with the wrong crowds in Florida. But though you had to look hard for it in my luxury community, she had found the wrong high school crowd to hang out with there as well.

I desperately wanted to help her, but it was useless. Too much time and distance had separated our values and lives. Now our relationship seemed unfamiliar. Our lives had been dissected and strewn in completely different directions. The feeling of glue bonding our sisterly ties evaporated into thin air. I wearily tucked both feet under my chair, knowing that flesh and blood were challenging one another. It seemed unnatural, maybe even against God's law, to go against kin.

My mother sat in the corner, smug in her outfit, sitting high in her chair with her shoulders back, determined to use her vanity to persuade the judge, and casting contemptuous glances across the courtroom table in my direction. Her facial muscles tensed and her eyes darted with a chronic air of suspicion. Her helmet of white hair was sprayed heavily against her pale face, and she telegraphed her disapproval with raised eyebrows. Her mouth was tight lipped, as if ready to explode words all over the wall. From mom's perspective, this would be an all-out family war. She was the one who could be counted on to drum up the negative energy and to keep it going all the time. She thrived on it.

Jeanine was one of her warriors. She wouldn't let anyone take Dallas away from her. She wouldn't let me take Dallas away from her. In the past two hearings, Mom had won both guardianship battles, and she was sure that she would win this one, too. Each of us felt we had Dallas's best interest in mind. We were each there to defend our case to the Judge. We each felt more qualified than the other to manage Dallas's life. But if Jeanine won this case, it meant that Dallas would be right back with Mom, unprotected.

My husband sat to my side leaning forward to get a view of the judge. I was always proud to have Blake next to me. He was everything good in my life. The first time she met him, my mother had been taken with his good looks and humility, but also by how he possessed a commanding presence.

The judge entered the chamber and called the hearing to order. The attorneys discussed the matter before the judge, and the legal protocols were reviewed. The director kept her commitment to support me. The community center and team captain were on board to support me, too. Their letters had been set on the judge's desk before the hearing began.

Dallas was represented by the state-appointed guardian ad litem. He had made the decision to not have Dallas present in the courtroom. Dallas's attorney opened his file folder and leaned forward.

My attorney rose from her chair. The judge acknowledged her and asked, "What capacity are you appearing in?"

"I'm appearing on behalf of the petitioner who has filed to become guardian," she said.

"And you are here on behalf of the ward?" the judge inquired of Dallas's appointed attorney. "Your Honor, the court reports have been filed and all copies indicate that Dallas suffers from mental retardation. He's unable to care for himself," the guardian ad litem said.

"It would appear uniform throughout those reports that Dallas is in need of a guardian," the judge looked around the table. "Does everybody agree with that?"

215

"That's correct." All three attorneys spoke in unison for the court record.

"So there's no objection to the Order of Incapacity?" the judge continued.

"None," the attorneys agreed again simultaneously.

Jeanine was sworn in, raising her hand before the judge. Her attorney established her background in owning a residential care home for the elderly in her home. Jeanine pressed her shoulders back and appeared confident that owning her own business qualified her to have guardianship of Dallas.

Jeanine's attorney continued to discuss Jeanine's involvement in Dallas's life. Then my sister spoke. "Uh . . .at first my mother was trying to care for Dallas, but then she couldn't," Jeanine said. "So they asked me. I live here in Spring Hill. Every time Dallas has to go to the hospital, I go. If he ran away from my mother's when he was living there, I went out and found him. Uh . . . when the police were involved, I picked him up. When he was raped by a neighbor, I took him to the hospital. So it's always been my phone call. This last time he was removed from my mother..." She stopped, realizing that she had just admitted that she was aware of Dallas's plight, but had not reported his abuse to the authorities.

My surroundings became fuzzy. The room felt as if the air had been sucked out. I was stunned by Jeanine's testimony that Dallas had been raped. I had never heard this before. No evidence was presented as to who did this heinous act to my mentally disabled brother. No evidence was presented to hold anyone accountable for this act. With this questionable background Jeanine was presenting to the judge, wasn't it clear that she had not been able to protect Dallas all these years? She wasn't able to protect him from my mother and from the outside world.

My attorney interrupted, "Jeanine, are you aware that when Dallas entered the group home that he, as part of his contract—this is based upon information from his residential team leader—that he specifically requested no contact with you or your mother? No telephone calls, no personal visits?"

Her voice shaking from the negative exposure, Jeanine responded, "The first phone call that I made to the group home, they had not . . . they said that he wanted no contact with my mother. Then they came back later and they told me that he wanted no contact with nobody." She drew in a deep breath.

My attorney further inquired, "Okay. Are you aware there was a guardianship hearing at one time in Illinois and a guardian ad litem was appointed for that hearing?" She was referring to Diane's petition for guardianship.

"Yes."

"Who later submitted a report," my attorney added.

"Yes," Jeanine answered.

"Did she in—" my attorney began.

"—and her and I have been working together," Jeanine interrupted

"And she interviewed you?" my attorney continued, ignoring Jeanine's interjection.

"Yes," Jeanine answered, hopeful this would establish her long involvement in Dallas's case.

"Okay. And do you remember telling her that based on information, there were some allegations made by your mother that Dallas had been sexually abused on another occasion while he was in your care?"

Jeanine lowered her eyes, and didn't respond.

"Okay. And during these proceedings where the guardian ad litem was appointed, when she interviewed you, you said you did not ever wish to file for guardianship. You said this specifically when she confronted you about ever becoming guardian. You said you were afraid of things your mother might do if you filed for guardianship."

Jeanine looked up at my attorney, her face burning with redness.

"Okay. And are you aware that in the exam committee report that was filed, your application at that time was the only application that was pending, and the exam committee, made of three members, recommended an independent guardian over you, even though yours was the only application that was pending at that time?"

Jeanine didn't respond.

"So at one point you didn't want to do this at all because you had concerns about what might . . . what your mother might do if you filed for guardianship." My attorney paused. "I have no further questions."

I was asked a few questions regarding my preparations for Dallas's move to California. I was not fully prepared to answer the judge's questions on the transfer of benefits, though I had researched the issue, nor did my attorney have the answers. I didn't see why this couldn't be worked out after I was awarded guardianship of Dallas.

217

Dallas's attorney affirmed that Dallas wished to live with me in California.

From the corner of my eye, I could see my mother beginning to stick out her chin—the warrior stance she carried during battle.

"Your Honor," she hissed in the judge's direction, her impatient tone instantly familiar.

There was contempt in her manner, and the judge sternly glanced at her and shook his head. It seemed there had been an agreement with her attorney that if Mom spoke a word, she was to leave. Mom sprang to her feet with her hands clenched, flushed and breathing hard, in insolent defiance of authority. She stamped toward the court door. Her determined tread shook the floor as she hastily left the courtroom. This was the drama of our personal lives playing out in the courtroom, just as mom would have it.

The hearing was coming to a conclusion. The judge adjusted his body back against the chair and upward, readying to make his decision. I braced myself, and I felt my nerves being pulled tight like a noose around my neck. He cleared his throat and announced, "Dallas will go to state care."

My eyes briefly glanced at the courtroom walls as my mind moved through the span of dead silence. My heart was in my throat. From within, I screamed silently about the chaos, my irrational mother, and the helplessness. There was no approval, nor movement in the room. A dull sinking feeling represented the conclusion I didn't want to hear in words. I drew in my breath and bowed my head, putting both hands over my mouth.

I slumped in my wooden chair, feeling the hardness of the shiny wood, thinking of the price Dallas would pay. This incomplete justice would leave Dallas open in the future to a perilous situation. Events would change; the people involved in his life would change. The abuse would just come by another name. Dallas would eventually not be protected in Florida. There were too many collaborators working together against Dallas's best interests, no matter how well intentioned they were. The hearing should have been a triumph for me.

As the hearing ended, the enormity of the judge's decision overwhelmed me. Dallas had lost his rights and would be assigned a state-appointed guardian to oversee his concerns. If only the judge could have seen Dallas's horrific life, a video replay of the abuse he had suffered during his lifetime. *Please judge, tear open my head and see what I saw.* Then the judge would have known to locate him out of this town and away from the possibility of my mother reuniting with him against his wishes.

This wasn't the outcome I had planned. It was as if some hope for Dallas had slipped out of my grasp. At least he wouldn't be with my mom --- that part was a small win. But he also wouldn't be with a functional family member who would love and protect him. Dallas's future was uncertain, and now it was out of our hands. My heart swelled up with misery until it felt too large for my bosom. A feeling of impending disaster overcame me. We have lost him to the system. Though it was filled with well-intended people, they might be inconsistent in their delivery and understanding of Dallas's needs and history, making him vulnerable. I would have to untangle this decision, but it would take time.

We left the courtroom, and Jeanine announced loudly to my mother that Dallas had gone to the state. Mom stared incredulously at the judge through the open chamber door. She had always prevailed over the legal system, keeping Dallas under her control. She had hoped Jeanine would win the case so Dallas could move back and forth between her world and Jeanine's world, leaving him vulnerable to abuse. I couldn't grapple with their senseless behavior.

I sat frozen still, conscious of nothing but pain. I looked for a touch of meaning in our broken family, unhealed for many years, unable to connect and communicate even for Dallas's sake. Glancing at a jagged crack in the courtroom wall, I saw the shape of a shipwreck. I wondered how this family would heal from the deep chasm between us that was growing deeper as if an earthquake was splitting our earth apart. We might never recover from this divide.

In the midst of the courtroom wreckage, I climbed on top of the heap to get a clearer view of our future. I felt like my hope for Dallas had slipped out of my grasp. But this was only our first try at rescuing Dallas. My sister Diane had made a noble effort before and had failed. From Jeanine's perspective, she thought she was doing the right thing. With the limited information the judge had before him, he had made what he thought was the best decision for Dallas, considering the lack of clarity about transferring Dallas's benefits to California.

The judge was trying to be thorough and fair. My being out of state made me unfavorable in the court's eyes. We knew coming to Florida that our address would work against us. Putting Dallas in a neutral situation with the state would diffuse things for a while.

My mother's control over Dallas had been taken away, but what would Dallas's future look like in state care? Was he headed for a slippery slope to an unknown future? He would be assigned to an institution --- or shifted from institution to institution --- where he would be surrounded by strangers who did not have a full comprehension of his history or understand why he acted the way he did.

My attorney said that we had an opportunity to meet a potential guardian and present him or her to the judge for approval. She said she had chosen a guardian for me to meet, but that I could either go with her choice or let the court make the choice. Without many options, I gave my approval for her to present her choice of a guardian. This was someone I had not met. She would present him or her to the judge for approval. My attorney set up a meeting at her office for us to meet the guardian.

Blake and I exited the courtroom, and we walked toward Jeanine.

"Can we take you out to lunch?" Blake asked in a cheery voice.

"No!" Jeanine said, and she turned on her heel away from us.

As we left the lobby, a restless energy filled my whole body. I moved anxiously from the courthouse back to our rental car. Outside, the rain had grown in intensity. Blake closed the car door and walked to the driver's side. I sat blankly, looking through the windshield, as thin streaks of rain streamed down the window. He was soaked from the rain, but Blake gently put his arms around my shoulders, soothing me. He was my oxygen during times like these. This retreat allowed me to collect my thoughts. Gradually, the sickening feeling began to dissipate.

"Would you like to be my date for dinner?" Blake asked sweetly, distracting me from my thoughts.

"No, but thank you. Let's go back to the hotel. I'm not hungry just now."

We entered our hotel room, and I threw my files on the desk, spilling the papers in a large heap. I stooped to pick them up, but Blake held my shoulders. "Honey, I'll pick them up," he said, bending down to gather the papers.

I removed my clothes, letting them fall to the floor, and I opened the shower door. I stepped into the glass enclosure and stared at the confined box, turning the handle to hot and back to cold, sterilizing my body and everything toxic in my life. I wrapped a towel around me and lay on the bed, placing a cover over my eyes, blocking out the light.

The dark shade calmed me. I was sorry that my sisters had focused on me as the threat rather than on my mother, the abuser, the cause of the chaos and dysfunction in our family. I heard my sister's words and saw their actions, but I could not allow myself to hate them. Nevertheless, I was confused by their actions. I felt no anger toward anyone, or about the gossip that I endured. I could think of nothing to say to alleviate their pain. My sentiments toward my family were filled with love in spite of our differences.

My absence from my family for years didn't mean I didn't care or know what was going on with everyone. Over the years, I took intermittent trips to visit my family members, but I wasn't part of the daily bonding or the ebb and flow of chaos and conflict between my mom and sisters. They were often at odds with one another, not communicating for long periods of time. As for Dallas, the information from my family members regarding his abuse fit with what I remembered from the past. It wasn't hard to connect the dots.

At that moment, I felt an immoveable certainty within that echoed a pattern of repeating pain in our childhood through the years that followed. My family swung between loving each other and then dividing each other, never able to look to the greater good.

God divined our family as a whole body to be supported and held together by its ligaments and sinews, and to grow together as He wanted us to grow. Malevolence crept into our world and broke us apart, pitting us against one another, upsetting God's plan for us to be together in this world. I had looked forward to the future when, as a family, we could face our memories differently.

Now I was exiled by the family, never to return to the fold, never to be united with them again, never to share childhood memories, and never to laugh together. My sisters disliked me, not because I did things badly but because I did them well—because I made choices in my life to better my future. We were cast from the same mold, but our viewpoints and solutions were different. My mother had taught certain family members to live unhappily, to enjoy the nobility of suffering over Dallas's issues.

Any clear-thinking person or family could not grasp the complexity of our family, the abuse toward Dallas, or the total dysfunction of one human, our mother, affecting every family member in a compelling and destructive way. She used the power divined to her by God to divide her family instead of teaching love and giving support. In my stable and loving life and with my values, I could not allow myself to fail to rescue Dallas.

How would we ever establish peace and harmony among us? How would we live as a family under God? I concluded that, my family be damned, Dallas must prevail.

The next morning, I called my sister Jeanine to make a peace offering. "Would you like to go to the beach and meet for lunch?" I asked. "I'll pick up a picnic. We could talk things out."

221

"That could be a possibility. Let me call you back," she said.

I lay my head on the pillow, and a lazy somnolence descended upon me. As the hours passed by, I fell into a deep sleep. By early evening, the sky had darkened. I checked my cell phone for a call from my sister, but she hadn't called. Perhaps I had slept through the ring. I dialed voicemail, but no calls had come through.

Blake stood before the mirror combing his hair, slender in his Tommy Bahama pants.

"Can I take you to dinner?" Blake looked at me with a smile that one contemplates with longing and desire, his eyes twinkling, putting a positive twist to the evening. Blake was what was right about the world. I wished I could sprinkle his magical dust around the world, making it a more harmonious and joyful place.

"I'd loved to, if you're my date!" It took me a moment to breathe, realizing how much he meant to me and how solid his support had been throughout the whole process of rescuing Dallas.

My attorney reaffirmed her recommendation of the guardian. In fact, she had worked with this guardian on other cases before. They had a social connection and closeness outside the office. I thought this would be beneficial for Dallas, since my attorney knew the extent of Dallas's issues, and I could be a conduit for further information. The guardian could be helpful in our bid for guardianship of my brother in the next few months.

Seated in my attorney's conference room was a fat, pallid woman, who appeared indifferent when she was introduced to my husband and me. She spoke with a soft voice. As we discussed Dallas's issues, she appeared to be too inexperienced to be handling such a complicated case. It would take someone more astute to understand the family dynamics and to respect Dallas's wishes to keep my mother away. I was eager to share Dallas's life and my hopes to end the abuse he had endured. I poured my feelings out to her so as to impress upon her the importance of protecting him. I expressed how important it was to never go against Dallas's refusal to see my mother, and to keep Dallas insulated from the family chaos.

I handed the state-appointed guardian a short list of Dallas's medical issues that needed to be followed up on. His teeth needed work. He needed a speech therapist to help him articulate his needs and feelings. I offered to pay for speech lessons and behavior modification therapy, but she would have to schedule that here in Florida. She just sat there listening without much reaction. She had no questions.

"We would like to have Dallas out for a vacation in California. He wants to visit us," I said.

"I will consider it," the guardian replied in a noncommittal voice. Her tone bothered me. She didn't sound like someone who was all too interested in what Dallas wanted.

Since my attorney had introduced the guardian to this case, I didn't understand her attitude. Not feeling the need to go into detail about my siblings, I informed her that our family was complex in its issues and interests when it came to Dallas, but that I hoped Dallas's interests would be placed above the politics of our family. Our meeting ended, and we said we would be back in a few weeks.

Something didn't feel right about the meeting with the guardian. She appeared distant and oblivious to my words. Perhaps it was my imagination.

From the beginning, Dallas's residential care home had set up contractual agreements with Dallas on a daily basis that documented his desire not see my mother. The staff would check in with him every day and would ask Dallas again, if he wanted to see Mommy. He would always respond with a resounding, "No." His responses were documented for the court records.

At the residential care home, Dallas had found it difficult to make adjustments. He would demonstrate undesirable behaviors such as acting out, leaving the property, and stealing things when he went to stores. He was upset that my mother refused to bring him his bible, his Nintendo, and his large collection of pens at the care home. These things defined his interest, his life.

Over time, the team captain built a trust with Dallas. He genuinely had Dallas's best interest at heart. Ken took the time to understand the family dynamics and to determine what was best for Dallas. He was a big influence in Dallas's new life away from my mother. And Dallas trusted him. Ken set up appointments with Dallas's psychiatrist to try to balance his medications. Dallas's acting out, myriad medications, and trust issues, presented an uphill battle. Dallas needed continuity and predictability with someone who could guide him with a tender hand into the future. Ken fit the bill.

My immediate concerns for Dallas's life did not have to do with the care Ken provided, but with what would happen in Dallas's future if he changed jobs, or the staff changed?

I called Dallas often. He always asked me the same question: "Shirlee, when you coming?"

"Soon, Dallas," I promised him. "Soon."

Six weeks later, we arrived back in Florida to visit Dallas and to take care of some legal issues. Outside the hotel window, an impending storm loomed in the distance. Suddenly, there was a downpour from the sky. The trees washed across the large window and bent low to the ground, dripping rain like a curtain of green liquid onto the grass. I watched as thin branches of tree limbs twisted in the strong winds and waved helplessly back and forth.

We had arranged to have Dallas's guardian meet us for breakfast at a restaurant of her choice. We wanted to discuss plans for Dallas's future. She recommended a restaurant near her home. We arrived early, and we seated ourselves next to the window. Thirty minutes later, the guardian arrived in the parking lot. I greeted her at the front entry with a hug, and I led her back to our table.

After deciding on our orders, an emaciated waitress arrived at our table with bloodshot eyes, looking high on drugs. She tried to balance the pen in her shaky hand. She took our order and then left for the kitchen.

After pleasantries were exchanged with the guardian, Blake and I reviewed what kind of people we were and what our interests in Dallas were, and we went over our resume of life accomplishments. Soon, the waitress came back and asked for our order again. We wondered if the manager had noticed the waitress's bizarre behavior, or if the restaurant was too short handed and had to keep her working anyway. The waitress came back again five different times to ask us what we wanted. This day was off to a precarious start.

During our conversation with the guardian, we asked how Dallas was doing. She gave us a brief update. He was making progress, but he still needed to correct his behavioral issues. Even though Dallas was adamant about never seeing my mother, the guardian said she was considering reconciliation with my mother. This was exactly what I had feared. The guardian didn't understand the breadth of the Dallas's abuse, nor his desire to not see my mother. She just wasn't getting it.

"But Dallas is adamant about not seeing her!" I exclaimed.

Another waitress interrupted our conversation to clarify the last part of our order. And, at last, she was followed by the restaurant manager who was carrying our breakfast. He poured a round of hot coffee.

"Dallas has made it clear that he does not want to see my mother," I repeated.

She looked down and did not respond for the second time. The guardian's body language seemed guarded, and she acted distant and cool toward us. Had a family member said negative things to her about my husband and me?

I handed the guardian another copy of Dallas's health concerns that needed to be followed up on, since I had not heard back from her after our first meeting at my attorney's office. She must not have reviewed the list of concerns. I restated our commitment to help Dallas pay for any services not covered by the state.

The guardian took the list without looking at it or saying anything.

"I believe Dallas should be evaluated and that he should receive speech therapy to learn to communicate, along with behavioral therapy to learn to cope with his past and present issues," I insisted. "Blake and I would personally like to pay for a qualified speech therapist to teach him to communicate with his words, and for a behavioral modification therapist to reframe his behaviors. But more urgently, could you look into the large five-inch mass on his stomach?" I restated the health issues that needed immediate attention, just in case she misplaced my list again.

Again, the guardian was not responsive.

"Please let me know what resources are available, and together we can help Dallas," I begged.

I asked that she call me in a few weeks with an update.

After arriving late to our meeting, the guardian seemed to be in a hurry to race out of the restaurant. We paid the bill, and we said we would stay in touch with her.

Blake looked down at the table, and then our eyes met.

"I believe certain family members have ganged up on you and that the guardian has bought into their lies," Blake said.

"Yes. I believe you are right," I said, draining my coffee cup.

There was no explanation for this. We had only met the guardian once at my attorney's office. Maybe I was too passionate too soon in sharing Dallas's history and concerns. Maybe she took my concerns the wrong way and felt that I was infringing on her territory. But wouldn't a guardian want this information about Dallas's background? Blake was puzzled as well.

We had told her of our interest in having Dallas visit California—that it was Dallas's wish to spend a lot of time with us. She wouldn't commit to a visit with us. Why would she react in such a strange way? Something had influenced her reaction to us.

I waited for a call from the guardian about Dallas's health issues. Months went by, but I received no phone call on the progress of his medical issues.

Disney World was celebrating its thirty-fourth anniversary. We were going to visit Dallas for the week, and we would set aside any legal concerns. Dallas always looked forward to our visit to the Magic Kingdom. On this trip, we would focus only on fun, not on court hearings, attorneys, guardians, or concerns about the future.

The Disney hotel was positioned along the river that ran to Disney Town. Dallas loved riding in boats, so we took Disney's man-made river to different destination points. We made an appointment at one of the Disney hotel spas to give Dallas a full-body massage.

Blake reserved tickets for Cirque du Soleil in Disney town. The high-performing artists, with their colorful costumes and acrobatics, dazzled Dallas. He laughed at the clowns and their silly antics. Temporarily, he was removed from his complex life, and he was enjoying every minute.

Blake had a special relationship with Dallas. He had the ability to animate humor and scenarios so Dallas could understand him. After a week of fun, Blake and I returned to California.

We called Dallas twice weekly, once on weekends, and once in the middle of the week. It was routine and predictable, and it was the first time in years that I had consistent contact with my brother. With his limited vocabulary, our conversations were brief, but we had a strong connection. He would always ask when we were coming back.

On our next trip to visit Dallas a few weeks later, we planned to take him boating. While driving in the car, I asked Dallas if he wanted to see my mother. It had been seven months since he had refused to go back to her home.

"Dallas, do you want to see Mommy?"

He gave a resounding, "No!"

"Do you want to see Jeanine?" Again, a resounding, "No!"

He now had seen a hint of life without the chaos, and he was beginning to put his chaotic past behind him.

"Dallas, would you like to go to the beach?"

"Yeah!"

Up ahead, while driving on a narrow country road, Dallas asked Blake to slow down. Dallas had spotted a turtle crossing the road. "Stop, turtle!" he cried.

Blake checked his rearview mirror and brought the car to a sudden stop.

Dallas opened the back passenger door and walked in front of the car toward the turtle. In the distance, a car was traveling from the opposite side of the road. Dallas bent down, and with both hands, he gently picked up the turtle and held it firmly at his side. He looked again in both directions. The car was closing in. Dallas walked the turtle to the opposite side of the road and carefully placed it in the trench. He returned to the car, and he closed the car door hard.

"No hurt," Dallas said.

The next day, we rented a small powerboat to take Dallas down the river. I brought a picnic since we didn't know how far down the river we wanted to go. We packed our picnic basket and swimming gear in the boat, and we headed down the lazy winding river.

Trees dripping with moss lined both sides of the river, shading the way. Manatees swam gently along the river in small groups. Manatees were a protected species that could be admired from a distance in the clear waters of the river. Our boat, a safe distance away, flowed alongside the manatees as their round flesh moved so gingerly down the river.

Up ahead was a swimming area with a sandy beach. It was just the right spot to break for lunch. We jumped out of the boat, and we began splashing one another. We sat dripping on the side of the bank and ate our lunch. We were hungry, and Dallas enjoyed the fried chicken, mashed potatoes, and corn.

After a couple hours, I took the helm of the boat drove us further down the river. Cruising through narrow passages, I spotted an oncoming speedboat. The bow of the boat rose up, and water sprayed in the air. The boat appeared to be out of control. The manatees were a few feet away and were in the path of the boat. I furiously waved my hand at the driver, signaling him to slow down.

"Manatees!" I yelled at him.

I quickly maneuvered to the first inlet allowing enough room for the boat to steer clear of the manatees. Pulled into the inlet, I steered the boat to the edge of the bank. As I turned the boat toward the bank, I accidentally turned the motor too hard and too fast, thrusting the boat uphill into the sandy embankment, and we slammed into a tree trunk. The sudden impact startled all of us.

I was concerned about Dallas's reaction. Alarmed, I asked him, "Are you alright?"

"Yeah, tree!" Then he started to laugh, and his laugh grew louder until he bent forward and then backward, laughing uncontrollably.

"Blake drive!" Dallas pointed at Blake to take the controls.

Driving back to the dock, we realized what a fun and relaxed day it had been. We ended the day with dinner at a restaurant. Dallas ordered a sandwich. When the sandwich came, we saw that the chef had placed a decorative green tree on the top bun. Dallas pointed to the sandwich and said, "Shirlee, boat!" and it brought out his laughter again.

The evening, after our visit with Dallas, I learned that a dark van with tinted windows had pulled up in front of the residential care home, just far enough away from the driveway. A minute before, Dallas had received a telephone call from someone. The dark-colored van moved slightly forward along the curb out front.

Dallas stood at the front door and was summoned by a loud voice from the car. He walked out on the lawn to the front curb toward the van. A staff member observed closely as Dallas reached the van.

Upon approaching the car, Dallas became visibly upset by the person inside. Someone's hand held up a book: It was Dallas's bible. Dallas quickly reached for the Bible, but whoever was holding it pulled it back into the van. There was loud conversation. Dallas raised his voice to whoever was in the van and said, "No! No, Shirlee not bad!" Dallas's voice sounded distressed and defensive.

The window lowered further, and Dallas quickly reached both hands in the van, grabbing his bible, tightly holding it against his body. He turned around and ran back toward the front door of the house, shaking his head sideways in distress.

"No! Shirlee not bad!" he repeated.

The staff member still standing at the open door moved aside as Dallas came swiftly through the front door. The dark van drove away quickly down to the end of the street and out of sight. The staff member observed the entire incident, and she walked toward Dallas and began to tenderly massage his shoulders. Dallas explained to the staff member that he was upset that the person sitting in the van was saying bad things about Shirlee.

Dallas felt tricked. He didn't want to hear bad things about Blake and me. The staff member could only speculate from Dallas's reaction that it had been Jeanine in the van and possibly my mother. But Dallas was visibly shaken and so the staff member didn't want to press the issue further. She called me that evening, to inform me of the incident.

When we saw Dallas the next day, his hands were clasped tightly around his bible. I knew that this was his favorite bible from my mother's house, and a family member in town had found this opportunity to use his bible as bait to change Dallas's mind about his affection toward us. Frustrated by the manipulation, Dallas was agitated over the incident. According to the staff members at the residential care home, this incident had repercussions for weeks.

Once again, Dallas had been exposed to the chaos and manipulation of the family and suffered as a result. He acted out by running away from the facility. His behavior became more erratic. Dallas walked into the garage of a nearby neighbor, which frightened her. Dallas was no threat, but leaving the property grounds was a violation of house rules.

After the van incident, the team captain worked hard to regain Dallas's trust in order to calm him down and make him feel safe at the care home. Ken also helped Dallas communicate his fears and regain trust by spending hours in counseling with Dallas. After several weeks, Dallas began to recover from the episode.

Learning of the trickery, I only yearned harder to be able to rewind my family's history and change our childhood. I felt powerless to change the past that led to these moments. Time, circumstance, distance, chaos, and the legal system all played into it. Just like the diseased limbs of a tree, our practice of gossiping and lying had to be cut out of our lives before it destroyed us.

After a year and half, Dallas was progressing well in the care home. But in the fall, without advanced warning or notice, the guardian moved Dallas to another residential care home. As family members, we expected we would be given a legal document informing us of the move, along with Dallas's new address. The legal document was withheld from us.

Several weeks later, the guardian contacted us. She said that my husband and I were not allowed to speak to Dallas or visit him for many weeks.

"Dallas is orienting to his new environment, so you can have no contact with him."

I will call you later and let you know where he is," she said. And then she hung up, cutting off all of our questions.

In the previous care home, we had spoken to Dallas consistently on the weekends and during the week. We had established a routine with Dallas, and he had looked forward to our calls. We were Dallas's lifeline. And it was established by the previous care home that Dallas trusted my husband and me above the other family members.

My husband and I consistently visited Dallas in Florida every three months at the other care home, and we had already booked our flight to see him in the fall. Now we would have to cancel our nonrefundable flight. We would have to delay our trip until sometime after the New Year, meaning that it would be six months before we would see Dallas again.

Two and half months later, after Thanksgiving, the guardian called and said we could finally talk to Dallas. In the meantime, I had discovered that other family members had been calling him and had visited him on Thanksgiving.

Why were we forbidden to see Dallas or have contact with him in the new residential care home? What could be happening?

Due to work constraints, the earliest we could book our flight to see Dallas was in February. It had been seven months since our last visit with him. I did not know how to explain to Dallas our absence from his life. He might have felt that we had abandoned him. But I didn't want to complicate his life by explaining the issues.

We arrived in Florida to a sunny and cool breeze. We planned dinner with a few friends in town who could help us better understand Dallas's situation. We wanted to know the reasons why Dallas was moved to another care home, and we wanted to understand the relationships he had in town.

We found out that Dallas had been moved to a care home that was only a few blocks away from my sister's home. Dallas was living with two women who took in special needs residents. These women had been working with my sister and the guardian; in fact, they said they knew my sister from high school, and they were all friends. Dallas was under my sister's control, and she was going against his wishes. Together, the guardian, my sister, and the care home controlled access to Dallas, preventing him from spending time with my husband and me even though he wanted to.

What was the state-appointed guardian's interest in carrying the water for my sister? It turned out that they all worked for the same interest: referral of residents. I was up against a sisterhood of women in town who were best friends and were associates working together to keep my sister in control.

Blake and I requested that the attorney help us with Dallas's visit to California. "You will need approval in writing from all of your siblings to take him out of state," our attorney said. Given that some of our family members were against our bid for guardianship, this requirement seemed inexplicable to me.

"But how could that be?" I asked her. "We are a dysfunctional family who doesn't look at the management of Dallas's life in the same way, and you want me to get their approval?"

"You are being adversarial," my attorney remarked.

"I am only interested in the welfare of my brother. He is living in the same town as his mother who abused him for forty years, and his sister who never protected him as an adult," I exalted with passion.

"That's the way it is!" She ended the call. We ended the legal relationship.

I learned during this conversation that my attorney was also representing Dallas's guardian, which posed a potential conflict of interest. She had given me no letter severing our legal relationship, yet I freely continued to discuss our strategy with her regarding our future guardianship plans with Dallas. We never knew that she was representing the guardian as well. It seemed the sisterhood against our interest in guardianship of Dallas was expanding.

"Airplane. Airplane," Dallas begged, each time we called. He wanted to fly to California to be with us. I could only assure him that I was working on it. I couldn't explain the obstacles we were dealing with in his life.

My schedule at the office became busier, but we knew it was time to visit Dallas again in Florida. We visited him again in May. In early August, I sent an email to the guardian saying that we would like to have Dallas visit us in California. I waited for her reply, but I received none. I phoned her. She didn't have time to talk. She was always busy when I called,

231

either standing in line at the bank, or rushing off to frequent vacations or weekend trips. While she was enjoying her vacations, Dallas was sitting at the residential home.

In mid October, we finally received an email from the guardian. The guardian said Dallas was afraid of flying. Where did this come from? Dallas was excited to take a plane to come to California when I had talked to him about it. He trusted my husband and me. What source had she drawn this from? She also said she was required to give the other family members notice and ask for their approval before Dallas could come to California. She wrote that we would need these letters of approval for Dallas to travel out of state.

I didn't hear back from the guardian about the family letters until Christmas. We discussed the letters from family members while keeping the intentions of the guardian in mind. Two of my brothers, Lynn and Roland, along with other relatives, including my cousin were very much in favor of the visit and felt Dallas would benefit from being with Blake and me. The guardian said that three family letters were scathing and had indicated untruths about my husband and me. My three sisters objected, saying that we would not return Dallas to Florida again and that we would kidnap him.

I asked myself how certain family members were allowed to document such lies. We had always returned Dallas after our many visits in Florida. Like clockwork, Blake and I would visit Dallas every three months. It gave Dallas the connection and security by having family members who consistently promised to visit him and who would follow through. Other family members would rarely visit—they'd only come out every two or three years. They would not take him away from the care home because of his incontinence issues. Some did not see him at all.

The guardian, her attorney, and certain family members were preventing Dallas from coming to California. It became clear that anyone who had power over Dallas used that power in a way that prevented good from coming to him. Mom held Dallas from the family, and now the guardian was holding Blake and me from Dallas.

On my next trip to Florida, I traveled alone. Since Blake had scheduled prior business meetings, he couldn't join me on my visit. I pulled into the driveway of the new residential care home. Dallas was standing at the front door ready with his suitcase, anxious to leave the house. Beside him on the floor was his pen collection solidly packed in his backpack. Through gifts and shopping, he had accumulated quite a pen collection in the two years since mom refused to return his old collection. Now Dallas never left anywhere without his heavy load of pens. Wherever he went, his pens went too.

I planned a day at the MOMI Science museum in Tampa. The drive would take about an hour and a half. I turned on Dallas's favorite radio station, and he relaxed back in his seat. Ten minutes later, Dallas's head fell to the side. He had fallen into a deep sleep. It wasn't like Dallas to fall asleep when he was in a car. Dallas loved being in the car, and he loved going anywhere. He loved to observe the scenery, watching the motion of life that he seldom could be a part of. He looked forward to playing a road game I called Mustang. Dallas was fond of Mustang cars. Whoever spotted the first Mustang received a point. Dallas always won.

Thirty minutes later, perspiration welled up on Dallas's face. I wiped it gently with a tissue. His breathing was labored. I turned the air conditioner up.

"Dallas, are you feeling okay?"

"Dizzy," he said as he touched his forehead.

I pulled into the parking lot of a fast food restaurant.

"Stay there, Dallas, I want to check something."

I opened the back door, and I quickly unzipped his suitcase. On top were his medications in a clear plastic bag. The unidentified pills separated in small plastic bags were to be administered later in the afternoon and evening. There were almost three times the number of pills as there had been at the previous home. Why was he taking so many?

I pulled into the museum parking lot and parked while he slept another hour. Then, it was lunchtime, and I woke Dallas.

"Dallas, let's get something in your stomach."

Dallas ordered his meal, but he soon lay down on the banquet bench and slept until his meal came. He wasn't fully awake until late in the afternoon. We spent a couple hours at the museum, but he had to sit down every fifteen minutes.

"Dizzy," he repeated.

Later that night, I studied the medication list before I gave Dallas his night medications. The medications on the list didn't seem to fit the written information. I counted out several mandatory prescription pills for Dallas, including sleeping pills. My brother was overmedicated. There were too many psychotropic medications for any human. Chills raced up my spine like cold fire. I considered not giving them to him. But there could be medical and legal consequences. I could be held liable. If he was taken off his medications too fast, he could have seizures or other

233

complications. I reluctantly placed the pills in Dallas's hand and gave him a drink of water. I called the guardian.

"I'm concerned about the accuracy of the pills dispensed to me," I said. "There doesn't seem to be a match with the quantities and the pills I have in my possession. Dallas has been acting strangely today, feeling dizzy and sleeping all day. "

"You have to give him his medication." Her voice lacked any concern as to how he was feeling. I was mandated to give them to him.

"But . . ."

"I'm sorry. This is the way it is," the guardian insisted.

I hung the phone up, not believing my ears.

I looked at the medication list again. There were sleeping pills that I was required to give to him. I would not give those to him. Dallas didn't need to be put to sleep. He had slept perfectly well the last two years without them. I laid the clear plastic bag down on the nightstand, and I closed my eyes.

The next morning, I went by a pharmacist and expressed my concerns about the medication list. I wanted him to verify the medication list against the pills. One by one, he found errors in the pills that had been dispensed to Dallas. A few pills he could not even identify.

"This is wrong and maybe criminal to be dispensing these pills in this way," the pharmacist commented. He recommended I scatter the administration of the pills throughout the day to ease the effects on Dallas until I could change the situation.

Dallas had been "Baker Acted" in the past due to the chaos in his life. This meant that he had been deemed emotionally unstable, thus permitting mental health professionals or law enforcement to perform an involuntary emergency examination. But in this residential care home, his caregivers were over-prescribing him with pills, and we were assured that they had no Baker Acts on the record. Overmedicating Dallas would assure his inability to act out. He would be compliant under any circumstance.

The second day of my visit, I planned a trip to the Tampa Zoo. Dallas woke up clearheaded. He would need help showering and dressing. The clothes he was wearing the day before had smelled of urine. I selected a set of clothes for the day, but they also were dirty and smelled like urine. I used the hotel laundry to wash and dry his clothes.

"Would you like to go out for breakfast?" I asked.

"Yeah!"

"Would you like to join me at the zoo?"

"Yeah!"

I gave Dallas one pill after breakfast, instead of several pills at once, as was required by the medication list. I waited a couple hours and then gave him one more. He seemed to be more functional.

We arrived at the Tampa Zoo. Dallas walked excitedly ahead of me, opening each door and holding it until I walked through. We walked to all the animal exhibits. Dallas had learned to appreciate animals. He was fascinated by the lions and tigers. "Power!" Dallas said as he looked at them. They were powerful, but they couldn't get away. He identified with them.

After taking the same number of pills, but spread throughout the day, Dallas seemed to function a little better. So what had happened the morning before? Had someone given him sleeping pills or some other drugs in the morning before I picked him up? Could someone have drugged him before his California sister picked him up? So he was unable to enjoy his first day with me?

On every visit to see Dallas at the residential care home, on the day I picked him up, he was totally drugged until late afternoon. I spoke several times to the guardian about possible overmedication. But to my knowledge, nothing was done to investigate the issue, and this practice continued throughout my following visits.

The time had come to get another attorney and begin the process for gaining guardianship of Dallas in Florida. One of the male attorneys I had initially called was now available. He had recovered from his surgery and could take on our case.

This would be our second hearing, and the new attorney filed a petition with the court so Dallas could visit us in California. We would hold off on the petition for guardianship until a later date. During the meeting, our attorney reviewed our file and detailed the strategy for our court hearing.

In my previous phone conversation with the attorney, I had explained Dallas's situation: that he was overmedicated, that the mass on his belly had not been taken care of, and that he suffered from poor hygiene. I further explained the obstacles we faced in communicating by telephone with Dallas since his move to another residential care home. We discussed the guardian's refusal to allow Dallas visits to California and how she required legal notice from all family members to approve of his visit.

"There is no legal requirement for her to do that," he stated firmly.

For this upcoming hearing, we discussed a new tactic: we would first petition for visitation to California. If we were successful, our chances for full guardianship would be greater. My attorney advised me that out-of-state guardianship was difficult to obtain in Florida due to the neglect of guardians assigned by the court. We would have to prove to a judge that we were absolutely committed to bettering Dallas's life. We would need to show some success first. I felt confident with my attorney's approach. He would be the attorney to represent me in the hearing.

Blake dropped me off at the front door of the courthouse, and parked the car. I walked slowly toward the tall glass doors, and a glitter of light reflected off the glass, blinding my eyes. I caught a glimpse of my figure: my spine was straight, my shoulders were back, and my hands were folded tightly in fists. I pressed the door handle, entering the courtroom lobby.

My eyes glanced around the lobby, as if getting acquainted with my surroundings. The rigid orderly lines of the interior walls and the sharp edged wooden furniture contrasted with the chaos of my family.

I needed to break through the barrier of nervousness. I inhaled deeply, and I exhaled loudly. This would be my second court hearing to try to get approval from the judge to take Dallas for a vacation visit to California. I reminded myself that I was here to advocate for Dallas's rights, decency, dignity, and safety. Dallas couldn't control anything in his life, not even his ability to speak.

I wanted Dallas to have a better life. Since my initial bid for guardianship, it had become clear that my sisters' answers for his life seemed harder to find. But I could not give up on my family no matter how poorly conceived their ideas for Dallas's life were. Of course, some of my family members had their own agendas for inheritances; they'd maintain unity with certain family members while sacrificing the abused for the gain. I wouldn't stop just because they might fear or loathe me; I wouldn't surrender to the massive barrage of misinformation. I would be there to protect Dallas's best interest.

Seated on a bench outside the courtroom was my sister Jeanine, who had also applied for guardianship of Dallas again. Jeanine, along with my other two sisters, objected to Dallas's visit to California. It was inexplicable.

Diane had come from Indiana to support Jeanine. Both of them seemed misinformed or misguided about the bad things occurring in Dallas's life. I breathed deeply, and I walked toward my sisters; my arms reached out and gave them each a hug. Their response to me was cold. They seemed to take pleasure in rejecting me; it formed their common bond. It became a conquest to them. But I felt no animosity toward them. They were there because they thought their plan for Dallas was better than mine.

The guardian walked into the lobby and sat near my sisters; her face was pudgy with malice. She had ignored my pleas to fix Dallas's issues: his overmedication and his need for stomach surgery and help with his urine-stained pants. She had ignored Dallas's dissatisfaction with the unkind people assigned to help him. Yet, she was there to object to Dallas's visit to California to see his sister. She was there to defend my sister and her friends because of their business associations, and by doing so, she was complicit in keeping Dallas from a better life.

The bailiff announced that the court session was beginning. We took our seats in the small courtroom next to our attorney. The guardian sat next to the judge, in the chair prized by my ex-attorney, and then positioned her body to face the judge, looking smug in her made-up look that she wore to impress him. She went for the same winning strategy, obviously planned by the female attorney and shared with the guardian.

The courtroom fell silent. The judge adjusted himself in his seat, and drew in a deep breath and leaned forward. He opened the case file with the flat of his hand, and tapped the paper's edge. The hearing had begun. We were now on the record.

The Court: I believe we are here in the matter of Dallas. There is a petition pending for visitation with family members.

My Attorney: This is my client, Shirlee. She is Dallas's oldest sister.

The Court: Dallas was previously appointed an attorney as counsel for the ward?

Dallas's Attorney: Yes, sir.

The Court: And you are the Guardian.

Female Attorney: I am counsel for the Guardian.

My Attorney: Well, Judge, the first thing I would like to do is suggest that I don't see why we are having this hearing. Her brother had apparently been abused by his mother. The family separated. Basically, most of the family members were estranged from each other. Shirlee was a petitioner to serve as his guardian when this hearing initially came up.

237

The Court was concerned about Dallas's benefits transferring to the State of California. And so the court determined that Dallas should have a local guardian to assure that those benefits would continue.

Shirlee and her husband have impeccable reputations. She has been coming to Florida to visit with her brother, and she's made not less than twelve visits here where they have taken him to any number of places. They have taken him to Disney World and Don Cesar, and on boating and fishing trips. Any number of things.

The Court: All without incident?

My Attorney: All without incident! They have picked him up on time and returned him on time without incident!

The Court to the Guardian's Attorney: You don't have any issue in regard to the family members being qualified for visitation?

Guardian's Attorney: No, no. In our opinion, her character, her integrity is not in question. She has visited him here. We would have never entrusted him to her care to begin with.

The Court: Okay.

My Attorney: But she has always brought him back without incident. As I say, there is no reason why my client should not be able to take him to California.

The Court: Is it your understanding that the impediment presented to your client is one of concern for the safety of the ward during travel? Is that your understanding of the hang-up?

My Attorney: That's my understanding of the hang-up. But we don't feel that there is any legitimate basis for that.

The Court to the Guardian's Attorney: You certainly don't take issue with Mrs. Scribner's integrity, character, and ability to adequately protect your client when they're visiting and having these, you know, family times?

Guardian's Attorney: No, Sir. No, Sir.

The Court: Okay. And so that certainly is an issue that's resolved.

My Attorney: Judge, also if I could say one other thing?

The Court: Sure.

238

My Attorney: They have been coming here regularly for the last four years. They've spent in excess of $50,000 on their brother.

Guardian's Attorney: The only concern that we've expressed—and I'm not sure where it was misconstrued that we had a concern about Mrs. Scribner or her husband or their character, because that just simply has nothing to do with it. They do come here. We've had no problems with the visits here in Florida. Dallas has expressed to not only the guardian but also to numerous people that provide him care that he doesn't want to go to California. The state-appointed guardian has been in a very difficult position as a guardian saying, "I don't feel that I should force him to do something." We have had numerous Baker Acts due to behavioral issues.

Guardian: Well, when he decides that he's . . . (she paused) ... his determination . . . when he decides that you're not allowing him to do what he wants to do—I don't know if you recall, but he was Baker Acted for jumping out of a moving vehicle on Highway 50 because it was going the wrong direction.

Listening to the Guardian stumble through her explanation, I closed my eyes and bowed my head in disbelief. *Let me understand this: Dallas was fearful of an impending car crash because the driver was in the wrong lane on Highway 50, a highly busy road, and out of fear for his life, he tried to get out of the car. He showed some recognition he might die. He was Baker Acted for the driver's wrong decision?*

Guardian: But the bottom line is, Dallas expressed that he does not wish to go to California, and that's why we've provided, you know... all family members have equal access here to him in Florida.

The Court: The question I have though, and I certainly assume, that this is your only concern. That as guardian of the ward ---

Guardian: Absolutely.

The Court: --- and I understand everyone's position. But let me ask this. There's really not a lot of qualitative difference between going to Disney World here or going to Disneyland in California is there? Because travel is travel. I mean, you know, you get on a plane and in three hours—

Guardian: It's not really the plane, and I think everybody's misunderstanding. It's not the plane. It's not whether he would know the difference between Disney World and Disneyland. When he goes, sometimes—and maybe this has not happened with you, and I'm not saying this—and he has said, "I want to go home now."

The Court: But my point is that if we don't—I'm just speaking in terms of conjecture—if we don't at least exercise the option, how are we going to know how he's going to respond?

Guardian's Attorney: You're right. We don't know.

The Court: How are we going to know unless we undertake it at least once? But the guardian is well positioned to put it on the Court's shoulders.

My Attorney: Basically, all the relatives are located all over the country. Okay?

Guardian: There are two that are here.

Guardian's Attorney: We're talking about immediate siblings. We're not talking about distant cousins.

My Attorney: Well, he has one sister here.

Guardian's Attorney: Correct.

My Attorney: And his mother is here, who was abusing him. The other side of it is that Dallas has expressed to my clients that he wants to go. Okay? I got copies of letters that said Shirlee and Blake would not bring him back. I said, this is ridiculous because they're not going to imperil their lives.

The Court: And so his personal feeling about that—and that's inconsistent with the twelve visitations that the client had with him. At least on twelve occasions, he has gone and been with the sister and apparently had an appropriate experience—a good time, for lack of a better term.

My Attorney: Here's a list of the visits.

The Court: Okay. Please provide that to counsel.

My Attorney to Guardian: Here's another thing I have. I have copies of emails from you to Shirlee, saying time after time that Dallas is looking forward to her visit.

Guardian: And he does. Judge, we have other siblings that have come from out of town to visit. They've come great distances.

The Court: Well, are they potential witnesses?

Guardian's Attorney: The two sisters present outside the courtroom have concerns based on whether or not Mrs. Scribner would return him to the State of Florida. Our concerns ---

The Court: Well you know, if she didn't do that it would be a crime. Looking at this file, Mrs. Scribner was the one who first reported the abuse.

My Attorney: Her sister, Jeanine, did not report it.

The Court: But the bottom line is Mrs. Scribner, on behalf of her brother, came to court and took up the banner, so to speak, in opposition to her mother who apparently ultimately—does anybody take issue with the fact that the mother was abusive? Does anybody take issue with that?

Guardian: No, she was abusive.

The Court: So that's a fact, the mother was abusive. So Mrs. Scribner is really, in the eyes of the Court, a very important person who got this thing started. Was there ever any issue or determination of the benefits and the impact of moving? Was that issue ever resolved?

My Attorney: Judge, we believe, though we haven't filed a petition for that, that he would be qualified for those benefits.

The Court: Okay? The point is she would have every right, as a sibling, a qualified petitioner, to come before this court in proper fashion with proper notice and ask to be appointed successor guardian at any time.

Guardian's Attorney: As would the rest of the siblings.

The Court: Exactly.

Guardian's Attorney: And nobody's objected to that.

The Court: So I don't see where the concern is coming from that she would try to jeopardize in any way her—-

Guardian's Attorney: We did not voice that concern.

The Court: Well, you did!

Guardian's Attorney: No. I said we did not. We never voiced a concern that he would not be returned. I said that was never a concern. The siblings voiced that.

At that moment, I felt a sense of beating tension overcome my body. "It's just a vacation to visit in California!" I uttered under my breath, my lips

241

mouthing my thoughts. All this objection coming from our ex-attorney who knew of our character and was now representing the guardian. It was my strength and determination they resented, the courage that none of them could conceive of, with which I stood up against the local machine that was trying desperately to grind me down.

My Attorney: I've got all these letters, Judge, that said initially she won't—

Guardian's Attorney: But those did not come from my—I mean, in other words, we didn't—

My Attorney: They came from your office.

Guardian's Attorney: Okay. But they were sent to me, and I just passed them along.

The Court: I don't see these other siblings as interested parties at this point. None of them have responded to the petition.

My sisters were riding on the backs of the guardian and her attorney, our ex-attorney. This cinched my understanding of the closeness of the guardian to my sisters. The guardian bought into the imaginations of certain family members. She bought into the gossip, not into Dallas's best interest.

Guardian's Attorney: Again, we don't share the same concern.

The Court: How many are out there?

Guardian's Attorney: Two.

The Court: Two? Okay. I'll talk to them after the hearing.

The Court: I'll be willing to—I want to try it. That's just where I'm at. You know, I'll take responsibility if it goes badly for Dallas. But in all likelihood, it will be a positive experience for him. If we create a positive experience, that's all the better. Well, I'm prepared to do that. Why don't we do this: Why don't we do an order—and let's—I'm going to grant the request and allow him to have a visitation with his sister in California.

My Attorney: Okay.

The Court: I think Dallas will benefit from that.

The Guardian shifted in her seat, and her emotion shot to her face as she presented another barrier to Dallas's visit.

242

Guardian: There's an issue with the program right now. If he is gone for more than a certain number of days, they will only pay the home for the nights that he's there.

The Court: How long? What's the window they will pay?

Guardian: I don't know.

The Court: How much do they pay? What is the cost?

The guardian should have known the cost. It was her responsibility to know. Many times, we had taken Dallas away for a week from his first residential care home, and Dallas's rent payment to the home had never been an issue there.

Guardian: The program pays them directly.

The Court: What I don't understand is that during these other twelve visits when he was away, obviously arrangements were made.

Guardian: Yes. And they don't bill for those days when he's not there.

I later found out that this was not true.

Guardian: Fifteen days is a lot longer than three or four days. It's a longer window. I don't know what the window is.

The guardian's response showed her utter incompetence to make a case— she couldn't claim anything without knowing the number of days.

The Court: What I don't understand is, he has to be somewhere every night.

My Attorney: Correct.

The Court: So if he's not staying there, then wherever he is staying is entitled to get those funds.

Guardian: If this happens once, or twice, if it becomes—and you know, other family members are going to want equal access.

The Court: I take it one petition at a time.

Guardian: Okay. Just concerns.

The Court: I'm not going to prejudice Mrs. Scribner because of something that could potentially happen in the future, that somebody else may want to do.

Guardian: Okay.

The guardian sat lower in her chair, her face pale with resentment and defeat. There was a frank contempt coming from her; she seemed incapable of realizing what would be in Dallas's best interest. Why did she choose the wrong side?

My Attorney: And I don't know why it's now an issue when it hasn't been.

The Court: Given the ruling of the Court that we're going to do the visitation, I want everybody to get on board to try to make it happen, and make it happen in an appropriate fashion. If it works out, we may be broadening Dallas's horizons.

I stood up from my chair, and as I turned to leave, I suddenly turned back towards the judge.

"Thank you," I said. And I exited the courtroom.

The bailiff called my sisters Jeanine and Diane, and escorted them into the courtroom. Their eyes looked downward as they passed within inches of my face; their posture was confident of the results that their testimony would have against me. I sat down in the lobby area next to Blake.

Ten minutes later, both sisters exited the courtroom with their eyes smoldering. They looked at me with disdain because I'd prevailed with the judge and succeeded to have Dallas for a vacation to California.

To calm the waters, Blake stepped forward and approached them. "We would like to take you to dinner if you would join us," he said to them.

"No!" my sisters refused, walking fast across the lobby, and they exited the building in a fury.

The skies in Florida were clear and bright. There wasn't a cloud in the sky. It would be a safe day to fly in an airplane. We had booked a ticket for Dallas and Blake on a local flight from Orlando to Fort Lauderdale. The flight would be a way to test Dallas for his longer flight to California. Dallas had told us that the residential care home tried to frighten him about flying in an airplane. Had the words he heard frightened him about flying to California? Would they prevent him from boarding the airplane or, worse, would he become Baker Acted because he panicked in flight? Not wanting to risk any of the above scenarios, we planned the reservations so Dallas could back out and not board the airplane, if needed. This was all part of preparing Dallas for the long-awaited trip to visit us, and ultimately, to live with us in California.

I drove Blake and Dallas to the Orlando airport, dropped them off, and then drove a few more hours to the Fort Lauderdale airport to pick them up. We had only one cell phone between us on this trip, and Blake took it with him. As I drove the highway south, I was concerned about how Dallas and Blake were doing on the airplane. Would Dallas succumb to the words that had been spoken to him? Would I be in Fort Lauderdale, while Dallas and Blake were still at the Orlando airport?

At the airline ticket counter, Blake explained Dallas's situation to the airline ticket agent. They kindly upgraded Blake and Dallas to first class, making Dallas's trip calmer and more enjoyable.

Three hours later, I picked them up at the Fort Lauderdale airport. Dallas was beaming with pride. He was victorious over the words he'd heard. I thanked my husband, who made the trip enjoyable for Dallas. After that, we booked Dallas's trip to California.

Even though we requested from the court that Dallas visit us for a couple of weeks in California, and though the judge mandated cooperation from the guardian, she would only let us bring Dallas to California for five days. In the meantime, we booked Blake's flights. He would fly back and forth to Florida and California to accompany Dallas, and then would make a final return trip to California. We didn't fight it. This was just another step in the process to obtain guardianship of Dallas, another obstacle to overcome.

Throughout the entire trip, Dallas willingly entered the airplane with Blake without any trepidation, overcoming the fear instilled by people around him that it wasn't safe to fly and that he would crash in an airplane. Dallas trusted Blake and me to never put him in an unsafe situation or force him to do something he didn't want to do. Once again, the airline upgraded Blake and Dallas to first class, making Dallas comfortable and happy while flying in the large commercial plane to California.

Dallas's vacation to California was successful. He didn't ask to go back to Florida once. We returned him from California on time, just like we had done after our visits in Florida many times before. Now the implication presented before the court that we wouldn't return Dallas back to Florida was out the door. The excuses that Dallas wouldn't get on an airplane, and that we would not return him, were laid to rest.

After Dallas's successful visit to California, I contacted our attorney to set another guardianship hearing.

The grey of the day sparked with color in certain surrounding areas, the clouds cracked in various places for the width of a single sunray, and the clouds began to open wider. We arrived in Florida a week early so we could meet with our attorney and have time to spend with Dallas.

We picked Dallas up at his residential care home at eight in the morning and drove to the attorney's office for a nine o'clock meeting. On the way, we stopped at a store to pick up a magazine for Dallas. He would wait in the attorney's break room while we had our meeting.

At the end of our meeting, our attorney, Blake, and I walked into the break room. Dallas was passed out, face down, on the linoleum floor. We tried to wake him, but it was difficult to bring him out of his sleep. Finally he awoke, and we helped Dallas to his feet. He stood up, the large mass on his stomach protruding through his T-shirt. Dallas was once again overmedicated on the first day we picked him up. This had been happening on my visits to see him for months at this point, but in my letters to my attorney, it was difficult to prove. But now, in my attorney's office, he was seeing firsthand the issues that Dallas had endured for so long.

Our attorney stepped back, his face drawn. "This is worse than I imagined," he said.

While driving to the latest hearing for guardianship, Blake and I agreed that this would be our last court hearing. We agreed not to fight the family beyond this battle. If we did not prevail in this hearing, it would be the end of the road for us. Dallas would be in God's hands in the future to right the wrongs of the past, and to put Dallas in a safer place.

I firmly adjusted myself in the car, holding tightly to the armrest on the door. I felt an uneasiness and revulsion at Dallas's neglect by certain family members who chose to ignore the abuse. Did it not occur to them that maybe they were wrong, that they were misinformed about Dallas's situation? That they had been lied to?

Three aspects resided within certain siblings: their human compassion toward Dallas, their inability to see the truth, and their inability to control what brewed within them. There seemed to be more concern for their lives than for Dallas's life. Their case before the judge that it was more inconvenient to travel to California than to Florida, even though the distance was about equal for many family members, was a ridiculous one.

It was difficult to trust my family's motives. Did they really want a better life for Dallas? What were their standards for Dallas? Were they different from mine? Was this really about Dallas? What were Dallas's rights in all of this? Did they know what I knew about Dallas's birth? I studied intently for some revelation in my sisters that they could trust me with Dallas's life. I could not find it.

It was hard at first to confront my family's objections to becoming Dallas's guardian, but I now felt further validated to press harder for the guardianship, in light of the insanity and chaos surrounding Dallas's life. My thoughts raced to the past as if certain days were spread before me in live video demanding to be seen again. I knew what the lies and manipulations had done to me. I didn't want Dallas experiencing this anymore in his life.

I knew some family members would not rest until they got the better of me. Certain family members were so emotional that no coping mechanism would make them bearable at this time; their emotions short-circuited their rational processes.

The noose had tightened on me; I had many opponents: my sisters opposed me going for guardianship, my mother opposed me. The legal guardian that was appointed by the court opposed my guardianship of Dallas, as did my sister's friends at the residential care home where Dallas had strategically been moved to. There seemed to be obstacles everywhere. I knew there had to be support and information somewhere to connect the dot between Florida and California.

The conclusions of certain family members denouncing me with malice and without proof of wrong-doing held together like hardened glue. I felt a deep sense of betrayal from those who, earlier in their lives, had counted on me to take them in and to provide temporary sanctuary from my mother's chaos.

I could no longer grapple with the senseless behaviors and excuses that kept Dallas in a failing situation. There was a limit to the negligence the state-appointed guardian could get away with. Dallas deserved better than to be overmedicated and given sleeping pills each night. He was overmedicated to the point that he would not act out at his unhappiness, which would keep the care home from getting a Baker Act on their record. Neglecting the large protruding mass from his belly was an utterly inexcusable act by a guardian assigned to protect him. Vivid images came to mind of Dallas's bottom spackled with hardened feces, and my husband showering him to resolve this unhealthy state. Even when we reported the lack of hygiene to the guardian, she did not tend to it. Dallas's unhappiness in his situation had been ignored.

I felt a faint wrench of sadness for having to compete against my sisters in court again. But I had to stand guard of my feelings toward certain family members, as if some part of me had become a stranger to my family. I had to be numb to the accusations. I would hold the strength to stand against them, feeling God's divine power upon me, understanding the purity of my motives. I stayed rational so I could transform Dallas's situation.

Blake and I walked hand in hand into the lobby of the Hernando County courthouse. He squeezed my hand tightly, then released it. It was mid-afternoon, and the bailiff appeared in the lobby and announced our case. He instructed everyone to file into the courtroom. I stayed back while twenty or more of my sister's friends and co-workers filed in. Blake and I glanced at one another, surprised that my sister had invited so many witnesses. The door closed behind them.

I started for the door with Blake and my brother Lynn following behind me. Lynn was there to give Dallas a better life, too. Lynn said the best home he lived in was with me in California before my mother had ordered he and Dallas back to Chicago. Lynn also knew while visiting Dallas in Florida that the issues of overmedicating, poor hygiene, and the mass on his stomach had been neglected. He was aware of Dallas's unhappiness where he was residing. He was there in court for Dallas. He wanted the best for him. Lynn would be my sole support for earning guardianship of Dallas.

Grasping the handle of the heavy carved doors, I hesitated for a moment. I had one more obstacle in my way. I pushed hard through the double doors and walked down the aisle. The carpet flowed at an angle down the middle of the room like a rushing river, its power about to pull me under. The space exuded an air of silent malevolence, and it felt like historical legal decisions were made in this room. The high ceilings and the wide expanse of the room made me feel diminutive and alone.

My attorney seated himself on the left side of the room as protocol dictated. Blake, my brother, and I sat down beside him. My proud strength became a challenge to keep hold of as the courtroom filled on the opposing side. The right side of the room was stacked with my sister and her supporters in town. If the courtroom had been a yacht, it would have capsized on the starboard side. The other attorneys for my sisters filed in last and sat in the front row opposite my attorney. Dallas's state-appointed attorney sat next to the other attorneys. Dallas's guardian and her attorney sat close together with my sisters.

My sister Diane was absent from the courtroom. She had decided for personal reasons to not be present, but she was represented by a shared attorney with my sister, Sissy, from Texas. They had hired their own attorney to support Jeanine in her bid for guardianship; in other words, to stack the courtroom against me. My mother was not physically present, but her presence was felt in the courtroom

The bailiff announced the arrival of the judge. He seated himself before the large room. He was the same judge from the first three hearings.

Without hesitation, the judge and lawyers discussed procedural matters and affirmed my brother as incapacitated.

"Those who are not party to this case, please leave the courtroom now," The judge ordered.

The guardian and Jeanine's friends and coworkers filed out of the courtroom, leaving only the attorneys, my sister Jeanine, and me to battle it out.

Right out of the gate, procedural matters set forth between the judges and the attorneys pointed out that Dallas had been traveling to other states to visit other family members for quite sometime. Shamefully, I had been the only one denied a visit by Dallas to my home in California.

My attorney called me to the witness stand, and I raised my right hand in sworn testimony. I took a seat next to the judge, and the court reporter. My attorney assembled his notes and walked toward me. He was calm, confident, and in control.

As my attorney began his first question, a sense of expectation rose through my body slowly like a warm liquid, soothing me. A radiant aura suffused me that I couldn't identify. A glow surrounded me with utter calmness. From somewhere, a warm light seemed to permeate my body. I felt a confident benevolence. My words flowed with ease, mouthing all that I knew to be true. It was as if my will had vanished, and a divine power was present over me, guiding my every word calmly and truthfully. My purpose to rescue Dallas was clearer than ever. At that moment, I knew I was not in charge, but that a higher being had measured all that had happened in the recent years. I would sit there and be an instrument to all that was good.

My attorney stood before the judge and asked the court to take judicial notice of my sister's initial petition for the guardianship of Dallas. The legal process would provide notice to all family members of Jeanine's bid for guardianship. My attorney turned to me, his eyes fixed on the document he was holding.

"Does it list you as being one of Dallas's relatives?" he asked me.

"I don't see my name or my siblings' names anywhere," I announced.

"Okay. None of your names are listed on that document, nor are there any of your addresses?"

"No, nothing is attached."

"Okay, did your sister, Jeanine, know where you lived and know how to get in touch with you and your brothers and sisters?"

"Yes, she did."

"But you never got a copy of that?"

"No, Sir."

My sister thought she could waltz into the courtroom, file untrue documents, and petition the court for guardianship without notifying me and our other siblings, thus guaranteeing her guardianship of Dallas.

My attorney presented a document from Dallas's team captain. The team captain had explained to Dallas that there was an upcoming hearing for guardianship. Then, he explained to Dallas that his mother, his sister Jeanine, and his sister Shirlee wanted to be his guardian. He received only one answer: that Dallas wanted Shirlee to be his guardian. The team captain's letter went on to explain that Dallas had no contact, and wished not to have any contact with his mother, nor with his sister Jeanine. His letter of recommendation summed up his opinion: "It is my professional opinion that Shirlee should be guardian. It would best serve Dallas to have a guardian that he has a positive relationship with."

My attorney read a statement by Dallas's attorney ad litem appointed by the state. He reiterated that Dallas's preference was for me to be guardian.

The bailiff summoned Sissy from the lobby to the stand. She confidently sat down in the chair next to the judge. Her attorney stepped forward to ask her questions. She asked a few questions to establish who she was. What followed was a leading question by her attorney, and Sissy adjusted herself in her seat. Then her eyes narrowed, the dark pupils darted directly at me, and her pointed chin quivered in mockery, as she exclaimed, "Shirlee, never wanted to have Dallas in her home!"

Sissy sat forward in the seat, enjoying her performance in front of the judge. The bitter lines of her mouth sharpened with each word. I studied her face, and I studied her mood with detachment, knowing that she would at all costs fight me to the end. It was a childhood issue. Sissy had always felt competitive with my successful life. She would not let me have this win for Dallas.

Then she looked at me with a slight look of cunning. Her staring eyes filled with malicious thoughts, which were then etched in her face, and her chin was distorted by righteous indignation. Her lips grew light, and her features sharpened dramatically, her nose appearing more prominent than usual. I never thought hope could look so ugly in the face when it was mixed with cunning words, but it did. She had suffered the burden of words spoken against me, and she knew her words were deceptive. She continued to speak in flat assumptions.

"Shirlee doesn't want any family members in her home!" Sissy said.

Uncharacteristically, I played into it from a gut level, shaking my head side-to-side, denying an untruthful statement said before God and the judge. Sissy heard things I did not say. This was peculiar, coming from someone who I hadn't seen or talked to in years. Only a few months before the hearing, she had phoned me to feel out the direction I was taking with the hearings. It was a patronizing conversation to feel out what my strategy in the courtroom would be.

I observed as both sisters discarded my emotions, and I tried to observe and understand their misguided truths. There was a stab of pain and disappointment that untrue words could be spoken in a courtroom. I felt that some universal cop should vet words before their vibrations touched the air. My opponents were self-assured in their delivery, and they displayed an air of confidence that they were going to collectively win this hearing. Apparently, their path to glory to defeat me would be through lies, manipulation, and trickery.

As our family drama unfolded in the courtroom, our lives crashed harder against one another. I was struck by our past; memories I had once buried tore loose. I watched it all through a clear pane of glass, struggling through the toxic fog. My spirit was heated with compassion; I felt a sickening tightness in my stomach for having to beg for a decent standard of living for my brother. I just wanted Dallas not to be overmedicated, drugged night after night with sleeping pills, or to suffer feces spackled to his buttocks, or to be dressed in clothes that smelled of urine. I couldn't let my vision for Dallas's life be sabotaged by the ugliness of words and actions.

The hearing was coming to a close. Blake was called into the courtroom and was seated next to the judge. His main point about Dallas's life was summed up briefly:

"Dallas is swimming in a fish tank when he could be swimming in the ocean."

The judge looked down at his desk and nodded his head with approval.

Within minutes of my husband's testimony, the judge rendered his decision.

"Shirlee is qualified at all levels to be appointed Dallas's guardian," the judge said. And he ordered the hearing over.

251

The courtroom held a dead stillness. After five long years, Blake and I had prevailed in bringing Dallas to live in California. I was now his guardian—a decision granted to me from the court, not from my weaknesses but from my strengths. I rose from my seat in tortured triumph, denying the pain of this circus. I looked at Jeanine. Her cheeks seemed faintly drawn inward, as if deflated like a tire. Then, Jeanine's overblown body shrunk in weight, posture, and shape, as if the air to her balloon had been let out quickly. She looked back at me. We held our gaze without smiling, each thinking, forming, and fitting this decision into our lives.

Finally, the system had grasped the complexity of this family. The judge had grasped Dallas's plight. He had grasped this case. After four hearings, the judicial system served its purpose.

I moved swiftly in Jeanine's direction, throwing my arms around her, trying to comfort her.

"Jeanine, we will unite as a family," I said.

"No! It won't happen! It can't happen!" she exclaimed loudly.

"It will happen if you want it to," I replied.

Then Jeanine shot out of the courtroom like a lit torpedo, loudly shouting so the judge could hear as she slammed the courtroom doors aside. "It's all about money!" she screamed to her crowd of supporters, covering her prideful loss.

Outside the courtroom, buzzing broke out among my sisters and their friends. Among them, conversations grew hotter. They stood in a huddle together with incredulous shock on their faces, as if the enemy had tossed a grenade at them after they thought they had won the war. A war: That's how they portrayed it among themselves.

Contempt lay in the air, and Jeanine and Sissy behaved like a passel of fools, finding the judge's decision reprehensible. Their voices rose and fell together in disbelief and then were abruptly choked off. Sissy made a tightening sideways movement with her mouth and glared at me as I passed by. Then the talk died down to a whisper. They did not contemplate the universal consequences of their words and actions.

I exited the courtroom and stood at the entrance to the lobby, observing the drama unfolding. I felt their savage resentment at my win for Dallas.

Brute strength. That's what it took to fight these battles from afar. It took muscles to resist the temptation to quit. My struggle was seeking the truth, and the right was mine. I found great clarity in being beyond emotion and holding true to the great purpose of this decision. I held no malice toward my family members. I only despised their judgment about Dallas's life. Their standards for what was right for Dallas differed from my own. There was neither thought nor feeling left in me. I wanted to make the family right, to heal it. But we were a family left in a pile of rubble, with the support pillars collapsed in a heap. It would take a collective determination and a new blueprint to rebuild again. I refused to harbor negative thoughts or feelings about them. Forgiveness was about me.

In these battles, I felt spiritually equipped with special armor to protect against their flying bullets. No matter how many bullets they shot at me, my courage was renewed. The decision was to surrender to the victory for Dallas. Triumphant, I looked back at the courtroom; it now felt smaller.

All three sisters had been irrational and unreal in judging me. Roland and Roger lived in blind resentment, pegging me, not the dysfunction in our family, as the enemy. I wanted to scream at my family. *Can't you see I am not the enemy? I have never been your enemy! I am now Dallas's victor. You failed at your perceived war. Please drop your swords, and join in the victory party.* But no sound would reach them.

My parents created the whole sordid mess in our family in order to serve their own self-interests. The tragic sin in my family was the moral failure by my parents who should have known better. Their choices throughout our lives affected all of our lives. Later, Mom lived her life for malice and not for the sake of the family.

But I'd discovered you cannot live with pure evil and its twisted form of despair that never rises above animal instincts. I still loved my mother. But sadly, I would never be loved back in a way a functional mother can love. I missed out on that bonding, that joy that I'd seen in other mother-and-daughter relationships. I only lived foolishly in the hope that Mom could have been different. It was not meant to be on this earth.

But now, the issues I had endured over the last few years with certain family members receded into some outer fog, like pain so deeply felt that it has no more power to hurt. I didn't want to hear their arguments about Dallas's life. They had had their chance to make a difference.

I walked into the lobby, and I glanced in Sissy's direction. Her head was drawn downward into her shoulders in defeat. With the weight of the judge's decision fully understood, there was a brief stab of shock in her eyes, then tears. The look in her face was a look of self-defeat, not a win for Dallas. The wrinkles of her sharp chin trickled into a shape resembling a sneer. The righteous bitterness of her voice excoriated me,

"Shirlee, don't you dare put Dallas in another home," she threatened. "You have to keep him in your home." Her mouth then pinched in silence, and her eyes filled with tears, and she waited for my reaction to her solicitous demand.

Oh really! I said quietly under my breath.

The irony of her forbidding me from seeing Dallas, her terrible accusations that I would kidnap him, and her denying Dallas a simple vacation to visit me in California --- after all of this, she wanted him to live in my home, not a residential care home. Now that I had been qualified, I was good enough for Dallas to live with me.

"Dallas will be safe," I gently reassured her.

I understood her concerns. That was the point: We all loved and cared about him. But decisions in his life had to be managed with astuteness, in order to prevent evil from entering his life. I would manage that well. It was not the narrative I wished for my family, it was not the happy ending I had hoped for. But Dallas would be safe. My mother would never abuse Dallas again.

I was sure of my actions, and I was at peace with myself. My siblings who objected would need to rise to the new purpose. This journey had been a conflict of minds, bodies, spirits, and souls. I wished I could say, *Oh the heck with them.* But I loved them.

After everything he had been through, I wanted Dallas to know that real love existed in this world. I wanted his mind free of chaos so that he could enjoy the small, simple things in life: colorful flowers, humming birds, turtles. I wanted Dallas to hear musical notes, high and low and to experience happiness each day. *Dallas, I want you to live life to the fullest and to live free. Dallas, I will help you do that.*

As Blake and I left the courthouse and stood outside under the brightening sky, a flood of relief rushed through my body, as if a senseless burden had been lightened, as if a current of air had blown it all away. The final battle had ended with a victory for Dallas: He would never again be abused, his needs would never again be neglected, he would never again be overmedicated, and his spirit would never again be taken by force. Dallas's destiny was in God's hands, and I felt guided by an unseen force to rescue him without resentment or anger toward my family.

Standing on the steps, I caught Blake's eyes. His luminous spirit radiated and transcended all that was bad. He smiled at me, and I smiled back in triumph. He rushed closer to my side and scooped me into his arm. We held each other for a long time, standing still, so still. I tilted my head upwards and stood on my tiptoes, staring solidly into his clear blue eyes.

"Thank you so much, Blake," I whispered. He had been steadfast on this journey. The shock on Blake's face soothed into a calm serenity. He sat down in disbelief, and I sat next to him, seeing objects in the lobby for the first time.

"Dallas won today," he whispered in my ear, with a clarity in his voice.

Back at the hotel, I drew a bath, not too cold or too hot. Running water touched my skin, and I felt the warmth of the water to my bones. I had saved a package of plumeria bath crystals from an earlier trip to Hawaii. It reminded me of the good side of my mom. I threw a few crystals into the running water until they dissolved. Their fragrance permeated the air. It symbolized hope that Mom would one day change, and learn how to be a mother to all of us, to Dallas. That's all I had: hope.

Two weeks after the final hearing, Blake flew to Florida to pick Dallas up and move him to California. He arrived at the residential care home. Dallas's belongings were packed in boxes and ready to go. Dallas refused to take his belongings; instead he picked up his pen collection and headed for the front door. Blake stopped him.

"Dallas, would you like to say good-bye?" he asked.

Without raising his head, Dallas ignored the owners of the care home and kept walking in the direction of the front door. At the entrance, a large box sat blocking his way. He kicked the box with his foot and pushed opened the door, but he still couldn't get through. He tried pushing the door by bracing it with his arm, moving it a few inches further. Finally, he pushed the door open wide enough that he could fit himself and his pen collection through. He rushed outside into the fresh open air to the rental car, quickly opening the passenger side door and seating himself inside. Then he immediately locked the door.

Blake returned to the driver's seat and they drove off toward the Orlando airport. Dallas rolled his window down, leaned his head outside, and let his hair blow furiously in the wind. He was leaving his past behind.

At the airport, Blake led Dallas towards the gate. Dallas rushed ahead of him and swept through the ticket counter to the open airport gate. Dallas held his chin higher, his posture was straighter, and he carried his pen collection higher on his shoulder than he had before. All without incident.

Blake and Dallas arrived home in California. I stood outside our home waiting to greet them. When Dallas exited the car, I ran over to him and took him by the hand. Together, he and I walked through our carved entry doors to safety. We were home.

Epilogue

In the following weeks, I consulted physicians regarding Dallas's medical issues. The mass on his stomach that had been neglected for years was X-rayed and proved to be almost fatal. Emergency surgery was performed right away. I paid a private psychiatrist to wean Dallas off the myriad medications that had been prescribed in Florida.

Over the next few months, I set aside my business to take care of the issues in Dallas's life. Dallas sat quietly in front of the lit fireplace, unable to read, but with his bible laid out on the floor in front of him. He sat for hours each day, contemplating the quiet in his life, his gratitude, and the power he now possessed. Over time, the rigidity in his facial muscles relaxed, the creases in his face disappeared, and the texture of his skin smoothed on the surface with a luminosity. He displayed serenity and a spirit I had not seen before. He felt safe.

Since living in California, Dallas has lived without chaos and feels safe. He has not acted out and has not received a Baker Act on his record. Dallas lived with Blake and me for six months while he acclimated to California, and until I felt that his health issues were understood and taken care of. He later went to a residential care home nearby, where we would be a part of his life.

For Blake and me, the five years of expenses it took to rescue Dallas accumulated to $130,000. This included the expenses of traveling to

Florida every three months, hotels, car rentals, legal fees, necessities for Dallas, and entertainment to enrich his life. Later, we assumed the cost of medical fees and the legal fees to obtain conservatorship in California. This money would have been set aside for our retirement, but Blake and I knew the remaining years of Dallas's life needed to be better than his earlier years. It was a sacrifice we were willing to make. My wonderful husband gets the Best Husband award for supporting Dallas's situation. We will work a long time to make up my retirement savings.

I haven't seen my mother since the first hearing— seven years ago at the time of this writing. Recently, I received notice that Jeanine had obtained guardianship of my mother, who now is suffering with dementia and is living in a residential care home.

My birth father lost his wife of sixty years, and he came to live with us in California. A couple of years later, he was transferred to a residential care home after vascular surgery. After four years, living in California, he passed away at ninety years old. There was a DNA paternity test performed that showed he was my biological father. Our genealogy also revealed that George Washington, founder of our country and first president, is my sixth generation uncle.

Today, my son Scott is happily married to Iwona, and together they have a son, Dillon. Scott works as a software engineer for the hospital system that I had designed hospital interiors for many years before.

Recently, my brother, Lynn, called to tell me that a woman, Dolores, had come forth as our sister. The State of Illinois recently opened its adoption files for adoptees to find their parents. Apparently, my mother, at thirty one years old, had gotten pregnant and then given the baby up for adoption; at the time, she was living in Chicago and had seven children in foster homes. She never told anyone about the baby, and the father was not identified on the birth certificate. A couple weeks after talking with Dolores on the phone, Blake and I traveled to meet her and her family. We are proud to have them as a part of our life.

Upon Dallas's arrival to California, I sent out invitations to family members to visit Dallas. It's been three years, and no family members have called or visited Dallas except for my brother Lynn and his wife, Debbie, who supported us in court. Nevertheless, I continue to hope that one day we will be able to heal as a family.

12278838R10146

Made in the USA
San Bernardino, CA
14 June 2014